Safe Haven

Safe Haven

*The United Kingdom's Investigations
into Nazi Collaborators and
the Failure of Justice*

JON SILVERMAN AND ROBERT SHERWOOD

OXFORD
UNIVERSITY PRESS

OXFORD
UNIVERSITY PRESS

Great Clarendon Street, Oxford, OX2 6DP,
United Kingdom

Oxford University Press is a department of the University of Oxford.
It furthers the University's objective of excellence in research, scholarship,
and education by publishing worldwide. Oxford is a registered trade mark of
Oxford University Press in the UK and in certain other countries

Published in the United States of America by Oxford University Press
198 Madison Avenue, New York, NY 10016, United States of America

British Library Cataloguing in Publication Data
Data available

Library of Congress Control Number: 2023936574

ISBN 978-0-19-285517-6

DOI: 10.1093/oso/9780192855176.001.0001

Printed and bound in the UK by
Clays Ltd, Elcograf S.p.A.

Links to third party websites are provided by Oxford in good faith and
for information only. Oxford disclaims any responsibility for the materials
contained in any third party website referenced in this work.

Preface

> It falls to the historian to excavate the lost and forgotten parts of
> the past as well as the truths we don't want to remember.[1]

In the 1980s, when the UK woke up, or was woken up, to the realization
that it had been playing host for decades to men who had committed
crimes in the service of Nazi Germany, there was a feeding frenzy of
concern in Parliament and the public prints. This led eventually, as
David Cesarani has chronicled, to the passage of the War Crimes Act in
1991.[2] Necessarily, the criminal and legal investigations which followed
went on away from the public gaze. Yet, when the process came to an
end in 2000 after one trial and conviction, the giddy intensity of the initial interest dissipated with the speed of air escaping a balloon, leaving
behind many unexplored questions. Such as: Why was there only one
conviction when several hundred names came under scrutiny? Who
were the other suspects? Why did the Crown Prosecution Service rule
that perpetrators responsible for hundreds, if not thousands of deaths,
should not face charges? Why were the issues at trial narrowed by the
prosecution to the extent that the crimes were effectively 'decoupled'
from the Holocaust? And why do we know so little, in fact almost
nothing, about the thinking behind the decisions which were made,
particularly at the level of the Crown Prosecution Service and Attorney-
General's office?

It is the job of historiography to try to make sense of events through
empirical discovery and conceptual analysis. And to evaluate the causation
of behaviours which have momentous consequences. It may be thought
that an obvious answer to one of the questions posed above, namely,
why was there only one conviction in the 1990s, is that the evidential

[1] London, 2000 *Whitehall and the Jews, 1933–1948*, p. 14.
[2] Cesarani, 1992 *Justice Delayed*.

trail, after a lapse of half a century, had inevitably run cold. That is certainly not the whole story, as we explain, but even if it was, there are unexamined issues, characterized by incompetence and apathy, arising from the military inquiries which began within weeks of the ending of the war, when the accuracy of identification and the memories of witnesses could hardly have been fresher.

Although the focal point of this book is the investigations carried out by the UK, whether by the army in the British zone of post-war Germany or the Metropolitan Police in the 1990s, the experience of other jurisdictions, both behind the Iron Curtain and in the United States and in Commonwealth countries, such as Australia and Canada, throw light on some of the key issues, such as the tension between survivor memory and the requirements of forensic justice. Moreover, this is a story with contemporary relevance. Germany is still prosecuting elderly Nazis and violently different narratives of resistance and collaboration continue to be a fault line in many parts of Eastern Europe. Anti-Semitism is a growing reality in many parts of Europe. And remarkably, truths and myths about Britain and Europe rooted in the Second World War can still be, well into the twenty-first century, a touchstone for political dissension.

Acknowledgements

The progenitor of this book was Dan Stone, Professor of Modern History at the University of London's Royal Holloway College, who suggested in 2019 that Oxford University Press would be interested in the subject matter. But the inspiration for the research can be largely attributed to Eli Rosenbaum, former head of the Office of Special Investigations in Washington, who has been a steadfast source of encouragement to one of the authors, Jon Silverman, since the late 1990s when they first met. Sincere thanks are also due to Martin Dean, also Washington-based, who was one of the two historians attached to Scotland Yard's War Crimes Unit, and who has been unfailingly helpful in checking facts and ensuring that interpretations were based on evidence rather than supposition. Thomas Will, Chief Investigator of the *Zentrale Stelle* in Ludwigsburg, was most generous with his time and expertise when we visited Germany's war crimes hub in 2022.

In London, Philip Rubenstein, former secretary of the All-Party Parliamentary War Crimes Group, has been a good friend to the project, acting as a first reader of some of the chapters and offering sound advice. His then close colleague, Jon (now Lord) Mendelsohn, has provided invaluable recollections on the period immediately before and after the passage of the War Crimes Act in 1991. Stephen Ankier, an independent Holocaust historian, has been a willing sounding board when discussing names of suspects and thanks are owed to Efraim Zuroff, of the Simon Wiesenthal Center in Jerusalem, who has made it his life's work to track down Nazis and prod governments into taking legislative action. We're grateful for the input of the BBC reporter Nick Southall, whose own investigation into Stanislaw Chrzanowski has added depth to Chapter 7 on the Holocaust in Slonim.

It goes without saying that archival research underpins a book of this nature and we have benefited from the cooperation of the following institutions: the Special Collections at the Hartley Library, University of

Southampton; the Wiener Library in London; the National Archives at Kew; the National Archives of Scotland in Edinburgh; and the Shapell Center in Maryland, attached to the United States Holocaust Memorial Museum. Senior Treasury Counsel, Sir John (Jonny) Nutting and defence barrister, William Clegg, have shared their personal experiences of the two UK war crimes prosecutions, as have Paul Harrison, former head of the Special Casework Division at the Crown Prosecution Service and Martin Lee, the solicitor who represented Anthony Sawoniuk. A special thank you is owed to lawyer Nicholas Bowers, who represented Szymon Serafinowicz, for providing a cache of documents which opened up fruitful lines of inquiry.

Finally, we pay tribute to the late David Cesarani, from whose expertise in Holocaust history both authors have benefited. His ground-breaking book, *Justice Delayed*, published in 1992, explained how the War Crimes Act came to be passed. Our mission has been to reveal what happened after it was.

Contents

Contents

List of Illustrations

Maps

Figures

Map 1 Map of Belarus, showing its location in the 'bloodlands' of Eastern Europe.

Map 2 Map showing location of massacres in Belarus, including Mir, Domachevo, and Slutsk.

Introduction

Whither Justice?

Beyond Nuremberg

On the first day of the Jewish Passover in April 1999, an English jury returned a verdict of guilty of murder on a 78-year-old man, born in what is now Belarus. The crimes of which he stood convicted took place fifty-seven years earlier in a portion of Eastern Europe aptly described by Timothy Snyder as 'bloodlands'.[1] The defendant was a hitherto anonymous police auxiliary, far removed in status from Hitler's 'paladins and Nazi functionaries' called to account at Nuremberg for war crimes.[2] Yet, the so-called 'small fry' who murdered Jews in countless towns, villages, and hamlets for at least three years left as indelible an imprint on the Shoah as those who operated the gas chambers at Auschwitz-Birkenau.[3]

The long tail of the Second World War is still impacting on Eastern Europe, with the chimera of dismantling 'Nazism' one of the stated pretexts for Russia's invasion of Ukraine in 2022. Just as the crimes of Hitler's perpetrators have periodically played out in courtrooms—from Nuremberg to Frankfurt, Warsaw to Jerusalem and beyond—so Putin's may yet face the verdict of war crimes trials, both domestic and international. Whether that happens or not, the pursuit of justice will provide

---

[1] Snyder, 2010 *Bloodlands.*
[2] Westermann, 2010 'Killers', in *The Oxford Handbook of Holocaust Studies*, ed. Hayes and Roth, p. 143.
[3] The terms 'Shoah' and 'Holocaust' will both be used in this book without discussion of etymological distinctions.

Safe Haven: The United Kingdom's Investigations into Nazi Collaborators and the Failure of Justice.
Jon Silverman and Robert Sherwood, Oxford University Press. © Jon Silverman and Robert Sherwood 2023.
DOI: 10.1093/oso/9780192855176.003.0001

lawyers, investigators, and academic researchers with meat to chew on for years to come.

Justice is a word which slips seamlessly into everyday discourse ranging from the banality of a disputed parking fine to a wrongful conviction for murder. Despite, or perhaps because of, its common usage, there is an overwhelming sense of inadequacy when applied to the Holocaust, the outcome of an enterprise 'not merely massive in scale but also bureaucratically organized and state-directed'.[4] The roots of the term 'justice' can be traced back through Latin to Greek, while both the Old and New Testaments provide layers of commentary and interpretation. The biblical incantation, 'an eye for an eye', represents the infliction of 'reciprocal mimetic violence'[5] which was enacted in wartime Germany as *Lynchjustiz*. Churchill's version of 'victor's justice' was the proposal that fifty to a hundred of the leading Nazis should be 'shot to death without reference to higher authority'.[6] The United States Assistant Secretary of War, John McCloy, countered that 'summary execution without trial is contrary to the fundamental conception of justice'. And since the American view prevailed, the creation of a multinational tribunal constituted as a unique court of law at Nuremberg has defined war crimes justice in the decades since.

The corpus of historiography on the Holocaust grows year on year and within that there is a smaller, but far from negligible focus on war crimes trials from which much can be learned. David Ben-Gurion called the trial of Eichmann in Jerusalem the 'Nuremberg of the Jewish people'. But, in purely juridical terms, that is a misleading analogy. The landmark prosecutions of the surviving Nazi leadership at the International Military Tribunal (IMT) at Nuremberg sought evidence primarily from captured German documentation. The Eichmann trial foregrounded live witness testimony. Studies of other trials in Poland, Germany, and elsewhere have teased out the degree to which there is acknowledgement that the Jewish Holocaust was central to the case being tried. Examination of Soviet 'show' trials of the 1960s, some in person, some

---

[4] Pendas, 2006 *The Frankfurt Auschwitz Trial, 1963–1965*, p. 2.
[5] Redekop, 2008 'A Post-Genocidal Justice of Blessing as an Alternative to a Justice of Violence: The Case of Rwanda', in *Peacebuilding in Traumatized Societies*, ed. Hart, p. 206.
[6] Overy 2001 *Interrogations: The Nazi Elite in Allied Hands, 1945*.

in absentia, illustrate the role of ideological triumphalism in the face of perceived Western atrophy. And at least one trial, that of Klaus Barbie in France in 1987, was as much about the host country and its post-war politics as it was about the defendant.

Trials are necessarily a site of convergence between law and history. As Erich Haberer has written (of the West German Nazi trials), both disciplines have their own 'rules and discourses' which must be observed.[7] David Fraser rightly reminds us that 'the agenda of historians and political scientists is not the agenda of lawyers, police, and judges…Law and History have different aims, different methodologies, and different fates in mind for their subjects.'[8]

This work might be characterized as 'historico-legal' in intent, rooted in the British tradition of empiricism—for example channelling the spirit of authors such as Ian Kershaw and Richard Evans—and pursues a path less well-trodden than preceding studies. The courtroom trial is a piece of public theatre. Literally so in the case of Adolf Eichmann, which was reconceived as a play, *The Man in the Glass Booth* by the actor-writer, Robert Shaw. This research concerns itself not with the spectacle of trials nor with the performative strategies of advocates but with the pathway intended to lead to a trial. The route to Nuremberg, via the London Conference which prepared the charter of the IMT, has been exhaustively plotted by historians. But not so the two criminal prosecutions in the United Kingdom, which, as the opening line of this Introduction suggests, is the locus for our point of departure. Of course, no equivalence is implied in terms of legal significance between Nuremberg and the UK prosecutions but it is, perhaps, even more remarkable that Nazi collaborators were forced to submit to forensic scrutiny half a century later, in a country which had not been occupied (if one excludes the Channel Islands). But this came at a cost and it is undeniable that the due process flagrantly denied by the Nazis to their victims was the very reason that the UK's belated instrumentalizing of justice fell so short.

---

[7] Haberer, 2005 'History and Justice: Paradigms of the Prosecution of Nazi Crimes', p. 510.
[8] Fraser, 2010 *Daviborshch's Cart*, p. 45.

The two UK prosecutions were the fruits of several years of investigations by police officers and historians necessarily carried out below the radar of public scrutiny. How did the detectives from the Metropolitan Police War Crimes Unit (WCU) go about this task, and what incriminatory or exculpatory details were they searching for? What constraints on prosecutions were placed by lawyers from the Crown Prosecution Service (CPS) and Treasury Counsel? We are able to fill in many of the knowledge gaps by interrogating some of those intimately involved and by examining a hitherto untapped resource, tapes and transcripts of police interviews with some of the key suspects. These include a platoon captain of a notorious Latvian killing unit and several of the Belarusian police auxiliaries considered for prosecution as well as video and audio recorded interviews with Szymon Serafinowicz, the first person in the UK to be charged, whose prosecution was eventually abandoned on the grounds of his dementia. Here we see him in a suburban police station, shortly after he was identified as a prime suspect, a man evidently in possession of his faculties, seemingly comfortable with telling his story in a mixture of broken English and Russian, and with a remarkable grasp of recall given his eighty-three years. This is history unmediated by lawyers or historians, as vivid as the first-hand memories of survivors which have underpinned foundational works such as Martin Gilbert's *The Holocaust* (1986).

The UK Faces its Past

One interpretation of justice, transactional though it might seem, is the investigatory search for 'evidence', and the building of a jurisprudential case, with the purpose of placing alleged perpetrators before a court. In the 1940s, in the retributive aftermath of the war, that court was a tribunal of military judges sitting in the British occupied zone of Germany. In the 1990s, responsibility for a verdict rested with a civilian jury at the Old Bailey in London. The unexpected resumption of inquiries in the 1990s, strongly opposed by many, offers unique opportunities for research. Unique in a juridical sense because England (and Wales) was the only jurisdiction in the Commonwealth to achieve a conviction when, in a bout of belated reassessment, many hundreds of suspected elderly Nazi collaborators, mainly from Eastern Europe, became the subject of criminal inquiries in England, Canada, Australia, New Zealand, and Scotland.

Unique also in a cultural sense. There are many paradigms of identity which define Britain's self-image in the twenty-first century and one of the most enduring is the narrative of an island nation standing alone against European tyranny during the Second World War. It is imagined as an uncomplicated parable of 'goodness' set against the 'evil' of Nazism. By contrast, the 'failure' to prosecute and convict more former Nazis and their collaborators in the decades after 1945 has neither tarnished this image nor troubled the national conscience. Perhaps the mistaken belief that the survivors merely wanted to be left alone to get on with their lives without being reminded, and reminding others, of the past was too firmly rooted. Unlike France, and the nations of Central and Eastern Europe occupied by the Nazis, 'the Holocaust is not embedded in the landscape of the English countryside'.[9] In 1979, Yehuda Bauer could justifiably tell a conference that 'nothing at all has been done in Britain' to engage with the Holocaust.[10]

In the last four decades, tentative engagement has flowered into 'Holocaust consciousness', an umbrella term for a steady accretion of cultural initiatives around memorialization, and a toolkit of educational programmes, demonstrating that the Holocaust has both an 'intrinsic and an instrumentalist significance'.[11] And it is worth asking whether this process interacted in any way with legal efforts to prosecute some of the surviving perpetrators and if so, how? In 1995, teaching the Holocaust gained a new prominence in the revised National Curriculum, a development which underpinned Andy Pearce's contention that 'Britain was thus more aware and receptive to the Holocaust than any time previously'.[12] The year 1995 marked the fiftieth anniversary of the final defeat of Nazi Germany and of the liberation of Bergen-Belsen, the

---

[9] Smith, 2002 *Making Memory: Creating Britain's First Holocaust Centre*, p. 160.
[10] Cited by Pearce, 2014 *Holocaust Consciousness in Contemporary Britain*, p. 90.
[11] David Bloxham, speaking at a launch event at the Wiener Library, 19 April 2021, for the publication of *The Palgrave Handbook of Britain and the Holocaust*, ed. Lawson and Pearce.
[12] Pearce, 2014 *Holocaust Consciousness in Contemporary Britain*, p. 193.

signifier of the Holocaust in Britain's immediate post-war narrative, even though it was not a death camp. And in that same year, preparations for Britain's first war crimes trial gathered pace with the announcement of the first prosecution under the War Crimes Act 1991.

Yet, as we demonstrate, there was a striking dissonance between the rising tide of Holocaust 'awareness' and the thinking of those in pursuit of a juridical reckoning, whether police or lawyers. How then should we consider the one criminal conviction of a Nazi collaborator achieved in the UK? If it served the cause of justice to disinter a 57-year-old act of violence committed in the context of a world war and pronounce judgement, what chain of decisions led to that outcome? To frame one of the questions we ask in the terms expressed by Lawrence Douglas: did 'the law create a coherent, judicially manageable response to unprecedented crimes'?[13] Or did the law, and lawyers, contrive to turn the criticism that the war crimes legislation was 'too little, too late' into a self-fulfilling prophecy? We can best respond by parsing Douglas's reflection. 'Coherent' would be an over-generous description of the approach taken by the English legal authorities, as we explain. As for 'judicially manageable', the answer must be a heavily qualified 'yes' but achieved by effectively untethering the charges from the enormity of the Final Solution, as Weinert puts it, placing 'the crimes in a conventional dialogue of murder'.[14] This did not mean dismissing the geopolitical context in which the offences had been committed but rejecting the view taken by the United States, for example, through a Supreme Court ruling, that complicity could be assumed if a suspect had been a member of a notorious *Einsatzgruppen* squad.

Hannah Arendt famously critiqued the Eichmann prosecution on the grounds that a national court should not arrogate to itself for 'political' reasons the right to try genocide and crimes against humanity.[15] The Anglo-Saxon nations which faced the issue of prosecuting war crimes in the 1980s and 1990s grappled with this question in another way. In the case of Australia, the legislation which amended the 1945 War Crimes

---

[13]   Douglas, 2001 *The Memory of Judgment*, p. 5.
[14]   Weinert, 2004 'Cosmopolitan Law – and Cruelty – on Trial', pp. 38–9.
[15]   Arendt, 1977 *Eichmann in Jerusalem: A Report on the Banality of Evil*.

Act incorporated the crimes against humanity or genocide element of international law into the statute. Sub-section 3 specifies in terms 'that the act be done (1) in the course of political, racial or religious persecution; or (2) with intent to destroy in whole, or in part, a national, ethnic, racial or religious group'. The wording of the UK War Crimes Act 1991 is spare in the extreme but finds space to include the discourse of the Geneva Conventions which prohibit acts that contravene 'the laws and customs of war'.

But the linguistic formula deriving from internationally recognized norms does not change the fact that common law precedent was always paramount, meaning the need to convince a jury of a suspect's guilt in specific circumstances, at specific times, underpinned by credible eyewitness evidence. David Fraser, who examined the three Australian prosecutions, has described the 'Anglo-Saxon' approach as constructing 'a limited tale of *mens rea*, *actus reus*, identity and so forth in which the Shoah...is displaced somewhere near or beyond the boundary of legal practice'.[16]

For the UK prosecutors, developments in international law deriving from the Nuremberg tribunals were of contextual interest only. Rajka Vlahovic, who headed the Crown Prosecution Service casework team which prepared the trial of Andrzej Sawoniuk, said: 'At first, the CPS was looking at prosecutions from a war crimes perspective but then we took the decision that these were "straight" murder cases and proceeded accordingly.'[17]

When asked whether any members of the Metropolitan Police War Crimes Unit had any knowledge of the Holocaust, Detective Chief Inspector Dermot McDermott, replied: 'No, only from school. It was a murder investigation. Never lost sight of that.'[18]

From an instrumentalist viewpoint, this made sense. The investigators and prosecutors knew what they needed to do to mount a winnable courtroom contest in front of a jury. But it could be plausibly argued that the gain of one conviction was achieved at the cost of promoting a

---

[16] Fraser, 2010 *Daviborshch's Cart*, p. 312.
[17] Rajka Vlahovic interview with author, 25 February 2020.
[18] McDermott interview with author, 29 August 2017.

wider appreciation of how the actions of a cohort of Belorussian police-men fitted into the wider tableau of the Nazi Holocaust. In this, there are strong parallels with the planning and conduct of the post-war Belsen trial, in which, for the British public, the Jewish genocide was, at most, a spectral presence only discernible through newsreel footage.

There is little dispute that the Eichmann prosecution was the first to consciously put the Holocaust on trial, with the defendant cast as a vec-tor for the entire criminal enterprise. Douglas argues that it 'served to *create* the Holocaust.'[19] The Eichmann case opened the door to a second wave of juridical reckonings with the Nazi past in the Frankfurt Auschwitz trials. Israel's motivation in trying Eichmann was clear: to show the world that the Final Solution had failed and that a self-confident Jewish nation had emerged from the ashes of the European genocide. Whereas historians offer different interpretations of the stra-tegic approach taken by the West German courts in the 1960s and 1970s to the major concentration camp trials. For Mary Fulbrook, these pro-secutions 'generally chose to focus on the personal motivation and "excess deeds" of defendants, who were seen as being accused of com-mitting individual crimes rather than being part of a wider crime complex.'[20]

Erich Haberer, though, argues that West German prosecutors, follow-ing the lead of the first director of the Ludwigsburg *Zentrale Stelle*, Erwin Schüle, marshalled evidence according to a 'cluster approach' to demonstrate that a unit was operating to a systemic 'murder complex' (*Tatkomplex*) enforced by the Nazi state.[21]

What is indisputable is that since the reunification of Germany and, more particularly, since a landmark legal ruling of 2011 following the Demjanjuk case, the pendulum has swung decisively towards a focus on the 'wider crime complex' of the Final Solution, represented by the net-work of concentration and death camps and those who served in them, however 'minor' their role. As Mary Fulbrook points out, the impact on the fabric of the nation has been profound: 'Perhaps most striking of all

---

[19] Douglas, 2001 *The Memory of Judgment*, p. 6 (emphasis in the original).
[20] Fulbrook, 2018 *Reckonings*, p. 349.
[21] Haberer, 2005 'History and Justice: Paradigms of the Prosecution of Nazi Crimes'.

is the way the Holocaust has become central to the identity and culture of the Federal Republic of Germany, incorporated into its material and moral fiber [sic].'[22]

Even more remarkably, deep into the second decade of the twenty-first century, Germany's war crimes agency at Ludwigsburg gained approval to extend its jurisdictional reach to include a suspect who was not German, who had been investigated but not prosecuted in another country, and was living outside German borders, in this case, the United Kingdom. Recounted in Chapter 7, the story of German interest in Stanislaw Chrzanowski, a former auxiliary policeman (*Schutzmannschaft*) whose crimes were committed in Belarus, can be read either as a rebuke to the UK authorities, which declined to prosecute on the grounds of insufficient direct eyewitness evidence, or as an idiosyncratic interpretation of the principle of universal jurisdiction. As Andrej Umansky, a legal researcher at the University of Cologne commented in 2018: 'I would say we are pushing the law to its maximum and showing that crimes…will be punished even seventy years afterwards because they were so grave.'[23]

The process of legal accountability for the Nazi project has now out-lived the Second World War by nearly eight decades, though acknow-ledgement in Germany that the country bore a unique responsibility for the Holocaust did not begin to take shape until the trials of the 1960s and was not fully formed until the 1980s. *Vergangenheitsbewältigung* ('overcoming the past') is inevitably a work in progress. The continuing need to seek judicial expiation for the sins of the grandparents and great-grandparents—in this context, the sin of leaving unpunished many thousands of perpetrators in earlier decades—perhaps requires less deconstruction than does the United Kingdom's investigations of the 1990s. Which makes it all the more surprising that even those few scholars who have studied the two English prosecutions (Hirsh, Bloxham, Laputska) have not strayed far from the courtroom, sidestep-ping the more intriguing contextual questions. For example, how did the English legal authorities determine who merited prosecution, and

---

[22] Fulbrook, 2018 *Reckonings*, p. 4.
[23] https://www.bbc.co.uk/news/uk-england-shropshire-43441118 (accessed 30 March 2021).

which victims were deemed more worthy of juridical acknowledgement? In seeking to answer these questions, we lay bare in detail just how inconsistently the UK's 'normative' procedures were applied.

Command Responsibility and Jewish Victims

On 29 March 1999, as the jury was being sent out to consider its verdict in the case against Anthony (Andrzej) Sawoniuk, the press corps at the Old Bailey was handed a four-page document prepared by the Metropolitan Police War Crimes Unit.[24] It was intended to help those not immersed in the detail of eight years of war crimes inquiries appreciate the remit and magnitude of the task faced by the police as they conducted a global search for evidence. In fact, though, this utilitarian briefing document contained information which casts a fresh light on the methodology followed by the UK investigators, suggesting that the search for *prosecutable* war criminals was circumscribed from the very outset.

It sets out the four criteria 'to be met before a suspect was considered a serious candidate for prosecution'. The first three, relating to eyewitness evidence, identification, and provable allegations of mass murder of non-combatants, are uncontroversial. The fourth, though, is in a different category: 'iv) proof that the defendant was in a position of command, responsibility is also an important factor in deciding on the defendant's culpability'.

The clear implication of this criterion is that a jury would believe that a person 'in command' bore a greater degree of responsibility than those who were 'merely' following orders, though it stands in contrast to the Charter adopted by the International Military Tribunal at Nuremberg in 1946. Article 8 stated: 'The fact that the defendant acted pursuant to an order of his Government or of a *superior* [authors' emphasis] shall not free him from responsibility but may be considered in mitigation of punishment if the Tribunal determines that justice so requires.'

---

[24] *Briefing Re-War Crimes Unit—General Information.*

The 'command' criterion also appears to make a value judgement about culpability which is plainly at odds with the findings of historians who have studied collaboration in Belorussia and Ukraine. Martin Dean, the senior historian attached to Scotland Yard's War Crimes Unit, has written:

> Individual local policemen appear to have distinguished themselves, particularly in the subsequent search for and shooting of Jews who went into hiding.... The willingness to carry out such actions can be seen in the numerous descriptions from a wide variety of sources depicting local policemen *acting on their own initiative* [our emphasis] in accordance with the general policy.[25]

Seeking to prosecute only those who had a command role would necessarily have had a limiting effect on the number of potential trials because such suspects would, on the whole, have been older and thus, by the 1990s, frailer, that is, if they hadn't already died. Historian David Cesarani drew the conclusion that 'The exclusion of those who were not officers indicated that a decision was quietly made by law officers, presumably in concert with the then Home Office, to ignore so-called "small fry", no matter how bloody their hands.'[26]

Detective Chief Inspector Dermot McDermott was adamant that all WCU officers 'fully understood' the evidential criteria required: 'All four standards of evidence were, in my view, of equal importance. In reality, the vast majority of witnesses could only recall the details of the person "in command" of the mass murders and not the shooters, therefore failing to meet one or both of the first two criteria.'[27] However, McDermott's argument is undermined by the evidence given in the trial of Andrzej Sawoniuk by those who had known the defendant for many years and had no difficulty in identifying him (see Chapter 6).

William Clegg QC, who defended Andrzej Sawoniuk, added: 'I thought it [i.e. the command criterion] was a sensible decision because there

---

[25] Dean, 2000 *Collaboration in the Holocaust*, p. 101.
[26] Cesarani, 2001 'Getting Away with Murder', *The Guardian*, 25 April, p. 2.
[27] McDermott email to author, 5 March 2018.

were never going to be many trials and the prosecution was aware of how a jury might react to a foot soldier being tried.'[28]

It is impossible to know what weight should be placed on the 'command criterion' because there is no empirical evidence, or none which has been vouchsafed by the CPS, to show that a suspect 'failed' the prosecution test only on the grounds that his role or rank was too lowly. Somewhat confusingly, Sir John Nutting, the Treasury Counsel, whose advice to the Attorney-General was the determining factor in prosecutions, expressed astonishment when shown the police briefing document:

> I've never seen this note before and frankly I would have been very surprised if we had forborn to prosecute someone just because they were not of high enough rank. Certainly, there was no rubric about rank. If there had been, I doubt whether Sawoniuk would have been tried because he wasn't really a 'commander' in the sense one understands it.[29]

Nevertheless, it is a fact that at the point where a small handful of cases was being considered for prosecution—some six or seven—the 'command criterion' became highly significant. Paul Harrison, who became head of the war crimes Casework Division at the CPS in 1994, said:

We identified a small team from Treasury Counsel's room to advise us and the Attorney-General. During that process, a decision was made to only pursue cases that met the following criteria:

1. Allegations of murder only (no problems there)
2. Had strong ID evidence
3. Had eye witness evidence
4. *The suspect was in a position of authority* [our italics].[30]

The epistemic value of a study which links the military-led investigations of the immediate post-war period with the inquiries of the 1990s

[28] William Clegg interview with author, 28 April 2021.
[29] Nutting interview with author, 28 May 2021.   [30] Harrison email, 12 July 2021.

under the civilian authority of police and lawyers is that illuminating contrasts emerge. Seventy per cent of the inmates of Belsen at the time of its liberation by the British army in April 1945 were Jewish but the Royal Warrant issued in the summer of 1945 pointedly did not identify specific victim groups. As Donald Bloxham points out: 'Clearly and intentionally, it also prevented explicit jurisprudential recognition of the scale of the Jewish fate.'[31]

In comparison, in the 1990s, senior lawyers, known as Treasury Counsel, responsible for drawing up the ground rules for prosecution, made the decision—never publicized—to focus efforts only on those cases where the intended victims were Jews. Was this belated redress for the 'de-Judaicization' of the Belsen and other trials of the earlier era? No, British lawyers have a more transactional attitude towards the demands of the courtroom than that! Martin Dean explained that:

> The Metropolitan Police at an early stage found strong evidence in Belorussia against specific Belorussian local policemen for participation in anti-partisan reprisals against civilians but the lawyers consulted at that time were not prepared to prosecute in these cases. They feared that the clear evidence of 'partisan resistance' linked to these incidents would considerably weaken the prosecution case.... They were looking 'ideally' for clear-cut incidents, particularly the murder of Jewish civilians *purely for their race* [our italics].[32]

Sir John Nutting, whose principal decision it was, put it like this:

> We certainly decided at an early stage that we would not be looking at crimes perpetrated against [non-Jewish] civilians who lived in villages, even if the victims were innocent of partisan activity. We felt it would have unnecessarily complicated the prosecution because such crimes would have been called war reprisals.[33]

In most common law jurisdictions, the prosecutor's code invariably takes account of the likely winnability of any case brought to court and

---

[31] Bloxham, 2001 *Genocide on Trial*, p. 76. [32] Martin Dean email, 2 February 2001.
[33] Nutting interview with author, 28 May 2021.

this involves not only weighing the strength of evidence against the accused but also assessing how a jury might perceive the vulnerability of the victim. Looking at the war crimes cases through this narrowly focused perspective, it may be understandable that the murder of an unarmed Jewish civilian would appear more 'clear-cut' to a jury than the killing of a non-Jewish Belorussian partisan.[34] However, this was not the only possible lens through which the UK legal authorities could have approached prosecutions under the War Crimes Act.

It is sometimes forgotten that despite the sound and fury which accompanied the War Crimes Bill when it was presented to Parliament in 1990, the legislation did not create a new offence or offences. It merely conferred jurisdiction on English courts to try those who had not been British citizens at the times of the offence(s). And Section 1(1) contains two clauses which, under a less constrained interpretation from that applied by Treasury Counsel, would have widened considerably the scope of the evidential quest and the prosecution of perpetrators. The Act states that proceedings could be brought if the offence 'was committed during the period 1st September 1939 and ending 5th June 1945 in a place which, at the time, was part of Germany or under German occupation; and (a) constituted a violation of the laws and customs of war.'[35]

These clauses distinguish this piece of legislation from any other on the statute book and cast a different and more problematic light on the CPS decision to treat the prosecutions as 'straight' murder cases. For example, the legislation, though only a few brief clauses long, was sufficiently flexible to have embraced the killing of non-Jewish civilians as prosecutable crimes on at least two grounds. The phrase 'violations of the laws and customs of war' was taken directly from the Nuremberg IMT Charter, which had determined that 'murder, ill treatment or deportations of civilians in occupied territory' were war crimes. All of these crimes and many more had been committed in Belorussia, as

---

[34] The decision to exclude non-Jewish victims from the prosecution criteria has echoes of the argument between the historian Yehuda Bauer and Simon Wiesenthal in the late 1970s about whether to include non-Jews murdered by the Nazis among the victims of the Holocaust. Wiesenthal was in favour, Bauer against (see Zuroff, 1994 *Occupation: Nazi Hunter*, p. 9).

[35] Although the Western Allies recognized 8 May as Victory in Europe Day, the Soviet Union dated the formal end of hostilities from 5 June, when they accepted the German surrender in the Berlin Declaration.

illustrated in Chapter 7 by the recollections of a Catholic priest in the town of Slonim where the wave of slaughter during the Nazi occupation included almost as many non-Jews as Jews.[36]

Moreover, during the trial of Andrzej Sawoniuk, such crimes formed part of the 'admissible evidence' presented by the prosecution in order to point to a 'continuing course of conduct' by the defendant, leaving observers, and perhaps jurors, to wonder why these murders, of non-Jewish civilians, were sufficiently germane to the case but apparently not enough to be included in the indictment.

We touch on the issue of partisans in Belorussia in a later chapter, and, in particular, whether the 'moral ambiguity' of some of their actions provided a justifiable cover for Nazi atrocities. Alex J. Kay and David Stahel, in anatomizing the crimes of the Wehrmacht on the Eastern Front, have written of '[t]he organized and disciplined staging of executions of partisans, offering a feeble guise of legality to what were often nothing better than summary reprisals'.[37]

Captured German documents show that to instil compliance with the Occupation, orders were issued to deploy whatever violence against non-combatants local commanders thought appropriate: 'even very serious measures of force taken against the *population in general* [our emphasis] in order to force, if necessary, the people's willingness to take active steps against the partisans. Our principle must be "Fight terror with terror".'[38]

The reality was that neither the Germans nor their local police proxies regarded the partisans as legitimate military opponents due the protections afforded under International Humanitarian Law. In other words, they were civilians with access to weapons, and it was, at least, arguable, and justiciable, that their gruesome fates were covered by the 1991 War Crimes Act.

There is another significant point here which illustrates the interpretive gap separating lawyers from historians when addressing war crimes

---

[36] Interview with Father Kazimir Adamovitch in Slonim, March 1996.

[37] Kay and Stahel, 2020 'Crimes of the Wehrmacht: A Re-evaluation', p. 110.

[38] The head of *Einsatzgruppe* A, Dr Franz Stahlecker, Report, 29 September 1941, copy in Hartley Library Special Collections, University of Southampton, Collection MS 408_A1057 2/39, p. 468.

justice. The legal mind sees clear distinctions between those who committed atrocities, their victims, and, in the cases under consideration in this book, the 'partisans'. But the historical reality was far more fluid. Some of the *Schutzmannschaften*, when they could see they were backing the losing side in 1943–4, joined the partisans. Some of those labelled as 'collaborators' for helping the Nazis hunt Jews who had escaped *Aktionen*, also at other times and with varying motivations, acted as saviours. Indeed, there is evidence that Szymon Serafinowicz spared some of the Jewish civilians who were living in the Mir and Turets districts under his administrative authority.

These important nuances in patterns of behaviour are picked apart by Gorycki and Kapralsi in their study of persecution of the Roma, suggesting that some of the determinants of collaboration are located in the level of integration and social interaction between different groups.[39] Georgij Elper, who was a child in the Minsk ghetto, later recounted overhearing a *Schutzmann* warning a Jewish girl about an impending pogrom.[40] Without understanding the relational context, should he be classified as collaborator or rescuer or perhaps neither?

From a historical, if not a juridical perspective, the policy followed by the lawyers in valorizing the suffering of the Jews and relegating the 'others' in the hierarchy of victimhood could almost be seen as a riposte to the Soviet designation of all those killed, whether Jewish or not, as 'victims of fascism'. It is interesting to speculate on how the prosecution might have been framed had the War Crimes Act been passed a decade earlier because when Britain's first permanent cultural memorial to the Holocaust was inaugurated in London's Hyde Park in 1983, Jewish particularity was deliberately eschewed and the site was presented as a commemoration of eleven million victims, a decision 'in many ways emblematic of the position then held by the Holocaust in British culture and society. Neither completely specific nor wholly universalized.'[41] By 1995, the catalyst of a criminal trial had transformed this liminal status

[39] Gorycki and Kapralsi, 2019 'Patterns of Collaboration and Genocide Against the Roma: The Case of Poland during the Second World War', in *Collaboration in the Holocaust and World War II in Eastern Europe*, ed. Black et al.

[40] Cited by Baranova, 2016 'Collaborators, Bystanders or Rescuers: The Role of Local Citizens in the Holocaust in Nazi-Occupied Belarus', in *The Holocaust and European Societies*, ed. Löw and Bajohr, p. 98.

[41] Pearce, 2014 *Holocaust Consciousness in Contemporary Britain*, p. 95.

into the unequivocally Jewish Shoah, with the countless other casualties of German barbarism in Eastern Europe left on the margins.

These important shifts in perception reflect 'the law's struggle to locate terms of representation and judgment adequate to the task of doing justice to the Holocaust'.[42] The historian Christopher Browning, who appeared as an expert witness at the Sawoniuk trial (Chapter 5), has suggested that a way of making the task more manageable is to disaggregate the Holocaust into three 'clusters of genocidal projects', beginning with euthanasia and racial purification aimed at the Sinti and Roma within Germany's pre-1939 borders and ending with the Final Solution.[43] The second genocide, which was defined by the project known as *lebensraum*, was the removal, whether by enslavement, deportation, or mass murder, of the mainly Slav populations of Eastern Europe to make way for Germans of Aryan stock. As the political scientist, Charles King, puts it: 'Pulling apart the many threads of the Holocaust allows scholars to understand the origins and evolution of policy and practice in ways that thinking of it as a single happening does not.'[44]

Allowing for the fact that lawyers are not required to be historical scholars, a cogent criminal case could have been assembled which did not rely on Jewish 'exclusivity' but placed due weight on the racial persecution and destruction inflicted on the Slavic population of Belorussia which, in percentage terms, suffered more than in any occupied territory. Timothy Snyder has written: 'By the end of the war, half the population of Belarus had been either killed or moved. This cannot be said of any other European country.'[45]

The decision by the CPS to limit prosecutions to cases where the victims were Jews is hard to reconcile with the declaration that 'normative' criminal procedures were followed. The indictment was murder not racially aggravated murder, so focusing on the ethnic identity of the victim suggests strongly that the 'war crimes perspective', which the lawyers were keen to downplay, did indeed have some bearing on their thinking.

---

[42] Douglas, 2001 *The Memory of Judgment*, p. 5.
[43] Browning, 2010 'The Nazi Empire', in *The Oxford Handbook of Genocide Studies*, ed. Bloxham and Moses, p. 407.
[44] King, 2012 'Can There Be a Political Science of the Holocaust?', p. 327.
[45] Snyder, 2010 *Bloodlands*, p. 251.

Moreover, this approach may well have been grounded in the supposition that a juror of the 1990s, familiar with media images of dehumanized prisoners incarcerated behind the barbed wire of Serb-run concentration camps in Bosnia, would likely make the connection—as did some European policy makers—with the racialized persecution of the Jews half a century earlier. For example, readers of one of the bigger-selling newspapers would have noted the commentary which declared that 'the names Omarska and Trnopolje have been carved alongside Belsen, Buchenwald and Auschwitz on the bloody tombstone marking man's inhumanity in war'.[46]

As a comparison to the CPS policy, Australia's Special Investigations Unit (SIU) imposed no criteria on its inquiries into Nazi collaborators: 'The SIU did not concentrate on any particular group of victims, Jewish or otherwise, nor did it single out any ethnic group to investigate.'[47]

The Legal Director of the SIU, Graham Blewitt, expressed surprise when told that the CPS had worked to its own prescriptive formula. 'In Sydney, there was never any discussion along these lines, in fact, it never entered our minds.'[48] Had the legal authorities in the UK published a final report, as their Australian equivalent did, their decision-making might have become part of a wider public debate and required some justification. As it was, this creative and contestable interpretation of the War Crimes Act was quietly archived without comment.

It is important to stress that these unresolved questions are not of mere theoretical interest. As Martin Dean says, the Metropolitan Police found compelling evidence of killings committed by Belorussian *Schutzmannschaften* against civilians and hoped that some of the perpetrators could be charged (Fig. I.1). A reading of the transcripts of their police interviews leaves little doubt about guilt and it is arguable that at least one or two could have been taken to court had the prosecutors been prepared to place a greater degree of confidence in the jury to distinguish between partisans and unarmed civilians. However, the CPS feared that if the defence made a successful challenge over what

---

[46] *Daily Mirror*, 7 August 1992.
[47] From the *Report of the Investigations of War Criminals in Australia* (Sydney, NSW, 1993).
[48] Blewitt interview with author, Sydney, 17 February 2020.

Fig. I.1 German gendarmes and local police auxiliaries at the *Schutzmannschaftsposten* near Kiev, December 1942. Bundesarchiv, Bild 121-1500/Scherer.

constituted a 'war crime', a judge might rule in their favour, thus jeopardizing any further prosecutions.

Those who cite the War Crimes Act as the UK's admirable, if belated, repayment of a moral debt owed to the victims of Nazi-related war crimes should also acknowledge what Mary Fulbrook has called the 'significant disjuncture…between official myths about "dealing with the past" on the one hand and the extent to which the overwhelming majority of perpetrators actually evaded the net of justice on the other'.[49]

It is also noteworthy that, at the very time that the English prosecuting authorities were shrinking the contours of the War Crimes Act, the House of Lords in the Pinochet judgement was expanding the possibilities of punishing egregious breaches of laws and conventions.[50] And contemporaneously, the Treaty of Rome was establishing the ground rules of the first International Criminal Court.

---

[49] Fulbrook, 2018 *Reckonings*, p. 7.
[50] *R v. Bow St Metropolitan Stipendiary Magistrate, ex parte Pinochet Ugarte (no 2)* (House of Lords), 25 November 1998 [2000] 1 at 84. AC 61.

This self-imposed limitation on potential trials is but one example of an English exceptionalism which constitutes an abiding theme of this work. It is to be found in a palpable lack of transparency about the eight-year period of investigations between the passage of the War Crimes Act in 1991 and the successful prosecution of Sawoniuk in 1999, to the extent that it would be little exaggeration to say that more has been disclosed about Poland's war crimes prosecutions during an era of Communist rule, thanks to the work of researchers such as Finder and Prusin, than the UK's.[51]

On the 'credit' side, knowledge about the role played by the *Schutzmannschaften* in Belarus has been immeasurably enhanced by the access granted to archives hitherto closed to Western historians. Martin Dean's experience gained from working with the Australian SIU was put to excellent use when he made the transition to the War Crimes Unit at Scotland Yard, fulfilling, at least in part, a post-war UK commitment to 'provide... an authoritative and impartial record to which future historians may turn for truth'.[52]

However, when Canada's Justice Department organized a colloquium in Ottawa in November 1998 on 'war crimes cases as educational and historical tools', there was no representative present from either the Crown Prosecution Service or Scotland Yard, despite the participation of investigators and lawyers from Canada, the United States, and Australia.[53] Whether this was wholly attributable to the comment of the trial judge in the Serafinowicz and Sawoniuk prosecutions, Mr Justice Potts, who said, in terms, that he did not wish to preside over a 'history lesson', must be a matter of speculation.[54]

This reticence (to put it generously) is all the more striking given the tumultuous provenance of the war crimes legislation, which took place amid accusations of special pleading by 'a vindictive world-wide Jewish

---

[51] Finder and Prusin, 2018 *Justice Behind the Iron Curtain*.

[52] The words of Sir Hartley Shawcross, Britain's chief prosecutor at the International Military Tribunal at Nuremberg. *Trial of the Major War Criminals Before the International Military Tribunal Nuremberg, 14 November 1945–1 October 1946*, 42 vols. (Nuremberg Military Tribunal 1947), 3:92.

[53] Held 11–13 November 1998. One of the authors delivered a paper.

[54] Process hearing in the Serafinowicz case, March 1996.

lobby,'[55] as well as complaints about the un-Britishness of 'retrospective' law which led to a constitutional battle between the two Houses of Parliament before the legislation reached the statute book in 1991.[56] Yet, unlike the legal authorities in the other Commonwealth jurisdictions, Canada, Australia, and New Zealand, which conducted war crimes prosecutions in the 1980s and 1990s, the UK produced no concluding report, neither the Metropolitan Police nor the CPS placing anything in the public domain to mark a unique juridical enterprise. Even Scotland, which carried out its own inquiries under the aegis of the Crown Office, with a notable lack of success, produced a heavily redacted report (more of which later). This omission on the part of the English legal establishment—which mirrors the absence of a concluding report by the Judge Advocate General's office in the 1940s—will come as little surprise to researchers who, like the present authors, have become wearily accustomed to requests for access to government and police documents on matters of public interest and historical significance being refused. It does a signal disservice to scholarship which this book is intended to redress.

Investigating the Investigators

The collective focus of scholars on the trial as a litmus test for establishing the efficacy of war crimes 'justice' has drawn attention away from the investigators whose efforts form the first stage of the quest for evidence. This book provides the first comprehensive account from inside the Metropolitan Police War Crimes Unit through interviews with police officers who travelled the globe searching for surviving witnesses to crimes. Often they were accompanied by lawyers from the Special Casework Division of the Crown Prosecution Service, whose decisions were a crucial link in the chain of actions which led on to the trial advice of Treasury Counsel and ultimately to the Attorney-General, on whose

[55] Cesarani, 1992 *Justice Delayed*, p. 7.
[56] The Conservative government employed the rarely used Parliament Act to force through the legislation. See Cesarani, 1992 *Justice Delayed* for a full account.

authority alone a prosecution could be sanctioned. Although one or two of these sources have spoken about their role in the Sawoniuk case, there are wider insights to be learned to enable the drawing of informed comparisons between the legal efforts of the UK and those of other jurisdictions.

It can be said with certainty that the one case which led to a conviction in 1999 has left little or no mark on public awareness in the UK. One of the authors of this work had an abrasive confrontation with the suspect, Sawoniuk, captured on camera and shown on the main evening television news bulletin before he was charged, and a picture of Sawoniuk menacing a photographer with his walking stick appeared in newspapers but other than that there was no identifying trope to anchor the case in the public consciousness. By contrast, the images of the British army's liberation of Bergen-Belsen on 15 April 1945, showing the SS guards forced at gunpoint to carry skeletal corpses for disposal in giant pits, are part of the familiar iconography by which we have come to understand 'the nature of the Nazi regime and/or the German people'.[57] Thus we find no basis for David Fraser's, albeit tentative, suggestion that 'the Sawoniuk trial may nonetheless have played a broader ideological, ethical and pedagogical role in the construction of the Holocaust in British public memory'.[58]

Tony Kushner argued persuasively that precisely because Belsen was liberated by British troops it occupies a place in the national memory symbolic of Britain's honourable war rather than as a *lieu de mémoire* of Jewish suffering.[59] It also conveniently masks all those aspects of UK policy both before and during the war which prolonged rather than alleviated the agony of Europe's Jews. The post-war accounts of the official hangman, Albert Pierrepoint, dispatching the 'archetypal' Nazis, Josef Kramer and Irma Grese on the scaffold reinforced the false idea that the nation which ended the tyranny of enslavement and murder went on to deliver a purifying justice for the victims of Nazism. The reality was somewhat different. Although the first Belsen hearing, in a British

---

[57] Kushner, 2013 *Belsen for Beginners*, p. 230.
[58] Fraser, 2005 *Law After Auschwitz*, p. 296.
[59] Kushner, 1991 *Jews in British Society, Vol. 2.*

military court, took place only five months after the liberation of the camp, Donald Bloxham suggests that the British government remained, at best, lukewarm about trials and investigations and, at worst, apathetic.[60] In any case, the Royal Warrant, published on 18 June 1945, confined prosecutions to crimes committed against Allied victims. In a spirit of either cynicism or naivety, it was expected that the victimization of Jews would be left to German courts to address.[61] In a sense then, the process of detaching prosecution policy from the enormity of the Holocaust began at the outset and, after an interruption of half a century, resumed in the 1990s.

The common thread between the two eras can be seen at work in attitudes towards the disputed 'command' criterion to determine whether suspects were deemed worthy of charging. Sir John Nutting QC points to Churchill's often-quoted comment in the House of Commons in October 1948 that 'British policy should draw a sponge across the crimes and horrors of the past' and end trials.[62] Nutting gave this explanation for his own thinking when, half a century later, it fell to him to consider whether to recommend charges:

> We were very conscious of British policy as enunciated by Sir Winston, and what worried us was being criticized for going after the small fry, foot soldiers as it were, when much bigger fish had been allowed to go scot free after the war. And of course, one of the complaints made by opponents of the War Crimes Act was that to change the law to catch these little fish was wrong and unseemly.[63]

This explanation deserves further scrutiny on a number of counts. Churchill made his observation as British control over its zone of occupation in Germany was drawing to a close and a newly created Federal Republic of West Germany was waiting in the wings. It is clear that he

---

[60] Bloxham, 2003 'British War Crimes Trial Policy in Germany, 1945–1957: Implementation and Collapse', p. 118.

[61] Jones, 1990 'British Policy Towards German Crimes Against German Jews, 1939–45', p. 366.

[62] Hansard House of Commons Parliamentary Debates (hereafter HC Deb), 28 October 1948, vol. 457.

[63] Sir John Nutting interview with author, 31 August 2020.

was articulating a view, shared by the Labour government, that the UK should no longer assume responsibility for investigating and prosecuting war criminals before military courts in the British zone in Germany. There is nothing on the public record to suggest that Whitehall even contemplated, let alone dismissed, the possibility of trying ex-Nazis or collaborators who had somehow managed to arrive in Britain. The jurisdictional position was made clear in a debate in the Lords in May 1949 by Viscount Simon, the former Lord Chancellor, who said that the policy decision concerned only trials before international tribunals and stated 'we are not dealing with the administration of our own domestic criminal law'.[64]

Hence to 'pray in aid' Churchill shows, at the very least, a lack of historical literacy. Moreover, it was generally accepted both by supporters and opponents of the War Crimes Act that, with the possible exceptions of Antanas Gecas—whose case we discuss in Chapter 4 and Harijs Svikeris in Chapter 3—all of those collaborators likely to be caught in the net after 1991 would be 'little fish'. Nobody harboured the illusion that a major Nazi war criminal had survived unremarked in the UK into the 1990s. Though technically fitting the criterion of a commander, Szymon Serafinowicz, the first person to be prosecuted, was, in the words of William Clegg QC, 'little more than the equivalent of a desk sergeant in a British police station'.[65] Thus, to cite Churchill's declaration of 1948 as an influence on policy was tantamount to disavowing the legislation itself. Finally, as we recount in Chapter 6, none of the charges laid against Andrzej Sawoniuk related to his role as a 'commander'. All of them incriminated him by dint of his own individual responsibility for murders. So, it raises further questions as to why the police believed that they had to find irrefutable evidence that a suspect had been in a command role before the case could be submitted for a decision to prosecute.

At the time of the parliamentary debates about the proposed War Crimes Bill, there was a living link between the two eras in the form of Lord Shawcross. As the Attorney-General in the post-war Labour government, Sir Hartley Shawcross played a prominent role in prosecuting

---

[64] Hansard House of Lords Debates (hereafter HL Deb), 15 May 1949, vol. 612, cols. 376, 389–91.
[65] Clegg interview with author, 28 April 2021.

the so-called major criminals at the Nuremberg IMT. Forty-five years later he opposed the legislation put forward by the Thatcher government on the grounds that it would provide a badly flawed form of justice. Even so, he took exception to the depiction of the less infamous perpetrators as 'minor criminals', which he called 'a misdescription, for their individual crimes were often of enormous gravity'.[66]

Churchill's advice that a 'sponge' should be drawn across the past expressed, for many, a mood of national weariness with chasing war criminals. Tom Bower, in *Blind Eye to Murder* (1981) quoted Brigadier Richard Halse, a lawyer in the Judge Advocate General's office, as saying: 'everyone was tired at the end of the war and both JAG and the War Office felt that war crimes was not going to produce glory for anyone'.[67]

It is possible to detect a similar ennui behind a Crown Prosecution Service decision, not publicly articulated, to call an arbitrary halt to any fresh investigations early in 1995. Without denigrating the conscientiousness of some of those police investigators and lawyers who took up the baton, it was evident to all that putting an elderly Nazi acolyte or two on trial was unlikely to be seen as a career-enhancing achievement. The journalist Sol Littman had reached a similar conclusion a decade earlier in critiquing the efforts of the Royal Canadian Mounted Police in tracing Nazi collaborators: 'Canada's top federal officers see little glory in "getting their man" when he is an "old geezer who has kept his nose clean for forty years and hasn't committed any crime in Canada".'[68]

The Soviet Conundrum

It is a paradox that when the war crimes legislation was being debated inside and outside Parliament, the context was the Nazi programme of genocide but some of the most vociferous opposition was expressed in implicit references to 'distasteful' Soviet practices. Thus, in *The Observer* newspaper, Lord Shawcross wrote: 'This is England. We do not indulge in show trials.'[69] The same words, 'show trials', were used by the former

[66] *The Observer*, 3 June 1990.   [67] Bower, 1981 *Blind Eye to Murder*, p. 129.
[68] Littman, 1983 *War Criminal on Trial: Rauca of Kaunas*, p. 169.
[69] *The Observer*, 3 June 1990.

Prime Minister Edward Heath, when he spoke against the bill in the House of Commons, thereby conjuring an image of Stalinist-era repression all too readily understood, especially by those veteran statesmen who had cut their political teeth during the early years of the Cold War.[70] One of the younger generation of opponents of the legislation, the Conservative MP Ivor Stanbrook, spoke derisively in a radio debate of 'evidence which has now been miraculously produced in Russia'.[71]

This illustration of the lengthy shadow cast by the Soviet Union over the whole issue of Eastern European collaborators who escaped or emigrated at the war's end is given insufficient weight in 'Western' accounts of the UK's war crimes process (the writings of Martin Dean and David Fraser excepted). In November 1942, the Soviet Praesidium established the Extraordinary State Commission on the Atrocities of the German Fascists and their Accomplices (ChGK) to document what crimes had been committed in every locality which had been occupied.[72] Under the direction of NKVD units, teams of investigators were sent to record the names of those killed, as well as gather information on their killers, and conduct an audit of property destroyed. According to George Ginsburgs, over seven million people participated in this unprecedented trawl for evidence.[73] Their handwritten reports were organized geographically by republic, county, and town. In all, some two million pages of material were contained in a so-called 'Black Book' and stored in the Central State Archive of the October Revolution in Moscow, with copies in the archives of the republics. They cover 1,450 localities.

Whilst acknowledging that the Soviet records of the number of victims is often at odds with Western estimates and appear to be exaggerated, the importance of this audit for future criminal proceedings can hardly be overstated. Many of the accounts were contemporaneous and identification of perpetrators by fellow villagers who had lived alongside them could not easily be contested. Future prosecutors could hardly

---

[70] HC Deb, 18 March 1991, vol. 188, cols. 23–112.

[71] The Brian Hayes phone-in programme on LBC Radio, 26 March 1990.

[72] Though set up in late 1942, the Commission did not begin work in earnest until March 1943, after the Battle of Stalingrad.

[73] Ginsburgs, 1966 Moscow's Road to Nuremberg, pp. 38–9.

have wished for more information on a suspected collaborator. Each file had to contain:

> The most complete description possible of the crimes committed...minutes of interrogations, statements by citizens, the conclusion of medical experts, films, letters from Soviet citizens carted off to Germany, German documents etc. The documents had to be drawn up at the scene of the crime within one month following the locality's liberation.[74]

John and Carol Garrard argue in their biography of Vasily Grossman that the codification of this material generally reflects Soviet ideological interests in identifying the Jewish victims euphemistically as 'peaceful Soviet citizens' rather than by their race.[75] However, this is not the whole story. As Kiril Feferman points out, the interrogators often asked specifically about the fate of Jewish victims: 'This fact is very important since it may testify to the Soviet desire to ascertain that there took place the genocide of the Jews.'[76]

After providing evidence for Soviet prosecutors in the first Nuremberg trials, this exhaustive record disappeared into Communist Party vaults with heavily restricted access. But since the collapse of the Soviet Union and the opening up of the archives to researchers, it has become clear that within two years of the German retreat from Western Belarus and Poland, Moscow had intelligence from witness interviews that a number of suspects had fled westwards.

In Chapter 5, we recount the case of the first person to face prosecution in the UK under the 1991 War Crimes Act, Szymon Serafinowicz, who was denounced as a war criminal at the end of 1946. There followed two missed opportunities to take action against him, first when he was interrogated at the London Cage in 1947 and then when he faced a court martial in 1948. The Serafinowicz case underscores the point that there

---

[74] Sorokina, 2005 'People and Procedures: Toward a History of the Investigation of Nazi Crimes in the USSR', p. 802.

[75] Garrard and Garrard, 2012 *The Life and Fate of Vasily Grossman*, p. 181.

[76] Feferman, 2003 'Soviet Investigation of Nazi Crimes in the USSR: Documenting the Holocaust', p. 591.

was a deliberate policy not to test the evidence against a suspect, either by interview or by examining the witness documents, if supplied, in order to maintain the fixed principle that a war crimes suspect could not expect a 'fair trial' in the USSR. Nevertheless, correspondence which we reveal in Chapter 3 shows that behind the implacable governmental refusal to engage with Soviet extradition requests lay private misgivings about the role the UK was playing in providing a home for war criminals.

It was predictable that those accused of crimes often sought to discredit information originating from archives in Eastern Europe, playing on Western scepticism about the ideological use which the Soviet Union made of its prosecutions. Sawoniuk claimed the allegations against him were part of a KGB conspiracy and that witnesses had been suborned to give false evidence. But twenty-first-century historiography from researchers such as Dumitru (2016), Solonari (2007) and others has shown that reliable Soviet-held evidence, painstakingly gathered over the years, contributed to a number of investigations and trials in other countries. It was also of exculpatory value—one notable example being the documentary proof which showed that John Demjanjuk was not the Treblinka killer known as Ivan the Terrible.

The fact is that the Soviet Union was in possession of so many authenticated original documents captured from the Germans that there was no need to manufacture evidence. When Antanas Gecas made the familiar claim that he was the subject of fabricated KGB evidence, Neal Sher, the third director of the USA's Office of Special Investigations (OSI), pointed out that the Soviet authorities were only too aware that war crimes proceedings in the West would end if 'even a single document emanating from the Soviet Union was shown to be forged'.[77]

When the former Nazi *Gauleiter* of East Prussia and *Reichscommissar* of Ukraine, Erich Koch, stood trial in Warsaw in 1958, the Soviets sent Polish prosecutors documentary evidence to support their case.[78] A document which we discuss extensively in the chapter on Sawoniuk provides further confirmation of the accuracy of Soviet documentation.

---

[77] Quoted by Peter Watson, lawyer for Scottish Television during defamation proceedings brought by Gecas in 1992.

[78] Finder and Prusin, 2018 *Justice Behind the Iron Curtain*, p. 229.

Obtained from the archive of Group 10 of the First Directorate of the KGB in Brest, it is a thirteen-page dossier detailing interviews carried out periodically over a forty-year period to establish whether Sawoniuk was still alive and where he could be found. Long before the investigators of the Metropolitan Police WCU traced Sawoniuk, their Soviet counterparts knew that he was in the UK and where he could be located.

The Belorussian Context

In the dictatorial era of President Alexander Lukashenko, it is hard to recall that there was a period following the collapse of the Soviet Union when newly independent Belarus was willing to open its doors to criminal investigators from the UK. It is all the more remarkable that this cooperation came after forty years with no judicial or police contact between the two countries and it is a tribute to the painstaking work done by the Crown Prosecution Service in preparing the ground for this enterprise.

Initial contact was made with the Soviet Union but after 1990, Memoranda of Understanding had to be negotiated with all of the relevant constituent republics which had become independent states. The priorities included:

> Ensuring a level playing field for defence investigations, breaking down the barriers of distrust, suspicion and persuading people we were not spies. The Cold War had not long ended, *glasnost* and *perestroika* were still new concepts. The people, officials and governments were entrenched in the old system which was rapidly changing.[79]

But the fact that Britain's investigators were knocking at a half-open door may have as much to do with the post-war history of Belarus as to their own diligence. One possible explanation lay in the Belarusian need, post-1991, to slough off the all-encompassing Soviet narrative of purifying sacrifice, what Nikolay Kopasov calls 'the heroic resistance

[79] Robert Bland, CPS Special Casework lawyer, briefing note, 15 December 1998.

myth', leading to victory in the Great Patriotic War.[80] In this version, those killed by the Nazis and their collaborators were *martyrs* rather than victims. Simon Lewis explains that in the service of ideology, 'the Soviet discourse of victimhood fulfilled a clear political function: it ensured the hegemony of Soviet memory models and thus the Soviet identity of the Belarusian people'.[81]

That identity has since been reasserted in Lukashenko's desperate embrace of Putin but, for a brief period after Belarusian independence there was a greater emphasis on individual suffering and the release of what Lewis calls 'traumatic memories'. This was accompanied by revisionist histories which, for the first time since 1945, dared to speak of acts of collaboration, undermining the official war memory of an 'all-national partisan struggle [*vsenarodnaia partizanskaia bor'ba*]'.[82] Thus the timing of UK requests for help from the Procurator's Office in Minsk and access to former KGB archives, which held thousands of captured German wartime documents, could not have been more propitious. It was unfinished business, an abscess which needed to be lanced, as well as a propaganda opportunity to prove that the British had been harbouring war criminals for decades.

Conclusion

In Chapter 3 we interrogate the lessons learned from the Australian experience, where, unlike the UK, none of the three cases prosecuted resulted in a conviction and only one went to a full trial. But that one case, of a Ukrainian forester, Ivan Polyukhovich, opened a window into a deeper understanding of the role of collaborators in facilitating the Holocaust in Ukraine. Similarly, the two UK prosecutions and many other investigations of *Schutzmannschaften* in Belorussia have enriched our knowledge of relations between the German authorities and their

[80]   Kopasov, 2018 *Memory Laws, Memory Wars*, p. 135.
[81]   Lewis, 2015 'Overcoming Hegemonic Martyrdom: The Afterlife of Khatyn in Belarusian Memory', p. 8.
[82]   Ibid., p. 4.

helpers in a territory which has been under-researched in comparison with many other theatres of the Holocaust in Eastern Europe.

Timothy Snyder estimates that half a million Jews were killed on Belorussian territory during the war. Some calculations by historians put the figure at 800,000.[83] The death toll was roughly four in five of the pre-war Jewish population. The majority of the killings were perpetrated by the German *Einsatzgruppen* and Order Police battalions but as Dean notes: 'Nevertheless, the rounding up and escorting of large numbers of Jews would have been difficult without the active support of the local police units.... As with the German Order Police, there was no shortage of volunteers for such "Jew hunts" and firing squads.'[84]

Dean writes that 'a consistent pattern of local police participation' has been identified in the killings in the area of Jewish settlement in Western Belorussia and Ukraine. Nevertheless, regional variations suggest that the outcome was not necessarily the same in the two territories. The virulent strain of 'local nationalism' found in many parts of Ukraine in which the Jews were seen as alien to the polity, was not so uniformly prevalent in Belorussia. As an example, in one of the larger ghettoes, in Minsk, help from Belorussian citizens enabled a mass flight of Jews to the forests to join the partisans.[85]

The hundreds of investigations into suspected Nazi collaborators were unlooked for by the British legal system and the process of dovetailing the prosecutions of Serafinowicz and Sawoniuk with a normative jurid-ical template required a substantial degree of finessing and 'rough edges' to be planed off. The consequence was that many mass murderers found comfortable boltholes in the UK, disturbed only at the end of their lives by one or two visits to a police interview room followed by a letter say-ing they would not be prosecuted because of 'insufficient evidence'. We argue in this book that the unexpected coming together of criminal law and history in a British context should not be allowed to pass without proper scholarly interrogation.

---

[83] Wilson, 2011 *Belarus: The Last European Dictatorship*.
[84] Dean, 2000 *Collaboration in the Holocaust*, p. 101.
[85] Epstein, 2008 *The Minsk Ghetto, 1941–1943*.

1

Law Meets War

Responding to a New Kind of 'Conflict'

During the inter-war period, Polish jurists such as Raphael Lemkin and Emil Rappaport were prominent in efforts to erect a scaffolding of international criminal law which could deter aggressor states and punish the behaviour of individual perpetrators. It was fitting, then, that as the first country to feel the weight of German atrocities following the invasion of September 1939, Poland, through its Government-in-Exile, based in London, took the initiative in early lobbying for a commitment to post-war retribution. As Finder and Prusin point out, Poland 'was a leader among the exile governments of countries under German occupation in urging Great Britain and the United States to condemn Nazi war crimes, punish their perpetrators and formulate a policy to try war criminals after the war'.[1]

Although Britain had gone to war 'over Poland', it had not done so with the intention of committing to a policy of retribution, whether judicial or of any other kind. Thus, the pleas of the Polish exiled leadership received little encouragement from their British hosts. The tenor of Foreign Office sentiment can be gauged from a note written by an unnamed civil servant in February 1940: 'If the Poles remain obdurate it is their funeral... it would be unfortunate to commit ourselves to punishing Germans for atrocities.'[2]

Indeed, 'fake' atrocity stories from the Great War were still lodged in the institutional memory of the Foreign Office. As late as September 1941, by which time decrypted signals traffic was leaving little doubt

---

[1] Finder and Prusin, 2018 *Justice Behind the Iron Curtain*, pp. 14–15.
[2] UKNA FO 371 24422/C2901 26.2.40.

Safe Haven: The United Kingdom's Investigations into Nazi Collaborators and the Failure of Justice.
Jon Silverman and Robert Sherwood, Oxford University Press. © Jon Silverman and Robert Sherwood 2023.
DOI: 10.1093/oso/9780192855176.003.0002

that the Nazis were engaged in a campaign of wanton murder in the East, Victor Cavendish-Bentinck dismissed emerging reports of the Babyn Yar massacre: 'We ourselves put out rumours of atrocities and horrors for various purposes and I have no doubt this game is widely played.'[3]

One of the few senior figures to sense that a new kind of war was being waged, needing a conceptually different response, was Sir Robert Vansittart, who wrote to the Foreign Secretary, Lord Halifax in February 1940, that: 'It would seem to me unthinkable that we should, in any event whatsoever, pass a sponge over these wholesale horrors. Were we to do so, it would put a premium on international crime in the twentieth century.'[4]

But his was very much an isolated voice within government in the first phase of the war. More representative was a tart observation from the office of the Lord Chancellor, Lord Simon—a later supporter of war crimes trials: 'At the present time we are more fully occupied in beating the Germans rather than hanging them afterwards.'[5] These comments were a fair reflection of Whitehall's aversion to prioritizing anything other than the war effort but that position was gradually being put to the test by mounting evidence of the nature of German crimes. Andrew T. Williams makes it clear that by 1941:

> The Allies had already accumulated considerable information about atrocities against civilian populations and against Allied troops on and off the battlefield. Communiqués intercepted by the British codebreakers revealed a wealth of detail about atrocities.[6]

In October 1941, President Roosevelt, provoked by reports from governments-in-exile and intelligence briefings about the execution of hostages in France, declared that 'one day a frightful retribution' would be exacted. And Churchill announced in a speech that 'the

---

[3] UKNA FO 371/26540.
[4] Vansittart letter UKNA FO 371 24422/C2544, 17 February 1940.
[5] UKNA FO 371 26540/11999.   [6] A. T. Williams, 2006 *A Passing Fury*, p. 37.

punishment of these crimes should now be counted among the major goals of the war'.[7]

With the exception of Hitler, the rhetoric of Second World War leaders invariably ran ahead of their capacity—and sometimes their willingness—to take the action their words foreshadowed. Nearly sixty years later, the Hetherington-Chalmers report which set the UK on the road to its belated reckoning with the crimes of the war, delivered its own verdict on the delivery of these promises:

> Little effort was made at forward planning. Even by September 1944 little thought had been given to how evidence and the war criminals themselves would be found once Germany fell. The first war crimes investigation team was formed at Belsen, and other investigators later recruited. The army, however, did not recognise the war crimes group as a priority and so in its early days, the months immediately after the war, it had to fight for men, transport and resources.[8]

Allied military thinking in the early phases of the war still bore the imprint of some of the shibboleths of the Great War—belief in the impregnability of the Maginot Line being one—so the concept of war crimes trials, embryonic as it was, was also influenced by the earlier conflict and its aftermath. In 1921, the victors put pressure on Germany to hold a number of trials of 'war criminals' in Leipzig's Supreme Court (*Reichsgericht*). Of the prosecutions involving allegations of crimes against British victims, only five people were convicted and given what the Allies considered to be derisory sentences. None spent more than six months in custody. The proceedings, as a whole, were regarded as an embarrassing failure and dismissed as the Leipzig Farce.[9] Two decades later, the memory of this flawed exercise in retributive justice, 'a traumatic and humiliating nightmare', was still strong.[10] In a House of Lords debate, Lord Frederic Maugham, who had been Lord Chancellor in

---

[7] Cited in Tusa and Tusa, 2010 *The Nuremberg Trial*, p. 21.

[8] Sir Thomas Hetherington and William Chalmers, *War Crimes: Report of the War Crimes Inquiry* Cmd 744, 1989, p. 23.

[9] See Mullins, 1921 *The Leipzig Trials*.   [10] Bower, 1981 *Blind Eye to Murder*.

Neville Chamberlain's government, suggested that to prevent any repeat of perpetrators being tried in Germany, 'the serious crimes I have mentioned should be tried by the national Courts of the victim'.[11]

Any accounting of war crimes justice inevitably starts with the achievement of the Nuremberg tribunals and here, too, the strategic legacy of the First World War still cast a shadow. Within six years of the ending of hostilities, the military historian Basil Liddell Hart was writing: 'The idea that the General Staff had played a dominant part in Germany's aggressive course, as it did before 1918, still coloured the prosecution proceedings at the Nuremberg Trial.'[12]

Notwithstanding that misconception, Nuremberg remains the legal benchmark but in the early years of the war, the concept of an internationalized reckoning for crimes was barely a glimmer on the horizon and thinking was shaped by the hegemony of the nation state. Yet even if domestic courts were still seen as the natural forum for trials, there was growing support for the application of common legal grounds and evidence needed to support prosecutions. This can be traced to a Polish-initiated agreement reached between representatives of nine occupied states, designated the Inter-Allied Commission on the Punishment of War Crimes, meeting in London in November 1941.

What became known as the St James's Declaration was signed in January 1942 and, in breadth of ambition, it called for a holistic response, placing amongst 'their principal war aims...punishment through the channel of organised justice, of those guilty of or responsible for these crimes, whether they have ordered them, perpetrated them or participated in them'.

Despite providing the venue for the meeting, St James's Palace in London, the UK was officially an observer rather than a participant. The United States and Soviet Union representatives also enjoyed observer status only. The Foreign Office's somewhat leisurely response to the St James's Declaration was the publication of a paper on 22 June 1942, called 'Treatment of War Criminals'.[13] This document proposed that

---

[11] HL Deb, 7 October 1942, vol. 124, cc 585.

[12] Liddell Hart, 1951 *The Other Side of the Hill*, p. 8.

[13] The exiled governments were formed into the London International Assembly (LIA) and created a body to consider war crimes, compiling a 400-page report, *Treatment for War Crimes*.

existing laws were sufficient and that offenders should be tried by British military courts when hostilities were over. With reports of Nazi atrocities and the functioning of death camps in occupied Europe filtering through to London and Washington, the impetus for an international mechanism to deal with war crimes grew in intensity. In October 1942, in a debate in the House of Lords, Lord Simon, who had been tasked with chairing a ministerial committee to work out a policy on war crimes, announced the formation of the United Nations War Crimes Commission (UNWCC), the aims and purposes of which were:

> to collect material, supported wherever possible by depositions or by other documents, to establish such crimes, especially where they are systematically perpetrated, and to name and identify those responsible for their participation ... The investigation should cover war crimes of offenders *irrespective of rank* [authors' emphasis] ... In making this proposal for an investigating Commission the aim is not to promote the execution of enemy nationals wholesale; the aim is the punishment of individuals, obviously very few in number in relation to the total enemy population.[14]

As a foundational mandate for the prosecution and punishment of war crimes, this was something of a fudge. To satisfy those who were uneasy with the principle of war crimes trials, it envisaged punishing only a small number of perpetrators and 'ring-leaders'. Yet, at the same time, it acknowledged that lowliness of rank should not be a bar to retributive action (incidentally, a recommendation which was not followed by the Crown Prosecution Service in the 1990s). Nor was there any mention of who would be responsible for apprehending the guilty, assuming they could be found. As Ashman and Wagman have pointed out: 'The commission staff members were not policemen or detectives. They were bureaucrats who, in most cases, had been appointed because they could be spared by their governments from the more pressing duties of wartime planning.'[15]

---

[14]   HL Deb, 7 October 1942, vol. 124, cols. 583/584.
[15]   Ashman and Wagman, 1988 *The Nazi Hunters*, p. 53.

The UNWCC was officially established in October 1943 and under-pinned by the Moscow Declaration, signed by the foreign ministers of the UK, United States, and Soviet Union, promising to 'pursue them [the criminals] to the uttermost ends of the earth'.[16] One of the jurispru-dential tenets of the Moscow Declaration was a commitment to respect the sovereignty of any signatory nation on whose territory alleged war crimes were committed and its right to seek the return of perpetrators apprehended elsewhere. In the event, it was a commitment which barely survived Germany's defeat and by 1948 had been rendered worthless by Cold War *realpolitik*.

Judgement has been divided about the contribution the UNWCC made during the war and beyond. Guy Walters focused on its lack of wartime supporters:

The Foreign Office wished for it to be closed down, with one mandarin noting that it was a 'great bore and probably a great mistake'. By the beginning of 1945, the UNWCC was effectively marginalized, and became an embarrassing weekly reminder of the ineffectiveness of Allied war crimes policy.[17]

The UNWCC's own archives were sealed in 1949 but in 2014, the histor-ian Dan Plesch and others successfully persuaded the United States government to allow access to a documentary trove, hitherto unavailable to researchers. An examination of this material has led to a major re-evaluation of its achievements. These included supporting what Plesch calls 'a popular movement for global justice', expressed in trials in domestic courts in some sixteen countries, many of them beyond the borders of Europe, to punish Holocaust perpetrators. In Plesch's estima-tion, 'work that the UNWCC accomplished successfully during its brief existence was certainly the precursor to modern international jurisprudence'.[18]

[16] The Moscow Declaration, published 1 November 1943.
[17] Walters, 2009 *Hunting Evil*, p. 77.
[18] Plesch, 2017 *Human Rights After Hitler*, p. 203.

Earlier writers, such as Ann and John Tusa acknowledged that the Commission experienced early 'teething difficulties'. But they point out that: 'By June [1945] it was issuing thick bulletins at least once a fortnight giving names, last known addresses and charges against suspects.'[19] However, the Hetherington-Chalmers Inquiry concluded that the UNWCC was weakened from the outset because it did not include the Soviet Union:

> The greatest atrocities occurred on what had become Soviet controlled territory and it was there that the most documentary and eyewitness evidence was to be found. Although the Commission released material to the Soviet Union, the gesture was not reciprocated possibly because the Soviet Union realized that Western governments were not supplying the Commission with all the information they possessed, particularly that concerning Soviet occupied territory. As a consequence, UNWCC files were hopelessly inadequate as a master-list of war criminals.[20]

Moreover, its lack of an investigative capacity left the UNWCC:

> a passive recipient of information from national war crimes offices who, for various reasons, were not forthcoming with information.[21]

Why Not a Civilian Rather Than Military Inquiry?

Hindsight offers opportunities to critically evaluate both decisions taken and not taken, and, in view of the haphazard and often slipshod war crimes investigations carried out by military officers after hostilities had concluded, it is worth considering if there had been another, better, way of doing things. In the case of the UK, for example, the Corps of Military Police (CMP) might have been utilized, given that a Special Investigation

---

[19] Tusa and Tusa, 2010 *The Nuremberg Trial*, p. 96.
[20] *War Crimes: Report of the War Crimes Inquiry* 1989 Cm 744 para 3.33, p. 23.
[21] Reydams, Wouters, and Ryngaert 2012, 'Introduction', in *International Prosecutors*, ed. Reydams et al., p. 10.

Branch of the CMP had been formed in February 1940, staffed initially by nineteen detective sergeants from the Metropolitan Police. This followed a recommendation from an experienced detective, Chief Inspector George Hatherill, who had been sent to France by the Home Office to investigate systematic larceny from stores and ships amongst troops from the British Expeditionary Force.[22]

Hatherill's report found that:

> The military police had no knowledge in matters relating to the prevention, detection or investigation of crime. During my tour I spoke to several Sergeants of the CMP and found that they had very little, if any, idea how to take proper statements from witnesses, and no idea at all about the laws of evidence, etc. and so far as knowing how to deal with exhibits the position was hopeless.[23]

Since 1936, the world-renowned Metropolitan Police Detective Training School had been training detectives from most, if not all, British and overseas police forces in the investigation and collection of evidence concerning offences ranging from theft to murder.[24] Although there is no information about the nineteen who were seconded to the CMP in 1940, it can be assumed that they would have been suitably competent and able to pass their experience on to others. This is more than a tangential point because when the Royal Warrant (81/1945), conferring jurisdiction on British military courts to try war criminals was signed in June 1945, it made clear that the rules of evidence applicable in English (common law) courts applied to military courts. Detectives were more than conversant with Judges' Rules, rules of procedure and evidence and so on and would have inspired more confidence than the hastily assembled and often ill-suited cohort of army officers and NCOs to whom the war crimes investigations were assigned.[25]

---

[22] The Hatherill Report dated 3 January 1940, a copy of which was supplied by the Royal Military Police Museum, Hants.

[23] The Hatherill Report.

[24] Inquiries of the Metropolitan Police Crime Academy revealed that detectives from provincial police forces attended this course from 1937 onwards. Courses undertaken for the CMP were conducted at Gatton Park and Mytchett Hutmetts (Ash, Surrey).

[25] Perez, 2014 *Bergen Belsen Camp*, p. 102.

It is also worth making the point that the directory by which suspects were initially identified, CROWCASS—the Central Registry of War Criminals and Security Suspects—had benefited from the experience of both Scotland Yard and the FBI when it was established in 1944, so there was, at the very least, an implied acknowledgement that when it came to identifying and arresting criminal suspects, the expertise of police agencies might have a role to play.[26] If this were not the case, there is no obvious explanation for the decision, in September 1945, to send two former police officers (rather than military) to Bückeburg in Germany to initiate a search for the perpetrators of the murders of fifty airmen, half of them British, who were shot by the Gestapo as retribution for escaping from the Stalag Luft III prisoner of war camp in Silesia eighteen months earlier.[27]

In principle and conception, CROWCASS was of more obvious strategic use to war crimes investigators than was the UNWCC because it included far more names of suspects and a means of cross-referencing them with lists held in camps. However:

> In practice, it had too few staff, too little accommodation and insufficient machinery to cope with the grandiose plan. At first, it was even unable to get its list printed for circulation without a three-month delay. It soon began to collapse under the sheer volume of paper returns that it was receiving and lacked the capacity to process.[28]

From the late summer of 1944, the Allied commitments to punish those responsible for the worst crimes began to be put to the test. For the UK government, the practicality, rather than the principle, of holding trials occupied the agendas of departmental meetings and discussions involving, variously, the War Office, the Lord Chancellor, Treasury Solicitors, Judge Advocate General, and Directorate of Military Intelligence (DMI). Even at this relatively 'late' stage, it was not settled policy that trials should be held by military, rather than civil courts, as a memorandum from the DMI demonstrates:

---

[26] Bower, 1981 *Blind Eye to Murder*, p. 133.   [27] Ibid., p. 152.
[28] *War Crimes: Report of the War Crimes Inquiry* para 3.34, p. 23.

I understand that the question as to what types of courts are to be set up to hear charges against alleged War Criminals and as to the rules of evidence to be applied in these Courts are at present under consideration by the Lord Chancellor and the Law Officers of the Crown....My principal concern in the matter is that no War Criminal should evade punishment for his crimes in any case where his guilt can be established beyond reasonable doubt and I consider that two factors may well militate against this, viz:

1. Delay in bringing the Criminal to justice.
2. Insistence on unduly strict rules of evidence.[29]

Lists of war criminals were compiled, with a heavy emphasis on those who had committed crimes against British subjects. Thus, at this stage, relatively few names were collected. Even so, the DMI was anxious to ensure that any incriminating evidence was gathered as swiftly as possible without being over-scrupulous about 'due process':

> It cannot be sufficiently emphasised that returned prisoners (i.e. British POWs) will have themselves seen and heard of the most flagrant War Crimes and Criminals, and will have every justification for expecting to see speedy and exemplary retribution administered. I fear that there would be a public outcry if such retribution were shown to have been evaded through insistence on a code of rules which excluded written or even hearsay evidence.[30]

Responding to the DMI's concern, the Judge Advocate General (JAG), Sir Henry MacGeagh, produced a paper in September 1944, headed 'Trial of War Criminals' and marked 'Secret'. In it, he expressed his strong preference for trials to be held before military courts, along the lines of courts-martial, with Corps Commanders designating a 'jury' of five army officers ranging in rank from Major-General to Lieutenant Colonel, advised by a barrister, the Judge Advocate. MacGeagh made

---

[29] Memo written by GR Way, Deputy Director of Military Intelligence, 4 August 1944, WO 311/8 British Online Archive.
[30] Ibid.

plain his view that: 'it would indeed be lamentable if any such trials were not to succeed through failure to have the necessary machinery in readiness in due time'.[31]

The JAG was equally anxious to ensure that the 'right' outcome was not impeded by too rigid an interpretation of juridical procedure:

> Strict rules of evidence before Courts-Martial would have to be greatly relaxed and affidavits, written statements and hearsay evidence should be admissible, though the fact that direct oral evidence on oath was not given might detract from the weight of such evidence… There should be provisions to ensure that no Proceedings should fail because of technical errors if there has been no substantial miscarriage of justice.[32]

With the war's end only a matter of time and a strong steer from the organs of government that a satisfactory measure of retribution needed to be handed out, a British War Crimes Group was established to operate in soon-to-be occupied German territory.

The Discovery of Bergen-Belsen

On 4 April 1945 the United States 4th Armoured Division came across the abandoned labour camp at Ohrdruf-Nord, a sub-camp of Buchenwald, where they uncovered in excess of three thousand decomposed bodies plus a few emaciated survivors.[33] Ohrdruf-Nord, which featured in the documentary film *Nazi Concentration Camps*, shown during the principal Nuremberg trial, was the first camp liberated by the Western Allies although several other discoveries had been made of abandoned sites the previous autumn.[34]

The British army faced the unfiltered reality of the earlier wartime intelligence bulletins on atrocities when troops from 63 Anti-Tank

---

[31] JAG's office, 4 September 1944 WO 311/8.   [32] Ibid.
[33] UKNA WO 32/12202.
[34] See Bridgman, 1990 *The End of the Holocaust*; Abzug, 1985 *Inside the Viscous Heart*.

Regiment, Royal Artillery, discovered Bergen-Belsen, near the city of Hanover, on 15 April 1945. Much has been written about the horror which confronted the liberators, perhaps less on the existential despair which overwhelmed the survivors:

> For the greatest part of the liberated Jews of Bergen-Belsen, there was no ecstasy, no joy at our liberation. We had lost our families, our homes. We had no place to go, nobody to hug. Nobody was waiting for us anywhere. We had been liberated from death and the fear of death but not from the fear of life.[35]

The question of whether the authorities were aware beforehand of the existence of the camp remains unresolved. According to one historical assessment:

> The Foreign Office and Colonial Office knew about Bergen-Belsen camp because it was from there that many of the prominent Zionists who were exchanged for Germans in Palestine in July 1944 came. British consular officials in Lisbon and Istanbul were instructed to get information on the place in the early months of 1945.[36]

This view favours a narrative, promoted by wartime 'activists' such as the MP Eleanor Rathbone and publisher Victor Gollancz, that the British government knowingly neglected the plight of European Jewry despite the mounting evidence. The authorities had a vested interest in undermining that assertion and, according to Tony Kushner, 'a more comfortable counter-mythology developed that nothing was known and that only with the liberation of the camps did knowledge become available'.[37]

---

[35] Belsen survivor Dr Hadassah Rosensaft speaking at a conference in Washington in 1981 to mark The Liberation of the Nazi Concentration Camps 1945. *Eyewitness Accounts of the Liberators* US Holocaust Memorial Council 1987.

[36] Major Dick Williams, 2006 'The First Day in the Camp', in *Belsen 1945: New Historical Perspectives*, ed. Bardgett and Cesarani; Shephard, 2005 *After Daybreak*.

[37] Kushner, 2004 'Britain, the United States and the Holocaust', in *The Historiography of the Holocaust*, ed. Stone, p. 258.

There is no doubt that the liberating troops and their civilian masters were unprepared for the full horror of what emerged and the traumatic shock of Belsen was felt, both at a personal and a policy level. In the opinion of the writer Ben Shephard: 'And so the British came to Belsen— without a plan.'[38] An alternative interpretation is that there *was* a plan and it was to avoid confronting the wider genocide, in Donald Bloxham's assessment, focusing instead on aspects of the Nazi regime of abusive incarceration: 'The chief categories of defendant in the British trials were personnel from the German concentration camps, Gestapo prisons and so-called "work education camps" and, increasingly over time, murderers and maltreaters of British soldiers and airmen.'[39]

Three days after the liberation of Belsen, on 18 April, Lieutenant Colonel John Barraclough was appointed as head of 21 Group war crimes programme and six days later on the 24th, the establishment of a war crimes investigation team was proposed. In a secret memorandum, a request was made for eleven personnel and three vehicles, with the possibility that more resources might be needed. The memorandum stated:

Owing to the numbers of war criminals now being uncovered it is necessary to form as rapidly as possible War Crimes Investigation Teams for the purpose of eliciting and recording evidence required by the Judge Advocate General (JAG) in the preparation of the cases for trial of such criminals. It will be the responsibility of the special investigators to act as detectives or a recce party, to seek out evidence and witnesses for the remainder of the team, who will examine, sift and record the necessary evidence in a suitable form for use at trial. The assistant investigator acts as a cross examiner on behalf of the presumptive accused... It is proposed to implement two teams, together with the pool as soon as possible, although other teams may be required at a later date.[40]

[38] Shephard, 2005 *After Daybreak*, p. 32.
[39] Bloxham, 2004 'From Streicher to Sawoniuk: The Holocaust in the Courtroom', in *The Historiography of the Holocaust*, ed. Stone, p. 400.
[40] UKNA WO 309/1418.

The memorandum explained that each team would consist of six officers, supported by two staff sergeants and three drivers. Each team would be provided with one four-seater car and a fifteen hundredweight truck and photographic equipment. A 'War Crimes Investigation Team Specialist Pool' would be established, including a pathologist, two photographers, and two NCOs. To the desk-bound bureaucrats of the War Office, these paper preparations may have seemed satisfactory but against the enormity of the task which lay ahead at Belsen, they were anything but, according to Colonel Gerald Draper, on the JAG staff:

> The evidence flowed in like a deluge and we were submerged by it...our efforts then and later were like a man standing at the edge of the sea, dropping lumps of sugar into it and saying 'Behold it is sweet'....When Belsen was discovered, it was decided in a hurried manner that the Judge Advocate General's office should handle war crimes. We were not geared or trained or qualified or had enough resources to do the job. It was a makeshift, hurried and *ad hoc* decision and we had to do the best we could.[41]

For the war crimes units on the ground, at Belsen and elsewhere, sluggish decision-making by superiors far from the action was threatening to allow incriminatory evidence to seep away. On 24/25 April 1945, the British army's 30 Corps liberated Sandbostel concentration camp, near Hanover and a month later, on 22 May, an officer from the 30 Corps legal team felt impelled to write:

> In my opinion, it is important that a War Crimes Investigation Team should be sent down to Sandbostel immediately. While Mil. Gov. [military government] are doing valuable work, of which we should be able to make use, further work more directly relating to evidence of war crimes requires to be done, and unless a team arrives very shortly, it will find, when it does arrive, that all the best witnesses have been dispersed to their homes.[42]

---

[41] Colonel Gerald Draper (lawyer and member of JAG) interview with Tom Bower, cited in *Blind Eye to Murder*, p. 144.
[42] UKNA WO 309/1418.

To underline the point about the risks of delay, a letter sent by a senior officer from B Corps to 21 Army Group HQ, warned that: 'Unless expert assistance is given, many criminals will evade punishment on the grounds of insufficient evidence.'[43]

A newly created section of the Adjutant General's Department, AG3, attached to the Attorney-General's Office, was set up in March 1945 to coordinate war crimes work. Its head was Viscount Bridgeman, who admitted to the author Tom Bower nearly forty years later, that he was briefed that the British commitment to war crimes 'was not to be bigger than absolutely necessary.'[44] This candid admission could well apply to the war crimes effort of the 1990s, though government secrecy being what it is, another forty years may need to elapse before a definitive judgement can be attempted.

The existence of AG3 was not widely circulated and even the Secretary-General to the UNWCC, Hugh McKinnon-Wood, appeared to be in the dark, as evidenced when he wrote to Patrick Dean of the Foreign Office, a strong supporter of the war crimes programme, and received this response:

> In the last paragraph of your letter, you ask what are the organisations dealing with war criminals. Apart from those which you already know such as the Attorney General's Office, the Treasury Solicitor's Office and ourselves – the War Office set up, so far as I can discover: 1) AG3 (VW) meaning Adjutant-General's Department 3 (Violations of War)...2) J.A.G Department, meaning Judge Advocate General's Department.[45]

The phrase 'so far as I can discover' hardly suggests any certainty of knowledge in Whitehall about the provisions made for dealing with war crimes. AG3 had sent one of its team, Major V. A. R. Isham, to Brussels and Paris, from 26 April to 1 May 1945, on a scoping exercise in order 'To obtain answers to questions regarding Belsen and horror camps and to establish personal contacts, discuss respective functions, explain

[43] Ibid.   [44] Bower, 1981 *Blind Eye to Murder*, p. 146.
[45] UKNA WO 32/11726.

present position as exists in W.O. and other Government Departments and explain other ways and means.'[46]

The report he issued also made it clear that Major-General Maurice Chiltern, Deputy Adjutant General (DAG) to 21 Army Group, had received little or no direction about the types of cases the Group could try.[47] Isham's fact-finding trip would have yielded much more useful information had he visited Belsen and, indeed, other camps where British investigators were engaged in piecing together evidence and identifying suspects in the most trying of circumstances. The reason he did not, preferring instead the relative comfort of Brussels and Paris, is unclear. It is true that the war in Europe was not yet over but if safety was the obstacle one can point to the visit made by eight cross-party MPs to Buchenwald, earlier in April, as an example of true 'fact-finding'. A senior officer did not arrive to take charge of the Belsen investigation until 19 May 1945.

The paucity of purposeful communication between AG3 and the investigators of 21 Army Group, based in Bad Oeynhausen in Northern Germany, handicapped the early phase of the Belsen inquiry and the semi-detached Barraclough provided little useful oversight from his post in Brussels. Indeed, Barraclough appeared either not to have read the Royal Warrant, authorizing investigations, or if he had, not to have understood it, because he sent a telegram to AG3 on 30 May 1945, asking: 'May guidance also be given as to whether there is any responsibility upon 21 Army Group for the trial of persons who have committed gross horrors upon their own nationals, e.g. German political prisoners and German Jews.'[48]

Any familiarity with the content of the Royal Warrant would have established that it applied only to war crimes against citizens of Allied nations, in accordance with international law. Uncertainty about remit and responsibility is evidenced by telegram traffic between the Treasury Solicitor, Sir Thomas Barnes, and the Director of Personnel at the War Office, Major-General Russell Gurney, over whether 21 Army Group should share the investigative role with a team from the UNWCC. Barnes states:

---

[46] UKNA WO 32/12202.   [47] Ibid.   [48] UKNA WO 32/12202/27A.

It seems to me that it would be much better for 21 Army Group to establish on the spot Allied investigation teams which would naturally work in close cooperation with the British investigation staff rather than that the (UN) War Crimes Commission should themselves send out investigation teams.[49]

Gurney replied:

I think that their suggestion to send independent parties would lead to all sorts of difficulties and confusion. I imagine that the reaction of 21 Army Group to such proposals would be that we cannot have divided responsibility and either they should be responsible or the War Crimes Commission should take over entirely and relieve them altogether.[50]

Thus, even as the conflict was approaching its endgame and the apprehension and punishment of war criminals moved from an aspirational pledge to an imminent reality, a troubling lack of clarity in the line of responsibility between the Judge Advocate General's office and 21 Army Group was threatening to undermine the whole enterprise.

Becoming a War Crimes Investigator

Recruitment to the post of war crimes investigator was anything but a systematic and well thought-out process. Due to the lack of forward planning, investigators had to be appointed at speed, regardless of their background and experience. The randomness of selection was underlined by the reminiscence of Lieutenant Colonel Ian Neilson, whose position in the Signal Corps was becoming redundant at war's end. As the result of a chance encounter with another senior officer, he was invited to a meeting the following day at 9 a.m.: 'By 1000 am, I found

[49] UKNA WO 32/12202 10A.   [50] UKNA WO 32/12202 16A.

myself commanding no 3 War Crimes Investigation Unit in a field which, at this stage, I knew nothing about at all.'[51]

Other British junior officers and men fell into war crimes investigation work by networking or by being virtually 'press-ganged'. The former Labour MP and peer Greville Janner recounted in his autobiography that he was in an army canteen in Germany in late 1946 when he was approached by a friend attached to the war crimes unit, who asked, 'Don't you want to do something useful with your army life? Why don't you join us in War Crimes?' Janner embarked on a two-week crash course in German, had a brief interview with the then head, Colonel Alan Nightingale, and was duly appointed. Janner received no training whatsoever.[52]

The serendipitous and disjointed ways in which the investigative teams were put together is another link between the two eras of war crimes inquiries considered in this book. After the 1991 War Crimes Act reached the statute book, Detective Chief Superintendent Eddie Bathgate was appointed to head the Metropolitan Police War Crimes Unit (WCU). Bathgate was nearing retirement and got the job only because the original candidate had been promoted and was too senior to take up the war crimes position: 'I didn't want the job when I was first offered it. I had my thirty years [of service] and was going to retire in December 1991 but they sent me a "bag" with some of the evidence/allegations and I began to be attracted to it.'[53]

The usual method of recruiting personnel for such a unit would be to advertise in the twice-weekly internal publication, Police Orders. This approach wasn't followed. Instead, Bathgate asked fellow senior detectives to recommend 'suitable candidates'. According to David Drinkald, who joined the unit as a detective inspector: 'Bathgate assembled his team by ringing round the various areas of the Metropolitan Police and asking if there was anyone due a move. And when I was appointed, I was told to pick my own detective constable. It was as informal as that.'[54] Bathgate himself said that his selection criterion: 'was to find people

[51] Taped interview with Ian Neilson, Imperial War Museum, London, 18537, November 1998.
[52] Janner, 2006 To Life!, p. 30.   [53] Bathgate interview with author, 4 October 1996.
[54] Drinkald interview with authors, 25 August 2021.

who were sharp and wanted to do it as an investigation and an intellectual challenge'.[55] Carolyn Edgerton, a lawyer attached to the Canadian War Crimes Unit from 1990–3, commented, somewhat caustically: 'Selection required a transparent, competitive process and not your friends phoning up and asking if you wanted a job.'[56]

In defence of the process post-1991, the unique challenges of the tasks being assigned put a premium on tight team working and camaraderie. Senior officers believed that that was best achieved by assembling a unit with a core who knew and trusted each other. While in 1945, a time vividly captured in Evelyn Waugh's 'Sword of Honour' trilogy, random recruitment to jobs in military bureaucracy would not necessarily have stood out as unusual.[57]

Although there is little evidence of any clear-sighted policymaking at the war's end, the decision to make use of the language skills, insights, and personal commitment of German-Jewish refugees as investigators made sense even if those recruited had little idea why they had been chosen. A German-born Jewish officer, and former internee, Captain Mark Lynton, who had been a tank commander, was suddenly posted to the British Army 21 Group HQ based at Bad Oeynhausen. Ordered to report to a Colonel Newman, Lynton recalled: 'All I knew about Bad Oeynhausen was that it was the centre of the British Zone and housed the headquarters of the entire British Occupational apparatus. Why Newman had me transferred to his unit, and how or when he had heard of me before, are mysteries to this day.'[58] Garry Rogers, a Sergeant in the Royal Tank Regiment, another German-born refugee and internee, was suddenly posted, without notice, to a Civilian Internment Camp (CIC) based at Recklinghausen in Westphalia. Rogers commented in his auto-biography, 'We really had to make up the rules as we went along.'[59]

Hanns [Howard] Alexander was yet another Jewish German-born junior officer who emigrated to the UK in 1936 and worked in the City

[55] Bathgate conversation with author, 24 July 2017.

[56] Carolyn Edgerton, telephone conversation with author, 5 March 2018.

[57] The three books which made up 'Sword of Honour' were published between 1952 and 1961.

[58] Lynton, 1998 *Accidental Journey*, p. 207.

[59] Rogers, 1998 *Interesting Times*, p. 167.

of London prior to the outbreak of war. Alexander immediately enlisted and inevitably ended up in the Pioneer Corps.[60] At the end of April 1945, by then a Lieutenant, he was posted to 1 War Crimes Investigation Team (WCIT) under the command of Lt. Col. Leo Genn who oversaw the Bergen-Belsen investigation. Alexander was assigned the role of interpreter, though he had received no training nor even requested this specialized form of work. A fellow Jewish German-born NCO, Fred Warner, was summarily posted to the war crimes investigation unit and, although primarily employed as an interpreter, was allowed to undertake several interrogations of significance.[61]

Henry Tauber, who had been interned on the Isle of Man when the war broke out, joined the Pioneer Corps in 1944 and, as a native German speaker, was seconded to the Intelligence Corps. Tauber's experience was untypical in that, before the posting, he was given an eight-week intensive course in intelligence gathering at Harrogate. Tauber was, however, critical of the British approach towards war crimes investigations and in a 1997 interview, when asked whether incompetence or lack of interest were the principal reasons why so many leading Nazis escaped, commented:

[The war crimes team] did a very bad job of it, so many people got away, Eichmann for instance. They were lackadaisical and there was a lot of incompetence. They were taking it very lightly. I don't know whether they realised the enormous atrocities they committed. The ordinary British person never realised that, I don't think they had ever been told that if they let a man like Eichmann go and so on and so on. There were dozens of people who ended up in Brazil and South American countries who could have easily been found.[62]

That harsh judgement may be considered the wisdom of hindsight but a contemporary assessment captures equally well the limitations of

---

[60] It is estimated that of the 4,000 German and Austrian Jewish refugees who landed in the UK from 1933 to 1939 and joined the British army, most enlisted in the Pioneer Corps. Longden, 2007 *To the Victor the Spoils*, p. 20.
[61] Warner, 1985 *A Very Personal Account* (Private Publication).
[62] Interview with Henry Tauber, 8 April 1997, USC VHA 28006.

inquiries led by military officers, who, for the most part, were desperate to return to civilian life once the war was over. It came from Prince Yurka Galitzine, an SAS captain attached to the War Office, who witnessed at first hand a war crimes inquiry—into the murder of thirty SAS personnel in the Vosges region in 1944:

> The official British and US war crimes teams and the allied administration were all soldiers, most of whom had experienced conventional war with all its dangers but who had little knowledge of war crimes. To them their responsibility was a job of work which might delay their demobilisation.[63]

Despite Galitzine's broad-brush assessment, it is possible to detect a qualitative difference between the haphazard and reactive approach of the British war crimes effort and that of the United States, many of whose investigators came from the Counter Intelligence Corps (CIC), which had been collecting evidence on Nazi activities since 1934. According to Guy Walters, the men selected for the CIC war crimes teams 'were often expected to have some form of legal experience, although as the war went on, this requirement was waived and recruits were merely expected to have an "adequate" education, be of good character and loyal to the flag.'[64]

One of the appointments made by the US at the end of the war was to have a long-term legacy. Irving Rosenbaum, a German refugee, was sent back as part of a US army psychological warfare unit to interrogate leading Nazis. In the 1980s, his son, Eli, joined the Nazi-hunting unit within the Department of Justice, the Office of Special Investigations, and became a key figure in the US government's legal pursuit of Nazis and collaborators who emigrated to the States after the war.

The United States army had recognized as early as 1942 the value of exploiting the skills, background knowledge, and commitment of refugees from the Axis states—German, Italian, and Japanese—in the investigation and interrogation of suspects. On 19 June 1942, a dedicated camp, called the Military Intelligence Training Center, was established

---

[63] Kemp, 1986 *The Secret Hunters*, p. 14.   [64] Walters, 2009 *Hunting Evil*, pp. 97–8.

at Fort Richie, Maryland, the brainchild of the US Chief of Staff, General George C. Marshall. The recruits received training in methods of intelligence gathering, interrogation techniques, and psychological warfare. Once fully familiarized, they were widely used in the European theatre to interrogate prisoners and provide counter intelligence. Some 20,000 of these so-called 'Ritchie Boys' passed through the scheme. A considerable number of them were Jewish.[65] Unlike the British 'alien' investigators, none of the graduates from Camp Ritchie had been interned under the powers introduced by President Roosevelt following Pearl Harbor.[66]

The British methodology was more seat of the pants. In June 1945, Peter (later Lord) Eden, a German-born Jewish refugee, then in the Intelligence Corps, was given just three months' training to improve his language skill and knowledge of German military systems and command infrastructure at Kensington, London but crucially no training on how to be an investigator. Eden was then transferred to a Field Security Unit, having received no direction regarding any specific suspects to arrest and interrogate.[67] Asked whether the investigators chose who to target, he replied, 'We did our own thing.'[68]

Nevertheless, this lack of rigour didn't necessarily preclude effective contributions to the war crimes effort, especially by the refugee investigators with German roots. According to the historian Helen Fry, 'the majority of high-ranking Nazis that were captured by the British were, in fact, arrested by the German-speaking refugees.'[69]

And as she points out, the commitment of these men—many of whom had been interned earlier in the war and then joined the Pioneer Corps, affectionately known as 'the King's most loyal enemy aliens'—has not received the recognition that it deserves: 'in many cases, their work went beyond that of non-Jewish personnel in the forces. Because many had anglicised their names, their contribution as German/Jewish refugees has basically been missed by historians writing in this field.'[70] As for

---

[65] Guy Stern, a former 'Ritchie Boy', interview with author, 29 March 2017.
[66] Presidential proclamations 2655, 2656, 2657 which related to Japan, Germany, and Italy, respectively.
[67] Interview with Peter Eden, IWM 17971, 4 April 1998.
[68] Interview with author, 13 October 2016.   [69] Fry, 2010 *Denazification*, p. 38.
[70] Helen Fry email to author, 11 February 2019.

Scotland Yard's War Crimes Unit in the 1990s, there were no Jewish
officers, whether by accident or design is not clear, although one of the
WCU officers, Charlie Moore, said: 'I was asked by Eddie Bathgate
whether I was Jewish. It was obvious that he didn't want Jewish
investigators.'[71]

Whither Intelligence?

The contribution made by the Jewish investigators of German or
Austrian origin was, in a way, an implied rebuff to the cultural preju-
dices of those, whether in the army or Whitehall, who displayed an ani-
mus against aliens. This mote in the eye of the intelligence agencies, MI5
and MI6 (SIS), was a legacy of the Great War. As Tony Kushner points
out: 'The Security forces [i.e. MI5] had been in the forefront of the campaign to link Jews with international Bolshevism in the postwar world
and it does not seem that their views had totally changed in the Hitlerite
period.'[72]

Maxwell Knight, who was in charge of MI5's spying network in the
war, lost confidence in his agent codenamed 'Vicki' 'simply because she
had a Jewish lover'.[73] 'Establishment' anti-Semitism, which no doubt
nourished some of the leading pre-war appeasers, blinkered the intelligence focus so that, although the threat of German rearmament was
duly reported by SIS in the 1930s, there was a poor understanding of the
existential radicalism of Nazi thinking, and what it might lead to: 'there
was evidently little demand in London for secret intelligence about
internal German political developments. There is, for example, almost
nothing in SIS archives (both for this period and during the Second
World War) about the persecution of Jews generally or the Final
Solution.'[74]

However, it is known that information about Nazi atrocities during
the war was being extracted and assessed from decoded Enigma

---

[71]   Charlie Moore interview with author, 19 February 2018.
[72]   Kushner, 1991 *Jews in British Society, Vol. 2.*
[73]   Masters, 1984 *The Man Who Was M.*
[74]   Jeffery, 2010 *MI6: The History of the Secret Intelligence Service 1909–1949*, p. xiii.

messages at Bletchley Park and the sophisticated surveillance (bugging) operation carried out by the Combined Services Detailed Interrogation Centre (CSDIC), a branch of MI5 and MI19. As Helen Fry revealed in her account of the London Cage, the focus after D-Day shifted from intelligence gathering to hunting and arresting the perpetrators of crimes. It was an enterprise which called for specialist language skills which the 'legendary' commanding officer of the London Cage, Colonel Alexander Paterson Scotland acknowledged by turning to the German and Austrian Jewish émigrés, late of the Pioneer Corps, for their expertise and obvious commitment to the cause.[75]

Their contribution to the investigation and prosecution of war crimes was significant. One, Captain C. D. Macintosh became an interpreter at the Nuremberg tribunal and three others were commended in a report for having 'rendered outstanding service and developed considerable ability in the interrogation of prisoners, especially where the taking of statements was required.'[76] As another indication of the synergy between the two periods under scrutiny in this book, Colonel Scotland was responsible, in 1948, for overseeing an investigation—which ended inconclusively—into Szymon Serafinowicz, the first person to be prosecuted in the 1990s.

The active participation of continental aliens in war crimes investigations is further illustrated by the role of No. 10 (Inter-Allied) Commando, 3 Troop—dubbed by Winston Churchill 'X Troop'. This was a British fighting force made up overwhelmingly of Jewish refugees from Germany, Austria, the Netherlands, Hungary, and Czechoslovakia, who took part in decisive operations from D-Day onwards and some of whose surviving members remained in occupied Germany after the surrender: 'X Troopers, with their fluent German, local knowledge and intelligence training, ended up playing crucial roles hunting down and capturing Nazis and interrogating them and preparing documents for the Nuremberg trials.'[77]

The X Troopers had to forsake their birth names and adopt new British identities when they were recruited. One, Sergeant Major Oscar

---

[75] Fry, 2017 *The London Cage*.   [76] WO 311/61.
[77] Garrett, 2021 *X Troop*, p. 252.

O'Neill was involved in the arrest and interrogation of the infamous *aufsherin* at Belsen, Irma Grese (although there are a number of different versions of her arrest). Another, Geoffrey Dickson (Max Dobriner), questioned industrialists who had exploited slave labour for profit. And Sergeant Geoff Broadman (born Gottfried Conrad Sruh), secured a position with the UNWCC collecting and interpreting material for the Nuremberg trials.[78] Thus, the refugee aliens, whether willing recruits or not, brought something to the unfolding process of war crimes investigation which the military mindset, in the main, did not.

The Crime Club

The officer appointed to command No. 1 War Crimes Investigation Team (WCIT), Lieutenant Colonel Leo Genn, arrived at Belsen on 19 May 1945. The pessimism with which Genn approached the task ahead is reflected in a letter to the deputy Judge Advocate General, Brigadier Scott-Barrett: 'I will, of course, do my best but I feel it only right to say that I cannot feel any confidence in producing the right answer since...not only have many of the horses gone, but I doubt if I have available the necessary strength to shut the stable door on those that remain.'[79]

Genn's team was enlarged but remained relatively small for the scale of the task, with six officers, eight NCOs, two clerks, and some interpreters. It lacked strategic direction, perhaps not surprisingly since the head of 21 Group War Crimes, Lt. Col. Barraclough, stayed in Brussels, never venturing to Germany. Before Genn's arrival to take charge, some statements, which proved to have little evidential value, had been taken by officers from the Corps of Military Police under the direction of Major Geoffrey Smallwood, of the Judge Advocate General's Department, a practising barrister. Despite Smallwood's presumed familiarity with Judges Rules and criminal procedure, it was an unsatisfactory process according to William Hitchcock, which highlights the

---

[78] Ibid., pp. 256–8.   [79] UKNA, WO 309/1418; GWDN: 00213.

glaring inadequacies of placing a search for evidence in the hands of ill-prepared military officers rather than seasoned detectives:

> The war crimes group simply walked through the camp with a stack of photographs of guards and *kapos* and asked witnesses to come forward to make statements about them – few witnesses were produced in court and the prosecution [at the subsequent Belsen trial] had to rely on what amounted to hearsay. Such a proceeding would not have been accepted in an ordinary courtroom.[80]

Interpreters were in short supply so Smallwood turned to camp inmates who spoke the respective languages but, again, this hardly conformed to the principle of an investigation uncontaminated by pre-existing prejudice against the suspects. Smallwood's successor, Lt. Col. Savile Geoffrey Champion, who arrived in Belsen on 14 May as a member of the advance party of Genn's team, later recorded his thoughts on how chaotic, under-resourced and poorly directed the war crimes process had been:

> In the case of Belsen, twenty such units could well have been employed without being entirely adequate to cover the field. In addition, the lack of certainty as to the precise legal position has made the nature and scope of the investigation somewhat vague and has also contributed to the difficulty, as has been the time lag between the liberation of the camp and the presence of organised investigation on the spot.[81]

It is noticeable that none of the senior officers who had dealings with the Belsen investigation remained on the spot and actively involved for more than a month or so before seeking to be demobbed and return to civilian life, calling into question their commitment to the war crimes issue. Indeed, at the Belsen trial, prosecuting counsel, Colonel Backhouse, made a sarcastic comment following Smallwood's testimony:

> Major Smallwood should more properly have been described as late of the Judge Advocate General's Department, having now been

---

[80] Hitchcock, 2008 *Liberation*, p. 358.
[81] Imperial War Museum, taped interview with Champion, 1993 (catalogue no. 2323).

demobilised. He was brought over from England [somewhat reluctantly by all accounts—authors' note] yesterday and I have no doubt he is anxious to go back to his lucrative practice at the bar.[82]

Leo Genn also gave the impression that he would rather have been anywhere but Belsen. Genn was a well-connected actor in civilian life and appeared alongside Laurence Olivier in his stirringly patriotic film version of *Henry V*. Genn found time, while he was leading the war crimes team at Belsen, to write a play and some poetry and to make arrangements for Olivier and Sybil Thorndike to perform in a West End production of Shaw's *Arms and the Man*.

Perhaps it was the drama suggested by the war crimes investigation that encouraged Genn and his fellow officers to refer to themselves as the 'Crime Club' and to host social functions and hand round dinner menus inscribed with a 'club' motif. Genn interrogated Irma Grese, who was hanged on 13 December 1945. On the evening of the execution, a 'celebratory' dinner was held at the Officers' Club, at which a dated menu was signed by all present, including the hangman, Albert Pierrepoint.[83] Further ghoulish details about the occasion were added by a former inmate of Belsen (and Auschwitz), Pearl Fiegler, who attended the trial and recalled the post-trial events at the Officers' Club: 'They made a party for us in the club, the English, and they had a cake with a hanging thing and she [Grese] was hanging there.'[84]

Limiting the Scope of Investigations

Between 1945 and 1947, in the British occupied zone of Germany, 1,085 defendants were tried by military tribunals in Lüneburg, Hamburg, and Wuppertal under the mandate of the Judge Advocate General. Two hundred and forty were sentenced to death.[85] Undoubtedly, the military

---

[82] Backhouse comments on 26 September 1945, http://www.bergenbelsen.co.uk/pages/TrialTranscript_TrialContents.html.

[83] Collection of Major Peter Clapham, governor of Lüneberg Prison. United States Holocaust Memorial Museum, Accession no. 1994.A.0022.RG No.10.232.

[84] Pearl Fiegler interview, 6 March 1995, USC VHA 1293.

[85] National Archives JAG WO 309.

courts took a more relaxed view of the rules of evidence than would have been the case in the civil system. For example, in the Belsen trial, against objections from defence lawyers, the court allowed not only 'live' witness testimony but also hundreds of affidavits taken by British investigators from prisoners who had been liberated and since disappeared into displaced persons (DP) camps.

That there was no great relish for war crimes investigations in the immediate post-war period is evident from the abundance of government papers released to the scrutiny of historians. The secrecy still surrounding the decision-making which followed the War Crimes Act 1991 and denial of access to relevant documents is an inhibiting factor when making claims about attitudes in the politico-legal 'establishment'. But it can be said with confidence that there are parallels in the two eras in the restrictive frames placed around the authorizing war crimes legislation. Even before the Royal Warrant confirmed the parameters to be followed, the Second World War investigators were instructed to focus only on those crimes committed against British and Allied nationals.[86] Thus the charge sheet against Josef Kramer, the Commandant of Belsen, and his staff, related principally to Keith Mayer, a British inmate who died in their custody, ignoring the thousands of others who perished in the camp. In 1943, the Foreign Office legal adviser, Sir William Malkin, had said 'offences against German Jews are not war crimes'.[87] And as the historian and barrister Nancy Beresford has written: 'Crimes against Germans and other non-Allied Jews would be defined as "crimes of violence other than war crimes" to be dealt with by a postwar German government.'[88]

As noted in the Introduction, the lawyers of the 1990s placed *their* interpretive corset around the concept of 'crimes of war' by insisting that only those in a position of command should be pursued to prosecution. By unwavering adherence to the normative rules of a common law murder prosecution, they believed that 'justice' was best served, though whether it served the public interest is another matter. It is not

---

[86] Minutes from Cabinet meeting in November 1944, UKNA CAB 65/44.
[87] UKNA FO 371/34367.8796/31/62.
[88] Beresford, 2012 *The Belsen Trials, 1945–48*, p. 20.

stretching the parallel between the two eras too far to suggest that the latter-day Crown Prosecutors and police investigators would have had much sympathy with the (admittedly patronizing) view expressed by Lt. Col. Barratt of the Judge Advocate General's Office in 1947:

> For every man who demands to know why we are continuing to grind the faces of our former enemies, there is another who asks why we have not yet traced and arrested his son's murderer. But the average pre-occupied little man in the street passes by knowing very little on this subject and not caring very much.[89]

Conclusion

> Britain was a signatory to the Moscow Agreement on the pursuit of war criminals; it was a prosecuting power at Nuremberg. And it held trials in its zone of occupation. Thus, at a very real and official level, British legal memory and practice inscribed the Holocaust as an illegal event.[90]

David Fraser's judgement is indisputable. Yet, it is equally true that the British government failed to live up to its own expansive promises made during the war to call to account the perpetrators. Perhaps it was always an impossible task to reconcile the number of war crimes prosecutions with the unprecedented magnitude of Nazi criminality. Moreover, to do so in the wreckage of post-war Germany, with so many competing demands around reconstruction, would seem to offer some sort of 'alibi' for those responsible for dispensing justice. The failure to commit to an unequivocally clear strategy on war crimes, the sclerotic bureaucracy which inhibited effective coordination between departments, and the inexperience of military investigators played their part but perhaps not as much as the lack of will shown by those in the War Office and the higher echelons of the military, many of them weary veterans of the

[89] UKNA FO 371/64723 c15911/7675/180, 9 December 1947.
[90] Fraser, 2005 *Law after Auschwitz*, p. 253.

Great War, who were always reluctant to elevate the issue of war crimes to a status matching its significance.

The author John Le Carré, who later worked for British intelligence in Germany, captured the essence of the situation well when he wrote:

> The War Crimes Investigation units themselves were near to disbandment; there was pressure from London and Washington to bury the hatchet and hand over all responsibility to the German courts. It was chaos. While the Unit was trying to prepare charges, their Headquarters were preparing amnesties.[91]

This sense of pragmatism and morality pulling in different directions was reflected in Whitehall. The UK's chief prosecutor at the International Military Tribunal at Nuremberg, Sir Hartley Shawcross, perhaps foreshadowing his later opposition to the 1991 War Crimes Act, vented his frustration in a Cabinet minute recorded in 1948: 'I am myself thoroughly sick of these war crime trials but the inexcusably long delays which are now being used as an excuse for doing nothing are the fault of the army and War Office.'[92]

As later chapters of this book explain, delay and ambivalence have been the hallmarks of the war crimes process ever since.

[91] Le Carré, 1969 *A Small Town in Germany*, p. 272.
[92] CAB CM(48)47(3) and CP(48)151; CP(48)159; CP(48)165.

2

The Soviet Hunt for War Criminals Who Fled to the West

The Moscow Declaration

More than half of the 301 names examined by the Hetherington-Chalmers Inquiry were compiled from Soviet sources. This was testimony to that country's relentless pursuit of alleged war criminals, in the wake of Foreign Minister, Vyacheslav Molotov's 'Third Note on German Atrocities' published in April 1942. At the heart of this foundational statement was the allegation that the massacres of civilians and burning of villages were part of a deliberate German plan. As early as 1943, Soviet tribunals began to hand out sentences against defendants in the Krasnodar trial, and juridical retribution continued until the 1950s. Research by Alexander Prusin (2003) suggests that during this period, Soviet courts convicted some 31,000 German military personnel and as many as 400,000 Soviet citizens.[1] Much of the evidence came from the inquiries conducted by the NKVD-led teams working for the Extraordinary State Commission. Although it ceased its activities in 1946, its voluminous files were retained and in 1951 handed over to the Central State Archive of the October Revolution (TSGAOR), which remained closed to public view until 1989.[2]

The pursuit of those alleged war criminals who had fled abroad derived its legitimacy from the Moscow Declaration of October 1943

---

[1] Prusin, 2018 'The "Second" Wave of Soviet Justice: The 1960s War Crimes Trials', in *Rethinking Holocaust Justice*, ed. Goda, pp. 129–57.

[2] By then, *glasnost* was so advanced that Yad Vashem in Jerusalem was granted permission to photocopy documentation related to Jewish matters. https://portal.ehri-project.eu/units/il-002798-m_33.

Safe Haven: The United Kingdom's Investigations into Nazi Collaborators and the Failure of Justice.
Jon Silverman and Robert Sherwood, Oxford University Press. © Jon Silverman and Robert Sherwood 2023.
DOI: 10.1093/oso/9780192855176.003.0003

which gave primacy to national jurisdictions to try offenders: 'in order that they may be judged and punished according to the laws of these liberated countries and of free governments which will be erected therein'.[3]

In 1947, the Soviet Union made an official request for the repatriation of thirteen 'suspects' said to be in the UK, three of whom were located. With the contours of the Cold War taking shape, this was not a matter accorded any priority by the British government. The Hetherington-Chalmers Inquiry recorded that: 'The men were not interviewed, largely because the Home Office was unable to find a suitable interpreter.'[4] No action followed. As Martin Dean points out, one of the thirteen was amongst the suspects investigated in the 1990s by the Metropolitan Police WCU.[5]

Five more Soviet extradition requests were lodged with the UK after 1950. Most were made in the 1960s when, in Prusin's words 'War memories [in the Soviet Union] acquired a sacral form.'[6] The request in November 1960 for a former Estonian police chief, Ain Edwin Mere, living in Leicester, garnered considerable publicity. Mere had been in charge of the concentration camp at Jagala and allegedly responsible for the deaths of 125,000 people. In support of its case for his extradition, the Soviets specifically referenced the wartime Moscow Declaration, to which the UK was a signatory. Despite this, the request was rejected on the grounds that there was no extradition treaty between the two countries and, even if there had been, there was no confidence on the British side that a suspect could obtain a 'fair trial' in the Soviet Union.

An additional factor, as David Fraser points out, was that: 'The Balts were, for the British, victims of Communism who had fought against the enemy of democracy and the rule of law.'[7] Thus, the Hetherington-Chalmers Inquiry commented: 'It is unclear how seriously Britain took

---

[3] 'Declaration Concerning Atrocities' made at the Moscow Conference.
[4] *War Crimes: Report of the War Crimes Inquiry* (1989) Cmd 744 para 3.78.
[5] Dean, 2005 'Soviet War Crimes Lists and Their Role in the Investigation of Nazi War Criminals in the West, 1987–2000', in *NS-Gewaltherrschaft: Beiträge zur historischen Forschung und juristischen Aufarbeitung*, ed. Gottwaldt et al., p. 457.
[6] Prusin, 2018 'The "Second" Wave of Soviet Justice: The 1960s War Crimes Trials', p. 135.
[7] Fraser, 2005 *Law after Auschwitz*, p. 256.

such requests.'[8] Detective Superintendent David Sibley, of the Metropolitan Police War Crimes Unit of the 1990s, put it more bluntly: 'Apparently the Russians had been giving us info on suspects for a number of years but during the Cold War era it was filed in the "too hard bin."'[9]

In contrast to the persistent hostility shown by the UK to contact with Moscow over alleged war criminals, as early as 1980, the Office of Special Investigations (OSI) in the United States—the unit within the Department of Justice with powers to bring civil proceedings against Nazi collaborators—concluded an agreement with the Soviet Procurator-General's Office. This covered the deposition of witnesses living in the Soviet Union or its territories as well as access to archived interrogations from the end of the war onwards. According to a UK parliamentary group: 'No United States judge has ever found that a witness made available by the Soviet Union has ever lied in connection with his or her testimony.'[10]

The written evidence, including pay records, unit diaries, and other official correspondence, has been crucial in obtaining denaturalization rulings against suspects. Allan Ryan Jr., who negotiated the 1980 agreement on behalf of the OSI, wrote that: 'In none of our trials has there been any finding that these documents were anything other than what they appeared to be—records produced for administrative purposes during the war, undoctored, unchanged.'[11]

Some of this Soviet-sourced material was considered by the Australian authorities in the course of establishing a Special Investigations Unit (SIU) in 1987 to examine claims that some seventy named individuals from Eastern Europe were worthy of further scrutiny. After extensive inquiries about war crimes trials in Canada, the US, West Germany, Israel, and the Soviet Union itself, the director of the SIU, Robert Greenwood, wrote: 'I believe that there is available in foreign states, in particular the Soviet Union and some Eastern European countries,

---

[8]   *War Crimes: Report of the War Crimes Inquiry* (1989) Cmd 744 para 3.78 (p. 33).

[9]   Email to author, 3 February 2018.

[10]   The All-Party Parliamentary War Crimes Group, 1989 *Nazi War Criminals in the United Kingdom: The Law*, p. 36.

[11]   Ryan, Jr., 1984 *Quiet Neighbours*, p. 84.

material that is likely to be of sufficient evidentiary value to warrant the institution of some prosecutions.'[12]

The Zvarich Case

It has become accepted wisdom that, during the Cold War, the UK rebuffed Soviet requests summarily out of ideological disapproval. For example, the historian David Cesarani writes that when the USSR sought the extradition of a member of a Ukrainian police battalion, Kirill (Kyrylo) Stepanovich Zvarich in 1971, 'the FO [Foreign Office] did not even bother to reply: no inquiries into the allegations were made by officials in this country'.[13] It is true that no independent investigation of the allegations was made but classified Foreign Office documents released since the turn of the twenty-first century reveal that there was a reply, albeit a belated one. And they offer an insight into the internal conflicts between officials, aware that they could not sidestep the accusation that the UK was sheltering war criminals.

On 26 May 1972, the Soviet news agency, Tass, reported that the USSR Ministry of Foreign Affairs had delivered a note to the British embassy in Moscow requesting the extradition of Zvarich, who was living in the Lancashire town of Bolton under the name Stanislav Petrovsky (sometimes spelled Piotrowski). It even included his exact address—70 Bromwich Street. The note said that:

> the war criminal Zvarich, who had fled the USSR at the end of the war, regularly took part in punitive operations carried out by the Nazi occupationists against Soviet citizens. Forty people were arrested and shot dead in the summer of 1942 in the Zabolotievsky district of Volyn region in the Ukrainian Soviet Socialist Republic.[14]

---

[12] Quoted in the Report of the Senate Standing Committee on Legal and Constitutional Affairs, February 1988, p. 57, para 5.57.

[13] Cesarani, 1992 *Justice Delayed*, p. 196.

[14] Tass Eng.1648 FCO 28/2087 File no. ENs14/2.

The Foreign and Commonwealth Office (FCO) official responsible for drafting advice to ministers, Frank W. Willis, of the Eastern European and Soviet Department, admitted that 'our information about Zvarich is extremely limited'. Everything that was known came from the self-reported statement Zvarich had made to an immigration officer when he arrived in the UK at Dover in December 1946. It was the familiar sanitized history of the East European *Schutzmannschaft*. He said that after capture by the Germans: 'He was taken to Germany where he remained until the end of the war. When the war had finished, he was taken to Italy where he joined the Polish Red Cross...the information before us contains nothing to show that Zvarich, alias Poitrowski [*sic*] was implicated in war crimes.'[15]

In fact, Zvarich's crimes in Ukraine were so egregious that he had been dubbed 'The Beast of Borisov' by the Soviets. There was credible evidence from Zvarich's former neighbours in Zabaloyta and dozens of other eyewitnesses interviewed by Soviet interrogators that he had murdered both Jews and non-Jews, often using extreme sadism. In the 1980s, Zvarich's name appeared at the head of a list of thirty-four names of alleged war criminals living in the UK supplied to Scottish Television by the Soviet embassy in London. According to the First Secretary at the embassy, Guennadi Shabannikov:

> He murdered children in the presence of their mothers. Zvarich burnt down a house with people in it who were having a wedding celebration. He used to bury people alive. The people in Ukraine have been saying about him since that time, a wild beast, not a man. He perpetrated crimes against humanity.[16]

In 1979, the commander of the detachment in which he had served and two other *schuma* were found guilty of killing about a hundred Jews at the village of Tur in January 1943. Zvarich's name featured in the trial.[17]

---

[15] Note from RG Jones of the Home Office to Willis, 17 March 1972 HO Ref:Z40167 File ENs14/2.
[16] Cited in Hutchinson, 1994 *Crimes of War*, p. 41.
[17] Cesarani, 1992 *Justice Delayed*, p. 196.

The Soviet government made its first request for the return of Zvarich in 1971 and the delay in receiving a response can probably be attributed to the major breakdown in diplomatic relations provoked by the expulsion from Britain of 105 Soviet officials—many of them professional spies—in September 1971. The Soviet government had supported its extradition request by citing the first international commitment to punish war crimes, the St James's Declaration of January 1942 and the 'The Declaration on Responsibility of Hitlerites for Atrocities committed by them', signed in October 1943.[18] The request also referred to 'corresponding resolutions of UN General Assembly on war criminals—including a 1968 Convention adopted by the 23rd session of the General Assembly on non-application of statute of limitations to war criminals'.

If the policy dealing with Soviet extradition requests had been as routine as some have suggested, an early outright rejection might have been expected. But the files do not bear that out. Frank Willis felt obliged to apologize to an officer in the Moscow embassy, Michael Robinson, on 2 May 1972 for the delay in formulating an appropriate response on behalf of Her Majesty's Government (HMG): 'I am afraid that a certain amount of inter-departmental difference of opinion has arisen which I did not foresee.'[19]

The 'difference of opinion' arose from a suggestion by D. R. Gilmour, an FCO legal adviser, that the government should ask for more information from the Soviets in order to establish whether there might be a *prima facie* case against Zvarich. Willis did not agree:

I think such an approach would be a tactical mistake. The Russians might very well produce a welter of documentation which we would be in no better position to assess than the allegations already before us. We would then be placed in the embarrassing position of saying that the evidence was still insufficient. By shifting our ground, we might encourage the Russians to maintain their pressure, and give the impression that we *treated each case on its merits* [authors' emphasis]

[18] The Declaration was actually signed, by Churchill, Roosevelt, and Stalin, on 1 November 1943.
[19] Ref: ENs 14/2 FCO 28/2087.

and not as a matter of principle. It seems far better to establish the cut-off point from the very outset and not enter into further negotiations.[20]

Another possibility was introduced by Ian Ellison of the FCO's United Nations (Economic and Social) Department, though he admitted it would be an 'extreme course to adopt'. He wrote:

we have a third alternative to extradition and deportation. It would appear that Zvarich is a Stateless person who is in this country at the discretion of the Home Secretary. If a *prima facie* case against him is established, it would, I suggest, be open to us to withdraw his permission to remain in this country...If he is either a Polish or Russian national, he could be returned to either country.[21]

The files do not include a direct response to this suggestion but the Foreign Secretary at the time, Sir Alec Douglas-Home, would have been aware of a doctrine on war criminals enshrined in a Cabinet paper of September 1950, written by Lord Henderson, a junior Foreign Office minister:

Parliamentary and public opinion has been critical of the trial of war criminals long after the end of hostilities and it is considered that the time has long passed when it would have been possible to justify, as conducive to the public good of this country, the deportation of an alien at the request of a foreign government solely on the grounds that there appeared to be a *prima facie* case that he was a war criminal.[22]

Taking a cue from this position statement, Frank Willis was anxious that the agreed response to the Zvarich extradition request should remind the Soviets that HMG had informed Allied governments represented on the UN War Crimes Commission in 1950 (1 December) that: 'they would

---

[20]   Willis note, 3 May 1972, FCO 28/2087.

[21]   Ellison note, 18 April 1972, K150A MA4 FCO 28/2087.

[22]   Referenced by *War Crimes: Report of the War Crimes Inquiry* (1989) Cmd 744 para 3.71 (p. 32).

no longer regard themselves as under an obligation to deport an alien for alleged war crimes. And [referring to the Soviet note] the UK is not a party to the UN Convention of November 1968.'[23]

The manoeuvring towards a formula which encapsulated the government's position on extradition/deportation was largely legalistic, a matter of interpreting conventions and so on. But responding to Willis, the legal adviser, Gilmour, raised an argument which reflects the perennial undercurrent to war crimes policymaking:

> If there is any question of this correspondence becoming public, I would have thought it unwise to claim that we had no "obligation" to return him. To many people, that would seem simply a travesty of the thing you appear to be most concerned with, viz. justice. Alternatively, we lay ourselves open to the argument that there are various kinds of obligation, including the moral.[24]

Willis, while determined to hold the line which had seen off earlier Russian extradition requests, was candid enough to admit the weaknesses in the government's position:

> The Russians may well publish this Exchange of Notes, as they have done in the past. The charge will inevitably be made that HMG, as a matter of policy, is sheltering war criminals.... We do not have a clear policy on the general question of punishment of 1939–45 War Criminals. Whilst we sought in 1950 to release ourselves from an automatic obligation to surrender alleged war criminals, we might well feel obliged to bring a major Nazi war criminal to justice, in the unlikely event of such an individual coming to light in the UK. In practice, however, the few requests which we still receive refer to individuals who belonged to minority nationalities of the Soviet Union and appear to have been co-opted for military service with the German forces after being taken prisoner. It could be argued, *though not entirely convincingly* [authors' emphasis], that such circumstances should be a

[23] Willis note, 12 May 1972, FCO 28/2087.   [24] Gilmour note, FCO 28/2087.

mitigating factor in our consideration of the crimes alleged against these individuals. Our reluctance to provide for extradition arrangements with the Soviet Union, however, is based on the quite different criterion that the Soviet legal system is unlikely to provide for a fair trial for individuals who we might extradite.[25]

A further Soviet attempt to extradite Zvarich in 1983 was also rebuffed and he died in Bolton in January1984 without ever having to face questioning about his wartime role in the *Schutzmannschaft* in Ukraine. In 1970, the year before the USSR had first sought his extradition, they had made a similar request for Yuri Epifanovich Chapodze. Chapodze was living under the Anglicized name George Chapell (see Chapter 7 for full details on him), and was under the 'protection' of MI6. Frank Willis, despite his determination to maintain precedent, admitted to colleagues that the FCO's position would look weaker if the full facts were known:

by surrendering Zvarich to the Soviet Union, we would be departing from the policy established in Chapodze and earlier cases. However "lame" our line was in those instances, I think you will agree that it would look even "lamer" if we were to tell the Russians that the criteria previously applied were no longer relevant. During our discussion of this problem, you referred to the "special circumstances" of the Chapodze case. These circumstances did, of course, mean that the case had to be handled with *some delicacy* [authors' emphasis].[26]

The Secret Intelligence Service is not subject to the provisions of the Freedom of Information Act and thus there is no publicly available document to indicate what input it may have had into the discussion about Chapodze but it was self-evidently a sensitive case for the FCO. As to Chapodze's alleged crimes, the Zvarich case file contains a translation of an undated note received from the Soviet Ministry of Foreign Affairs about Chapodze, 'former detachment commander of the so-called Caucasian Company':

[25] Willis note, 12 May 1972.   [26] Willis note, 12 May 1972.

Investigations have established that Chapodze, being part of the above named company... took direct part in the mass execution of the civilian population in the territories of the Ukraine occupied by the forces of Hitler. Thus, in the summer of 1943, Chapodze, being a member of the company, took part in the liquidation of about 2000 persons confined in two Jewish ghettoes on the territory of Ternopolski Oblast [i.e. Ternopil]. On this occasion, Chapodze personally shot women, old people and children. In October 1943 [it was almost certainly November 1943], Chapodze was a participant in an operation to execute 3000 persons of Jewish nationality who were confined in Yanovskii [Yanowska Road] camp.[27]

At the time of the extradition request, Chapodze was 57. The Jewish Telegraphic Agency reported that his response was:

I refuse to comment any more until such time as some official approach is made to me. I don't worry if they (Soviet Union) have something against me. I cannot hide but there is nothing on my conscience.... These charges are definitely not true. I was in the Ukraine at the time but I was in the Soviet army.[28]

Two years before the request for Chapodze, his fellow Georgian, Avtandil (Avto) Pardzhadnadze, was also the subject of a Soviet extradition request which was refused. Unlike Chapodze, he was still alive when the War Crimes Act was passed and had the dubious distinction of being the last of the 376 war crimes investigations conducted by the WCU in England and Wales to be resolved.

Avto Pardzhadnadze and the Caucasian Company

On 13 October 1999, Scotland Yard said they had been advised by the Crown Prosecution Service that there was 'insufficient evidence' to

---

[27] FCO 28/2087 No. 2/2E.
[28] Jewish Telegraphic Agency (Historical Archive), 28 April 1970. https://www.jta.org/archive/britain-refuses-to-extradite-man-soviets-claim-murdered-ukrainian-jews-in-world-war-ii (accessed 18 April 2022).

prosecute a 78-year-old man living in Wales called Anton Husak for war crimes. Following the announcement, the CPS took the highly unusual step—in the context of war crimes inquiries—of publicly clarifying its advice. A statement said:

> War crimes are very complex. The CPS has to satisfy itself that there is sufficient admissible evidence that will provide a realistic prospect of conviction. This means:
>
> Credible, reliable admissible eye-witness accounts
>
> Clear, uncontroversial evidence of identification
>
> Clear, provable allegations of mass murder of non combatants
>
> Proof that the defendant was in a command position of responsibility
>
> The CPS has concluded that not *all of these criteria* [authors' emphasis] are met in this case and has advised the police accordingly.[29]

What the statement omitted to say—and what the CPS must have known—was that Husak, whose birth name was Avtandil Pardzhadnadze (the 'zh' in his name is sometimes rendered as 'j') came to the UK after the war with the approval of MI6, if not their direct assistance, a fact which would have caused great embarrassment to the British government had it come out in the course of a trial.

The case of Husak/Pardzhadnadze is significant on several other counts. The WCU inquiry led to the charging of a former Gestapo officer in Germany, who was subsequently convicted of mass murder. And the subtext of the CPS statement was that at least some of the criteria for prosecution *had* been met. This is noteworthy because it was an *Einsatzgruppen* case and, from the outset, lawyers and police believed that these would be the most difficult investigations to bring to a fruitful conclusion.

Pardzhadnadze was born in Tbilisi, the Georgian capital, and conscripted into the Red Army following the Nazi invasion of the Soviet Union in the summer of 1941. He served in the 51st Army in the Crimea which suffered heavy losses as the Nazi offensive codenamed 'Operation

---

[29]   *War Crimes: CPS Statement*, 13 October 1999.

Blue' punched south to Rostov-on-Don, with the aim of capturing the prize of Baku, the oil/petroleum capital of Azerbaijan. At some point in 1942, his unit surrendered, joining several hundred POWs from Georgia, Azerbaijan, and Armenia in captivity. According to one of the leading historians of the Holocaust in the Caucasus, Andrej Angrick, the Germans knew remarkably little about the region and recognized that these captives, fiercely anti-Bolshevist and familiar with the territory and its various minorities, could be useful to *Einsatzgruppe D*, whose task was to purge 'elements inimical to the Reich...This particularly meant all Jews without exception but also took in the Roma, "antisocial elements", communists and—as "parasites on the body of the German people" and bearers of "unworthy life"—anyone with physical or mental handicaps.'[30]

Two hundred or so of the POWs were recruited into the Caucasian Company which was split into three platoons based on ethnic origin— one Georgian, one Azerbaijani, and one a mixture of Armenians and Russians, with a sprinkling of others such as Ossetians. Training took place in Simferopol under the Caucasian Company's second com-mander, SS-Sergeant Walter Kehrer, who died in 1992 while on trial for the murders committed by the Company at three labour camps in Ukraine. Pardzhadnadze was drafted into the Georgian platoon and told the WCU, when interviewed, that he served for three years. He admitted witnessing many mass executions of Jews but denied having been a participant.[31] The Soviets believed otherwise and placed him on the 1988 list of alleged war criminals supplied to the British government. When the *Einsatzgruppen* reached the town of Georgievsk: 'the Caucasian Company surrounded the homes of Jewish residents, drove them out with great brutality, and executed them outside of town or sent them to the glassworks [where one of the *Einsatzkommando* units killed them]'.[32]

---

[30] Angrick, 2020 ' "Operation Blue," Einsatzgruppen D and the Genocide in the Caucasus', in *Beyond the Pale*, ed. Brooks and Feferman, p. 72.

[31] He refused to speak to one of the authors, Jon Silverman, when confronted at his home in the Welsh seaside village of Aberporth in May 1999.

[32] Angrick, 2020 ' "Operation Blue," Einsatzgruppen D and the Genocide in the Caucasus', p. 90.

Einsatzgruppe D, with a complement of 600 men, was the smallest of the four *Einsatzgruppen* which wreaked such devastation on the populations of the occupied territories. Testimony given in a Canadian trial supported a determination that its five *Einsatzkommando* (EK) units between them 'executed 55,000 civilians between June 1941 and mid-December 1941, and another 46,000 by April 1942, and many more thereafter.... By August 1942, EK10a had executed so many thousands of Jews that its operational area was declared *Judenrein* (Jew free).'[33]

This unprecedented killing spree has been called the 'Holocaust by bullets' to distinguish it from the more impersonal, mechanized murder of the gas chambers. But, in places, gas was also used by the mobile squads. In June 1942, under the direction of Walter Kehrer, a German from a Transcaucasian settlement in Azerbaijan, gas vans were deployed to kill Jews and others taken from the prison at Simferopol.[34] The Caucasian Company provided guards to prevent escapes and afterwards 'would shoot the corpse unloaders [usually Russian POWs—authors' note].'[35] In October 1963, during the 'Second Wave' of Soviet war crimes trials, eight former members of the Caucasian Company were sentenced to death by firing squad after a trial at Krasnodar.[36] And in December 1967, thirteen perpetrators were tried by a tribunal of the North Caucasian Military District. One of the defendants was Walter Kehrer, tried *in absentia*.[37]

Witness statements found in the archive of the Jewish Historical Institute in Warsaw and interviews with members of the Caucasian Company carried out by the OSI in the United States bolstered the view of British investigators that a credible case could be built against Pardzhadnadze though finding eyewitnesses prepared to testify in court would be difficult. After the Company retreated from the Caucasus, following the defeat at Stalingrad, it moved into the southern Ukraine and documentary evidence was found which placed the Caucasian Company

---

[33] Ruling by Canadian Federal Court judge Andrew MacKay in the case of Helmut Oberlander, 2000.

[34] Dean, 2008 'Soviet Ethnic Germans and the Holocaust in the Reich Commissariat Ukraine', in *The Shoah in Ukraine*, ed. Brandon and Lower, p. 262.

[35] Tyas, 2020 'The Kaukasier Kompanie ("Caucasian Company"): Soviet Ethnic Minorities, Collaborators and Mass Killers', in *Beyond the Pale*, ed. Brooks and Feferman, p. 100.

[36] Ibid., p. 97.   [37] Bundesarchiv Ludwigsburg, B162/2860.

THE SOVIET HUNT FOR WAR CRIMINALS

and the *Einsatzgruppen* at the site of three specific massacres in 1943. Two took place on the same day, 10 July, at the liquidation of two labour camps in the region of Ternopol, Kamionka, and Borki Wielki. Shmerele (Sam) Halpern, who was incarcerated at Kamionka for sixteen months, and one of the tiny handful to survive it, has written:

> Compared to the horrible death factories like Auschwitz, Maidanek, Treblinka and Belzec, the smaller labor camps like Kamionka and Stupke may have caused more prolonged suffering; proportionately more people died in the small labor camps. In a labor camp, life was a constant nightmare of gruelling work and brutality. It was only a matter of time before one could no longer go on. Some sixteen thousand people lived and worked in Kamionka…during the German occupation. Of these, only thirty-six survived the war.[38]

The fact that there were any survivors can be attributed to a leak of information on Friday 9 July that the camp, with its five thousand inmates, was to be liquidated the following day. Sam Halpern was one of about three hundred who crawled through a hole cut in the wire fence under cover of darkness and hid in a cornfield about two hundred yards from the camp:

> I could hear everything that happened. About seven thirty in the morning, people were ordered out of the barracks and shot where they stood. A woman was ordered to sing German *lieder* and play the violin while the massacre was carried out. Many of those who were hiding stood up to see what was happening and were shot down by the Germans and Ukrainian guards. I lay there in the corn as still and quiet as I could. The shooting went on for hours and hours. At the end of it, the Germans held a big party with singing and drinking. They were happy – they had done a wonderful job. They killed five thousand Jews.[39]

[38] Halpern, 1996 *Darkness and Hope*, pp. 56–7.
[39] Sam Halpern interview with Jon Silverman, 28 June 1999.

In addition to the five thousand who perished at Kamionka, a thousand inmates of the labour camp at Borki Wielki, who had been used as slave labourers on a road construction project, were slaughtered on the same day. The problem for the WCU lay in tracing a path through the generic evidence gleaned from decades of trials and interrogations incriminating the Caucasian Company in these massacres to arrive at a provable case against Pardzhadnadze as a killer. As Eli Rosenbaum, of the OSI, commented, while the investigation was ongoing:

> There are, of course, documents on the murderous role played by the Caucasian Company (for instance, in the liquidation of the Janowska Road concentration camp in Lvov/Lemberg). And there are documents that place the UK subject in that unit. We aren't in possession of documents that expressly disclose any of his activities while so serving.[40]

Janowska Road

Janowska, on the outskirts of Lvov (now Lviv) was established in September 1941, the site chosen deliberately because it had been a long-established Jewish cemetery. By the time one of the authors visited in 1999, the camp had been converted to a military prison but the watchtower and high walls topped with razor wire betrayed its wartime provenance. It was both a concentration camp and one of the largest forced labour camps in the Nazi carceral/industrial galaxy. After the first 'purpose-built' extermination camp, Belzec, opened in March 1942, Janowska became a transit point for those destined for the gas chamber there. Its first commandant was Fritz Gebauer, by all independent accounts a brutal sadist, who was sentenced to life imprisonment in a post-war trial. His deputy, who took over command in July 1942, was SS 2nd Lieutenant Gustav Wilhaus, whose reputation for overseeing a regime of wanton savagery was even worse. Robert Marshall wrote that:

---

[40] Eli Rosenbaum email to Jon Silverman, 28 April 1999.

Everywhere was a kind of mad hatred, a violence that beggared the imagination. As the temperature regularly dropped well below freezing during winter, people were often simply left outside to freeze, or placed in large barrels of water. In the morning, they would appear like elongated balls of snow on the ground, or their cadavers were chipped out of frozen barrels of ice.[41]

Anthony Chuwen, who made his home in the UK after the war, was one of those incarcerated in Janowska, mercifully for only six weeks before being sent to another labour camp. Eighteen members of his family died in Janowska, including his parents:

Janowska was supposed to be a labour camp but the idea was to work us to death. If you didn't move quickly enough for the guards' liking, you were beaten. And if you didn't succumb too quickly to the appalling conditions and ill treatment, they would help you along with a bullet or a rod. The commandant, Wilhaus, would sit on his verandah and shoot at prisoners for target practice. Anyone who came within range of his rifle was at risk.[42]

Some of the most remarkable, and macabre, testimony given at the Eichmann trial came from a prisoner at Janowska, Leon Wells, who became an American citizen after the war and a renowned scientist. He was initially part of a working brigade and survived an execution of 182 prisoners by running away from a guard and escaping from the camp. He told the court that German record-keeping required there to be 182 bodies so he was listed amongst the corpses. Later, he was sent back to Janowska and made a *Sonderkommando*, whose job was to remove all traces of the mass killings. Since each of the bodies was numbered, he and the other members of the party were forced to search for his own corpse![43]

---

[41] Marshall, 1990 *In the Sewers of Lvov*, p. 120.
[42] Chuwen interview with Jon Silverman, 14 May 1999.
[43] Wells, 1978 *The Death Brigade*, published in the United States in 1963 under the title *The Janowska Road*.

In November 1943, the decision was taken to liquidate the camp in compliance with SS Colonel Paul Blobel's instruction to destroy all remaining evidence of Nazi atrocities in the Lvov area. The German version of the *Encyclopaedia of the Holocaust* notes that the *Einsatzgruppen* encountered some resistance and a handful of prisoners escaped, amongst whom was Leon Wells. The documentary evidence confirmed the presence at the *Aktion* of the Caucasian Company which was 'primarily used in escorting prisoners to be shot rather than shooting on this occasion'.[44] About a thousand people were murdered on the day of the liquidation, 19 November, a number exceeded multiple times by those who perished at Janowska Road between 1941 and 1943, where the death toll reached two thousand a week at one point. The independent historian Stephen Tyas has done a reckoning of the calamitous impact of the violence inflicted by the Caucasians as they moved relentlessly, with the *Einsatzgruppen*, through Ukraine, parts of Belorussia, and eventually Poland: 'By the end of the war, the *Kaukasier Kompanie* may well have participated in the murder of at least 19,000 victims in the Pripet [marshes], Lemberg (Lvov), Lublin and Warsaw.'[45]

The jurisprudential problem facing the Crown Prosecution Service was the one which hamstrung the prosecution of the Latvian Harijs Svikeris, a platoon captain in the Arājs Kommando (see Chapter 3)—in other words, although the undisputed *raison d'être* of both the Caucasian Company and the Arājs Kommando was to kill and the voluntary membership of such an outfit could reasonably be described as an *actus reus*, the CPS insisted on having live eyewitness evidence of the individual act of killing by a suspect. And as pointed out elsewhere, this was always an improbability in *Einsatzgruppen* cases, not least because of issues of identification.

The only way to circumvent this obstacle was to find credible cohort witnesses and much of the effort expended by the WCU in pursuing Pardzhadnadze was in tracing surviving members of the Caucasian Company, a process which was severely hampered by the civil war in

---

[44]   Martin Dean email to author, 20 May 1999.
[45]   Tyas, 2020 'The Kaukasier Kompanie ("Caucasian Company"): Soviet Ethnic Minorities, Collaborators and Mass Killers', p. 100.

Georgia and conflict between Armenia and Azerbaijan in the early 1990s. Eventually, in 1995, detectives were able to travel to the capital, Tbilisi, to speak to people, some of whom had spent years in Soviet prisons for the crimes committed during the war. But there was a general reluctance to cooperate for fear of being tried again, whether in Georgia or another jurisdiction.

The Goetzfrid Case

The interconnectedness of war crimes inquiries, to which we have referred in the sharing of historical evidence by the Australian SIU and the WCU at Scotland Yard, was also evident in the Pardzhadnadze case. Amongst the material found in the Moscow Special Archive were several interviews conducted with a former Gestapo officer, Alfons Goetzfrid, when he was captured by the Soviets at the end of the war. According to the WCU historian Martin Dean:

> In one of these interviews, he specifically named Pardzhadnadze which clearly made him an important witness. Initially we believed that Goetzfrid was living in the Soviet Union/Russia. Then I was able to locate him in Germany through the WAST – the German Army records centre in Berlin.[46]

Goetzfrid was an ethnic German born in southern Ukraine, who had been attached to *Einsatzgruppe D*, with links to the Caucasian Company as it perpetrated atrocities in the Caucasus, Crimea, and Galicia. He had been arrested by the Soviets, tried in 1947 by a military court, and sentenced to twenty years' imprisonment. He served eleven years in a Siberian labour camp. In a statement made in 1973, he admitted that, as a member of the Caucasian Company, he had participated in the gas van operations in Simferopol: 'I helped in forming the corridor [i.e. the cordon through which the condemned passed] and also had to go into the

---

[46] Martin Dean email to author, 11 April 2022.

cell in order to hurry the people up. I also had to escort those people who had to bury the dead bodies.'[47]

After completing his sentence in Siberia, Goetzfrid moved to Kazakhstan where he lived for thirty years until the collapse of the Soviet Union in 1990. He then exercised his entitlement as an ethnic German to emigrate to Stuttgart. The war crimes investigators of the *Zentrale Stelle* at Ludwigsburg were unaware of his presence almost on their 'doorstep' until contacted by Scotland Yard's WCU in connection with the Pardzhadnadze case. In May 1996, Dean and WCU officers were able to interview Goetzfrid. He admitted serving with the Georgian but claimed that he could not recall the kind of details which would help the British investigation:

> These *Aktionen* were ordered by the KdS Lemberg [the Security Police or Gestapo] and then executed by the *Kaukasier Kompanie*. So, yes, they were involved but I cannot remember the details.
>
> Q. What was the goal of these *Aktionen*?
>
> A. To destroy the Jews. I don't know of any other goal.[48]

After confirming that the statements he had made previously to interrogators had been accurate, Goetzfrid refused to answer any further questions. Thus it was clear that he would not be of any use as a potential witness in a prosecution of Pardzhadnadze. However, he startled the German police officer present, Herr Detling, when, unprompted, he made an admission which led to him facing a fresh trial for murder in connection with one of the most notorious atrocities of the Nazi occupation.

In November 1943, an operation to which the Germans gave the codename 'Harvest Festival', began in the Lublin region to exterminate those Jews held in labour camps such as Poniatowa, Trawniki, and elsewhere, including the survivors of the Warsaw Ghetto uprising of April

---

[47] Dean, 2008 'Soviet Ethnic Germans and the Holocaust in the Reich Commissariat Ukraine', p. 262.

[48] Interview with Alfons Goetzfrid, 8 May 1996. Source: *Justiz und NS-Verbrechen* (Amsterdam: Amsterdam University Press, 2012), vol. 48, Lfd. Nr. 916, pp. 616–17.

that year. They were amassed at the Majdanek death camp and some 17–18,000 were shot in ditches behind the crematoria in twelve hours. At the war's end, the Chief Rabbi of Great Britain and the British Empire, J. H. Hertz, singled out the massacre in a letter to *The Times*: 'On one single day, 3 November 1943, at Maidanek, the central human slaughter-house in Poland, eighteen thousand Jews were done to death, accompanied by the music of bands playing tango marches in mockery of the agony of the victims.'[49]

During questioning about the Caucasian Company and Pardzhadnadze, Goetzfrid surprisingly confessed to shooting some five hundred people during 'Harvest Festival', when he had been assigned directly to the Gestapo in Lvov, and to participating in the whole slaughter by reloading weapons for the executioners. He went on trial in Stuttgart in April 1999 and Martin Dean gave evidence as an expert witness about the Caucasian Company and the *Aktionen* in which it was involved in Ukraine.[50] Goetzfrid received a ten-year sentence but went free because of the period already spent in prison in the Soviet Union. Thus perversely, the only person to be convicted as a result of the long and arduous UK investigation into Pardzhadnadze was an ethnic German who was freed immediately for time served.

Nikolai Popko

On 9 June 1988, the Soviet embassy in London handed a diplomatic note to the Foreign Office containing the names of ninety-six men said to have fled to the UK after the war and alleged to have committed war crimes. One was a man called Nikolai Arsentyevich Popko, a former *Schuma* from Zhukhoviche in Belorussia. During the investigations which followed the setting up of the War Crimes Unit in 1991, his name was consistently close to the top of the list of those who police and

---

[49] Hertz letter published on 28 May 1945 cited in Antero Holmila *Reporting the Holocaust in the British, Swedish and Finnish Press, 1945–50* (Basingstoke: Palgrave Macmillan, 2011), p. 34.

[50] Martin C. Dean papers, USHMM Document Accession No. 2015.449.1.

lawyers thought to be promising candidates for prosecution. According to Chief Superintendent Eddie Bathgate, who headed the unit: 'Popko was considered a strong case and got stronger as a result of the Serafinowicz investigation.'[51] By July 1994, a review of the cases still under active investigation placed Popko in Priority One category, along with Szymon Serafinowicz and Harijs Svikeris.[52]

Documents discovered in the Moscow archives showed that Popko was a member of the *Schutzmannschaft* from July 1941, shortly after the German invasion, and headed a *Jagdzug* (hunting group) which tracked down and murdered Jews who had escaped the *Aktionen* in Mir and Turets. A witness in the Serafinowicz investigation, Lev Abramovski, told police that: 'He was one of the most horrible killers in Mir. I saw how he walked with his shotgun on the day of the first pogrom and was yelling "We will kill all you Yids".'[53]

After a search of his home, Popko was first interviewed by officers from the WCU on 29 June 1993 at a police station in York, where he had lived, at the same address, for forty-six years. They put it to him that witnesses had told investigators from the Soviet Extraordinary State Commission on 26 May 1945 that 'a policeman named Nikolai Arsentyevich Popko assisted the German major called Pol in the abduction, forcible abduction of persons from Mir. On 9 November 1941 [the day of the first major *Aktion*], it is alleged that he shot and killed Jews attempting to escape from Mir.'[54]

As Martin Dean has written:

The willingness of the local policemen to carry out such actions can be seen from a wide variety of sources.... The example of the November 1941 massacre in Mir...demonstrates enthusiastic participation in a brutal slaughter conducted on the streets of the town. The numerous eye-witnesses leave no doubt as to the key role played by local police

[51] Bathgate conversation with Jon Silverman, 4 October 1996.
[52] Notes of case review by Martin Dean and DS David Sibley Hartley Library Special Collections, Archive file MS 408_A1057 2/35 p1011.
[53] From transcript of witness statements tendered in evidence in Serafinowicz case Hartley Library Special Collections, Archive file MS 408_A1057 1/9.
[54] Hartley Library Special Collections, Archive file MS 408_A1057 2/35 p1017.

collaborators, who were the only ones clearly able to identify their Jewish neighbours.[55]

It is one of those striking historical parallels that, while accurate identification, of Jews in the East, was critical to the Nazi mission of 'ethnic cleansing', identification of suspects was also of paramount importance for the war crimes inquiries half a century later. Neither Serafinowicz nor Sawoniuk, when interviewed, denied that they were the person alleged to have been prominent in the *Schutzmannschaft* in Mir and Domachevo, respectively. As already stated, the misidentification of John Demjanjuk as the notorious Treblinka killer, known as Ivan the Terrible, was an ever-present concern for the Crown Prosecution Service. It was accepted as a *sine qua non* of any potential prosecution that there should be no dispute about the identity of the suspect in the dock. Nikolai Popko adopted a strategy to frustrate his inquisitors and deny them the evidential certainty which they required.

What follows is taken from a nine-page transcript of his June 1993 interview with Detective Inspector Howard Chapman and Detective Constable David Lloyd in the company of his solicitor, Sandra Keen, and an interpreter. The interview was conducted in a mixture of English and Polish.

He answered fully questions about his pre-war service with the Polish cavalry and was, according to the police, 'very loquacious' about the various jobs he had done after immigrating to the UK through the port of Liverpool as a member of the Polish military police in 1946. He recounted in detail what uniform and type of pistol he was issued in the military police. But then his memory became 'faulty':

Q. Were you ever in Zukhoviche or the Mir region when the Germans were in occupation?

A. I am sorry, I no can answer that because I no can remember, I am sorry.

Q. Did you ever visit Mir in your youth?

---

[55] Dean, 2000 *Collaboration in the Holocaust*, p. 166.

A. Never.

Q. So you didn't go to Mir during the period of the war, let's say 1941–44?

A. Never, never.

Q. Can I just ask you, were you in Zukhoviche at all during the 1941–44 period of time of the German occupation of that area?

A. I'm sorry, I no can't answer that question, I'm just no can't remember my life around there you see, no can.

Q. ...you appear to be unable to remember things that occurred between 1939 and your time of joining the Polish army in Italy about 1945. Is there a reason for that loss of memory, do you think?

A. It's a good question.

Q. It seems that you have a block in your mind.[56]

The police made very little progress during several hours of questioning on 29 June, but they called Popko in again the following day and confronted him with allegations from witnesses that he had murdered 'Jews and *civilians*' (an interesting distinction) in Mir. He professed to be 'very shocked' and wanted to know where the information had come from, saying that his wife wouldn't want him back because 'he's a bandit'. His final comment was perhaps the most pertinent of all and has a resonance for all of the other war crimes interrogations which ended without a prosecution: 'Why didn't you come to me many years ago instead of waiting sixty years until I am old and can't remember any more?'[57]

In fact, Popko showed that he had been equally adept at weaving a false narrative about his wartime past decades earlier when he was interviewed as part of Operation Post Report. In November 1952, he was questioned by an immigration officer in York. The interview recorded that he was in the Polish army when war broke out and became a Soviet POW (for which there was no verification) and then 'he was taken prisoner by the Germans in 1942, released to his home where he stayed until

[56] Police Exhibit No. HC/128 Hartley Library Special Collections, Archive file MS 408_ A1057 2/5.
[57] Police Exhibit No. HC/128.

1944. Does not want to go back to Poland.' He was described as of 'no security interest'.[58]

The WCU persisted with the Popko investigation because there was strong circumstantial evidence not only that he had committed war crimes but also that he fulfilled the 'command criterion'. Thus, on 7 September 1993, he was again questioned by Chapman:

Q. I have a copy of a German document which is a recommendation for promotion of members of the *Schutzmannschaft* on December 30 1943 and promotion confirmed in January 1944. Number three on the list is Popko Nikolai d.o.b January 2 1916 in Zhukhoviche. Recommended for promotion to corporal [he had been a Lance Corporal since January 1943]. The citation reads 'Politically and professionally, he is reliable and energetic. Popko has already distinguished himself, particularly in the fight against bandits'.

A. I have nothing to say.

Q. Were you in Mir between July 1941 and September 1944?

A. No

Q. Where were you during those dates?

A. I'm not answering that.[59]

Documents discovered in the Moscow archives offered more proof that Popko was both in a command role and regarded highly by his German superiors. As evidence, the detectives put it to him that in June 1944, he was recommended for a further promotion to Junior Sergeant. The citation, signed by the head of the Baranoviche gendarmerie post, read: 'Popko is a very good junior leader, he knows how to assert himself with his subordinates, he is the local leader of the post and defensive village of Shimakovo and has proved his worth there.'

In response, Popko said, 'I am surprised, very surprised' and offered no further comment.[60] The following day, he was called back to the police station where DCI Chapman confronted him directly:

[58] Post Report no. 212543 Hartley Library Special Collections, Archive file MS 408_A1057 2/6.
[59] Police Exhibit No. HC/134.   [60] Ibid.

Q. It is alleged that on November 9 1941 in Mir you shot and indeed killed Jews. What do you have to say?

A. I never shoot nobody. I never shoot anyone.

Andrei Bakunovich

The police devoted considerable time and effort to the Mir and Turets war crimes cases once the opening up of files in Moscow and Minsk had established that a cohort of *Schutzmannschaft* had come to the UK in a similar fashion to Szymon Serafinowicz, the first person to be prosecuted in the UK. One was Andrei Bakunovich (there are several spellings of his surname), who lived in Sheffield and worked for British Steel for eleven years. As early as November 1991, the historian Martin Dean, in a report for the Australian SIU, wrote: 'Bakunovich may very well be an excellent case, for as a translator, he would have known everything about the activities of the German Gendarmerie and local police in Mir.'[61]

Like Popko, he was on the 1988 Soviet embassy list and was one of those recommended for further investigation by the Hetherington-Chalmers Inquiry on the strength of an archive report written by the Mir District Commission (NKVD) on 25 April 1945 'into crimes committed by the German-fascist occupying forces in Mir district, Baranovichi'. At the head of the list of 'main criminals' in the area were 'Serafimovitch Semion and Pankevich, commandants of district police. Bakunovich Andrei, interpreter of the gendarmerie and executioner. This gang of German accomplices burned down the village of Lyadki, 130 homesteads, killed and burned alive children, women, old people.'[62]

The merciless punitive *Aktion* at Lyadki, a village suspected of harbouring partisans, took place over two days between 12 and 14 January 1943. The village, in the Mir *rayon* (administrative district) was surrounded

---

[61] Dean Historical Briefing Paper dealing with the Mir and Turets Police Unit, 23 and 26 November 1991 Hartley Library Special Collections, Archive file MS 408_A1057 2/3.

[62] This material originated in the Oldenburg Public Prosecutor's Office in 1969 in connection with the trial of Max Eibner. Hartley Library Special Collections, Archive file MS 408_A1057 2/6, p. 342.

by a large group of *Schutzmannschaft* in the early hours of the morning to prevent any escapes. One of the few survivors of the massacre, a child, gave a graphic account of what happened when daylight arrived and the police entered her house:

> The two policemen ordered my father, mother and two sisters, one had her child with her, to lie down on the floor. They ordered Nina and me to climb down off the stove but then [policeman] M. fired at my mother, he shot her in the back and her chest exploded. They must have been firing explosive cartridges. Then they shot my sister, they shot off her right arm, then the child, they shot off his left arm.[63]

Witnesses, including two *Schuma* who later escaped to the West and were interviewed for the Australian and British inquiries, said that the bodies of the dead were left lying in the houses where they had been shot. Andrei Bakunovich was identified as one of the *Schuma* who participated in the executions. When a detachment of partisans appeared, the police were forced to retreat to Turets.[64] On another occasion, in February 1944, a witness, Jan Bunczuk, described seeing Bakunovich interrogating an unnamed man 'with his nose in a pair of pliers'.[65] The Mir District Commission inquiry in 1945 was told that 'he had power to recommend persons for execution following interrogation'. And, crucially for the WCU, he was said to be 'higher ranking than the ordinary policeman'.[66]

When Martin Dean was working on the historical background to the Australian war crimes cases, he found that Bakunovich's name appeared frequently in documents from the Moscow archive as 'translator and clerk for the auxiliary police'. A German personnel file, written in February 1944, recommended him for promotion from Lance Corporal to Corporal, and provided a flattering assessment of him: 'Bakunovich is a translator and looks after all the written work of the *Kreisschutzmannshaft*,

[63] WCU D3619, Dean, 2000 *Collaboration in the Holocaust*, p. 129.
[64] Witness statements SOBLP89; SOBLP289; SOBLPX88 Hartley Library Special Collections, Archive file MS 408_A1057 2/35, p. 1082.
[65] Witness statement BUNCJ594. Ibid., p. 1079.   [66] NS(HC169)#I ST2.

Mir. He is intelligent and very talented. Reliable politically and in his duties *very energetic* [authors' emphasis]. He has proved his courage in partisan war.'[67]

A month after their first interview with Popko, Chapman and Lloyd arrived at Sheffield's Woodseats police station on 27 July 1993 to question Bakunovich. Unlike Popko, he offered a detailed recollection of the wartime occupation of Belorussia, though the precision of his memories of what he called the 'NKVD terror' between 1939 and 1941 can be contrasted with the confected account he gave of his service in the *Schutzmannschaft*. He said that the Germans had 'taken him away in September or October 1942 and beat him up':

> They said why hadn't I volunteered for the police. In their opinion, anyone who didn't volunteer must be with the partisans. I was told to work on the telephone switchboard at the police station. I did that until the Russians arrived in 1944.
>
> Q. Were you actually involved in the murder of civilians in Byelorussia?
>
> A. No…I wish to add that I suffered through all these malicious rumours and I have lost, I have lost my parents because they have been shot by the Russian partisans. Actually, I am very pleased that it come to this interview because all this story is all based of malicious rumours.[68]

As more intelligence emerged from the archives, the claim by Bakunovich that he had spent his time as a *schuma* manning a telephone switchboard became increasingly untenable. All the evidence suggested that his command of German made him the obvious choice to replace the interpreter for the Mir *Schutzmannschaft*, Oswald Rufeisen (see Chapter 5 on Serafinowicz), after Rufeisen had escaped in the summer of 1942. And interpreters played a critical role in Jew-hunting missions.

If the first interview with the WCU was something of a scoping exercise, the second, on 16 November 1993, confronted him with a series of more explicit accusations. Once again, it took place in Sheffield. In the first interview, he claimed that he hadn't been required to wear a police

---

[67] NS(HC169)#ST2.   [68] Police Exhibit No. HC/151.

uniform because he was merely a lowly desk-bound recruit. But a witness had said that Bakunovich was equipped with a TT pistol (a semi-automatic Tokarev) whereas lower ranks were issued only with revolvers. This time, DI Chapman challenged him:

> Q. I put it to you that you did have a police uniform and that you had shoulder boards or epaulettes that indicated your rank was higher than an ordinary rank-and-file policeman.
>
> A. All that is total balderdash.
>
> Q. I put it to you that you were involved in an attack on Lyadki.
>
> A. No.
>
> Q. You were seen leaving houses in Lyadki [on 13 January 1941] and re-loading your gun.[69]

Chapman mentioned an incident which took place in the village of Liubna in 1943 where an old woman called Loiko was shot because her son was suspected of being a partisan.

> Q. It is alleged that you were the person who shot her.
>
> A. I categorically say it's, it's not the truth and that's a lie.[70]

Chapman later confronted Bakunovich with a German document which said:

> In the fight against the bandits [i.e. partisans], Bakunovich distinguished himself by particular courage and nerve.
>
> Q. You didn't do that, Mr. Bakunovich, by sitting in the police station, did you?[71]

It may have been more difficult to prosecute Bakunovich than Popko because the former did not join the Mir *Schutzmannschaft* until September 1942, after the two main *Aktionen* had all but wiped out the

---

[69] HC/165.   [70] Ibid.   [71] Ibid.

town's Jewish population. By contrast, Popko, seven years older, joined barely a month after the German invasion in July 1941 'and therefore most likely to be implicated in the major crimes against the Jews'.[72] But the wider point remains, that both were in a position of command and no less culpable of war crimes than Serafinowicz or Sawoniuk. 'Bakunovich was a strong case and we had quite strong evidence against Popko' in the words of Martin Dean.[73] It was only the normative requirement for credible testimony presented in person by live eyewitnesses that spared both him and Popko from a potential trial. However, Bakunovich was not spared embarrassment about his arrest as a Nazi collaborator. It upset his wife because he had told her that during the war, he fought on the Allied side!

Pavel Budarkevich

The name, Pavel (Paul) Budarkevich (sometimes spelled Budarkiewicz), appeared in a roster of the Mir *Schutzmannschaft* drawn up by the head of the Baranovichi gendarmerie, Max Eibner. Budarkevich was said to have been present and armed with a sub-machine gun at the notorious massacre at Lyadki—though possibly as one of those guarding the village perimeter rather than a shooter—and at Novoye Selo, another scene of mass killings where a group of villagers were herded into a barn which was set alight. A witness named Teda claimed that he participated in the slaughter of ninety-seven Jews at Yeremichi on 5 November 1941, a precursor to the first of the *Aktionen* against Mir's Jews on 9 November.

Budarkevich became head of the Turets *Schutzmannschaft* and in that role was alleged to have been involved in the murder of fifty-seven Jews on 28 October 1941 and responsible for the selection of 500 Jews who were shot in the town's Jewish cemetery just over a week later. In the 1980s, the Soviets knew that Budarkevich had emigrated to the UK—arriving at Liverpool in the autumn of 1946—and accordingly he was placed on the Soviet embassy list handed to the Foreign Office on 9 June

---

[72] Martin Dean review, 26 November 1991.
[73] Dean interview with authors, 20 September 2022.

1988. In March 1989, he was interviewed by Sir Thomas Hetherington himself as part of his inquiry and agreed that the police unit in which he served had taken part in the massacres at Lyadki and Novoye Selo: 'He said that he was in charge of the canteen at the police station and had taken part in none of these operations.'[74]

This claim to have been non-operational—like Bakunovich's claim to have merely been manning a telephone switchboard and like the insistence of other suspects that they had carried out guard duties only—posed considerable difficulties for the WCU in light of the strict criteria imposed by the Crown Prosecution Service. In May 1991, Martin Dean, in a review of the Turets cases, wrote:

> Summary – Substantial evidence that Pavel Budarkevich was a member of the police unit stationed at Turets which took part in mass murder of inhabitants of nearby villages. There is insufficient evidence that he took part in these operations although some witnesses apparently believe that he did.
>
> Conclusion: Further inquiries are necessary in Byelorussia to establish Budarkevich's duties in the police unit.... If evidence is forthcoming to rebut Budarkevich's claims to have been a non-operational canteen manager, the evidence might well be adequate to justify proceedings [i.e. a prosecution].[75]

In August 1993, Budarkevich was called to Hammersmith police station in West London, to face officers from the War Crimes Unit. Like Serafinowicz, he was intensely anti-Communist, having had close family members deported during the Russian occupation. He said his mother had died in Siberia: '[When the Russians came]...they started to talk about collective farms straight away, [there was]...propaganda...meetings.'[76]

He did not adopt the Popko tactic of claiming a total memory loss about the war years and nor did he deny being a member of the *Schutzmannschaft*, though his insistence that he had been confined to

[74] HC/182 Hartley Library Special Collections, Archive file MS 408_A1057 2/41, p. 219.
[75] Dean *Case report: Turets cases*, 8 May 1991, SIU copy (Case No. 177).
[76] WCU Exhibit no. HC/182 Budarkevich interview, 10 August 1993.

non-operational canteen duties began to crumble when the conversation turned to executions of Jews at a cemetery on the edge of Turets in 1943:

Q. Who was responsible for digging the graves?

A. Probably police. I was digging.

Q. How big was the hole you had to dig?

A. Quite a big…probably bigger than this room, longer than this room [the room was judged to be about twenty metres long].

Q. And how wide?

A. About two metres and six feet deep.[77]

Like Serafinowicz, Budarkevich was absorbed into the 30th Waffen SS Grenadier Division and accompanied the German forces westwards in the summer of 1944 in the face of the Red Army advance. He is recorded as going missing following a fierce Allied tank and infantry assault at Ballersdorf in Alsace on 26 November 1944. With his fellow *Schutzmänner*, he signed up with the 10th Polish Hussars and saw service in Italy and Egypt before entering the UK, his wartime collaboration with the Nazis seemingly expunged—until the passage of the War Crimes Act nearly half a century later.

Conclusion

The information disclosed in this chapter is significant because it is evidence that refuge in the UK acted as a centrifugal pull bringing members of the Mir/Turets *Schutzmannschaft* out of Europe in the aftermath of the war. Any assumption that the police were dealing with a mere handful of suspects is dispelled by a confidential report drawn up by Chief Superintendent Eddie Bathgate in June 1993. He identified six *Schuma*, including Serafinowicz, Popko, Bakunovich, and Budarkevich, against whom there were 'credible' allegations of war crimes. In addition,

[77] WCU Exhibit no. HC/182.

there was evidence that another seventeen people living in the UK had served in the Mir/Turets auxiliary police. Fifteen others were dead by the time the War Crimes Act was passed and eight others may have come but had not yet been traced.[78]

Historians have rightly commented on better-known examples of Britain's 'hospitality' towards collaborators in the 1940s, such as the transfer of an entire Ukrainian SS division to the UK, the 14th Galician Waffen Grenadier Division. David Cesarani has written that the decision 'under cover of the EVW [European Voluntary Workers] scheme was astounding in view of the unambiguous evidence that the majority of them had volunteered to fight for the Nazis'.[79] What then of the lack of scrutiny which allowed at least forty-six members of one of the most murderous auxiliary police units to have participated in the Holocaust in Belorussia to settle in the UK and find a secure home for life?

---

[78] Bathgate First Historical Report, 1 June 1993, Christopher Browning Papers Box 18, USHMM Collections, Shapell Center.
[79] Cesarani, 1992 *Justice Delayed*, p. 114.

3

The Latvian Death Commando

The Svikeris Case

The belief among promoters of the war crimes legislation that it would
signal an end to impunity for some of the more egregious perpetrators
who had sheltered in the UK, was always likely to prove illusory. The
post-1991 period is when hope came up against the immutability of a
common law iteration of justice requiring demonstrably probative evidence to be presented to a jury. As Paul Harrison, who became head of
the CPS Special Casework Division on war crimes in 1994, explained:
'I was not there at the very beginning but it was very clear to me when
I arrived that we were going to apply the Code for Crown Prosecutors to
these cases. We did not apply a higher or lower evidential test. I'm not
sure it would have been legal to do so.'[1]

No case is a starker illustration of the pursuit of 'legal truth' rather
than 'the truth' than that of Harijs Svikeris, who had been a senior officer
in the Latvian Auxiliary Security Police, known as the Arājs Kommando
(*Sonderkommando Arājs*) (Fig. 3.1). This force was involved in the murder of 26,000 Jews in and around Riga between July and December 1941
and committed atrocities in Belorussia in 1942. Svikeris, who lived in
the new town of Milton Keynes in Buckinghamshire, had been investigated by the Hetherington-Chalmers Inquiry after his name appeared
on a list of twenty Kommando members supplied by the Office of Special
Investigations in Washington in September 1988. He was one of the
handful of suspects about whom the inquiry recommended that there
was a *prima facie* case to investigate further: 'Consideration should be
given by the prosecuting authorities to prosecuting in three cases in

---

[1] Paul Harrison email to authors, 11 February 2022.

Safe Haven: The United Kingdom's Investigations into Nazi Collaborators and the Failure of Justice.
Jon Silverman and Robert Sherwood, Oxford University Press. © Jon Silverman and Robert Sherwood 2023.
DOI: 10.1093/oso/9780192855176.003.0004

Fig. 3.1 A group photograph of the Arājs Kommando, 1942. Victors Arājs is number 3 in the front row (the number is on his right sleeve). Harijs Svikeris, unidentified, is almost certainly in this photograph. SAL, 1986 Fund. Description 1. Case 45285, vol. 8, page 104. Latvian National Archive.

which there appears to us to be a realistic prospect of conviction on the evidence *already available* [our emphasis].[2]

For some time after becoming head of the Scotland Yard War Crimes Unit (WCU) in 1991, Detective Chief Superintendent Eddie Bathgate remained confident that the Svikeris investigation would lead to a trial:

> Svikeris was a powerful case and I would cheerfully have put him on the charge sheet. The more we [the WCU] investigated him, the stronger the case got. There was no dispute about identification, he was a volunteer and admitted during the interviews that he was present when massacres took place, without an actual confession of guilt. Moreover, he led the unit when its head [Victors Arājs] was away. Every time I saw Paul Harrison, I would say "What about Svikeris?"

---

[2] *War Crimes: Report of the War Crimes Inquiry* (1989) Cmd 744, para 9.14.

but the CPS wouldn't move off the fence and make a recommendation to prosecute.[3]

The Svikeris case deserves some granular analysis because it has much to tell us about how the War Crimes Act was interpreted, what constituted, in Bathgate's words, 'a powerful case', what undermined that presumption from the viewpoint of the Crown Prosecution Service, and the evidentiary value placed on documentation which divided the British from the American investigators. This chapter also explains how criminal inquiries into an under-researched aspect of the Holocaust, even if they did not lead to a trial in the UK, have made an invaluable contribution to historiography. As the historian of wartime Latvia Richard Plavnieks has written:

> Thus much of what we know about the Kommando is the result of decades of painstaking work by prosecutors around the globe who, to make their cases against that unit's killers, augmented the scarce wartime material at hand with witnesses of all stripes: survivors, bystanders, and the perpetrators themselves.[4]

When the Hetherington-Chalmers Inquiry reported in July 1989, it could not have anticipated that the unitary Soviet Union, with which it had dealt when organizing witness interviews, would implode within two years. This required the Crown Prosecution Service to negotiate individually with the Procuracies of the three Baltic states to formalize agreements on judicial cooperation.[5] In November 1991, after the War Crimes Act had reached the statute book, the acting Director of Public Prosecutions, Michael Bibby, sent a letter of request to the General Procurator of Latvia, Mr Y. Skrastinsh, regarding Svikeris, which was the most advanced of the War Crimes Unit's inquiries. The name

---

[3] Bathgate telephone interview with author, 4 October 1996.

[4] Plavnieks, 2013 'Nazi Collaborators on Trial during the Cold War: The Cases Against Viktors Arājs and the Latvian Auxiliary Security Police', PhD dissertation submitted to the University of North Carolina at Chapel Hill, p. 3.

[5] Though, in the immediate aftermath of the collapse of the Soviet Union, inquiries regarding cases in Belarus and Ukraine were handled by Moscow.

Svikeris has been redacted from the archive copy somewhat unnecessarily, one might think, after more than thirty years have elapsed:

> …re-advanced inquiries concerning a man called —— who was an officer in a police unit known as the Arājs Kommando, allegedly involved in a number of atrocities in Latvia.… You may be considering asking the question: as the alleged offences were committed in Latvian territory, why should not the Latvian authorities try the defendants? My answer is that the defendants will be persons who have made their homes in the UK for 40 years or more and who are now regarded as British. We think it right they should be tried according to our laws.[6]

As it turned out, of course, 'our laws' proved to be the insuperable obstacle to a trial in the UK and, had he lived beyond the mid-1990s, it was more likely that justice would have been applied in Riga rather than London.

Within three months of the letter, an agreement, largely modelled on one between the Australian Special Investigations Unit and the Latvian Procuracy, was in place but it was not until February 1993 that KGB file summaries on twenty UK-based suspects arrived at the WCU, including one on Svikeris, containing a number of serious allegations. At this point, he was a relatively healthy 75-year-old and considerably younger than Szymon Serafinowicz when he was prosecuted.

Soldiers or Murderers?

If one of the most frequently voiced arguments against late twentieth-century 'Nazi hunting' was that these were 'small fish', whose prosecution so long after the war would bring Western justice into disrepute, it could not reasonably be deployed in the case of the Arājs Kommando. The leader of the eponymous unit, Viktors Arājs, was a former law student and police officer whose 'hands were literally splattered with the

---

[6] UKNA DPP 2/13571.

blood and brains of those he shot as acts of "mercy".[7] He was tried in Hamburg in 1979, convicted of 13,000 murders and sentenced to life imprisonment. Another of his close associates, Captain Herberts Cukurs, described in court documents after the war as adjutant to Arājs, achieved an infamy expressed in the sobriquet 'the Hangman of Riga'. During the Eichmann trial in Jerusalem, witnesses accused him of acts of sadism such as killing babies by hurling them against buildings. He was assassinated by a team from The Mossad in Montevideo, Uruguay, in February 1965.[8] Thirty other members of the Arājs Kommando were executed for war crimes by the Soviet Union.

And what of Svikeris, whose signature was on documents describing himself variously as 'Head of Security, Kommando' and 'Battalion Commander'? He was born in 1918 in the historic town of Cēsis, north-east of Riga and, when war broke out, he served in a Latvian tank unit reaching the rank of lieutenant. In interviews with the British police he admitted to being an officer in the Kommando from September 1941. However, investigators believed this was a lie and that he joined in mid-July, only a fortnight after the invading German forces reached Riga on 1 July and decided to establish a 'native (*Einheimische*) auxiliary force whose assignment was to help the Nazis to kill Jews and other "undesirables".[9]

Many of these early recruits to the Kommando were drawn from an elite student fraternity called Lettonia, which espoused a radical nationalism.[10] Svikeris, like the other recruits, was a volunteer but as the historian Rudīte Vīksne writes, the choice to join was sometimes 'affected by pressures and threats that had placed the person's physical existence at risk. In the conditions of a twice-occupied country, it is difficult to establish a clear criterion of voluntary choice.'[11]

---

[7] Walters, 2009 *Hunting Evil*, pp. 333–4.

[8] Linda Kinstler in her excellent Latvian account *Come to This Court and Cry: How the Holocaust Ends* (2022), p. 24, points out that there is still historical and legal debate about Cukurs's precise role and level of culpability.

[9] Ezergailis, 1996 *The Holocaust in Latvia 1941–1944*, p. 173.

[10] Plavnieks, 2018 *Nazi Collaborators on Trial during the Cold War*, p. 30.

[11] Vīksne, 2005 'Members of the Arājs Kommando in Soviet Court Files', in *The Hidden and Forbidden History of Latvia under Soviet and Nazi Occupations, 1940–1991*, Symposium of the Commission of the Historians of Latvia, vol. 14, Institute of the History of Latvia, p. 195.

Whatever free will was exercised by putative members of the Kommando, the options for Riga's Jews were narrowing all the time. Already living in one of the worst residential areas of the city known as the 'Moscow Suburb', their number swelled as it became the designated Jewish ghetto. Most were deemed expendable by the Nazis, apart from, in the short-term, those with a skilled trade, such as glazers, plumbers, and stove fitters whose work was needed by the Wehrmacht. The Kommando 'cut its teeth' on the elimination of mainly Jewish prisoners during July, August, and September in organized executions in the Biķernieki Forest outside the city. Within three weeks of the occupation, up to 1,000 Jews had been killed there in *Aktionen* which sometimes went on all night and into the following day. By the end of August, that number had swelled to 4,000, with 1,000 Communists also killed. According to Andrew Ezergailis, a leading scholar of the Latvian Holocaust: 'Among the Latvian officers who commanded the shootings, the names that reappear most frequently in testimonies are Dibietis, Svikeris, Kalnins.'[12]

The Arājs force also took part in planned forays into the Latvian countryside to liquidate Jews living in the hinterland. These became known as the 'Blue Bus' *Aktionen*:

In a number of towns, Arājs men arrived in blue buses [the municipal buses of Riga co-opted by the Kommando] to shoot the Jews concentrated by local Latvian police. By mid-October, more than 30,000 Latvian Jews had been killed by German and Latvian police forces. Most of the remainder were shoved into a ghetto in Riga.[13]

A former member of the Kommando, Eriks Parups (designated a war criminal by the Soviets), was questioned about Svikeris in 1992: 'I would say that Svikeris was definitely in the Arājs Kommando in July 1941 but I cannot give you the exact date that he joined... The Arājs took over the

[12] Ezergailis, 1996 *The Holocaust in Latvia 1941–1944*, p. 190.
[13] Hilberg, 1993 *Perpetrators, Victims and Bystanders*, p. 101.

blue buses of Riga and used them to go to various places for executions and Harijs Svikeris was a commander of one of those buses.'[14]

The slaughter of the remaining Jews of Riga was the largest atrocity in which the Kommando participated. This followed an order to clear the ghetto in order to make room for an expected influx of thousands of Jews deported from the Reich and the Protectorate of Bohemia and Moravia. Two witnesses, questioned by the KGB in 1947 and 1952, placed Svikeris at Kommando headquarters in Riga during that period. The shootings, in two pitiless instalments on 30 November and 8 December, were carried out by as few as a dozen members of an execution commando (*Erschiessungkommando*) handpicked by General Friedrich Jeckeln, who had organized the massacre at Babyn Yar in Kyiv two months earlier. Jeckeln, who was hanged after the war by the Soviets, was personally present at the 30 November *Aktion*. The Arājs force performed an indispensable role in manning a cordon as the Riga Jews were forced to march from the city to the Rumbula Forest six miles away. About 1,000 Jews died along the route, their deaths witnessed by one of the few survivors, Frida Michelson: 'Corpses were scattered all over, rivulets of blood still oozing from the lifeless bodies. They were mostly old people, pregnant women, children, handicapped—all those who couldn't keep up with the inhuman tempo of the march.'[15]

The killings at Rumbula followed the gruesome choreography of the 'Jeckeln' system for mass executions: the Jews forced to undress, then lie face down, layer upon layer, in one of three vast pits pre-dug by 300 Russian prisoners of war (who were subsequently killed). The method was known as *Sardinenpackung*, which requires no translation, and the victims were shot in the back of the head. On 30 November, 13,000 were murdered in this fashion over the course of a long day.[16] On 8 December, another 12,000 were slaughtered. In a macabre coda, a witness recorded that: 'At the conclusion of the operation, Lieutenant Alberts Danskops of the Arājs Kommando was observed with a mandolin, playing Chopin's

---

[14] Hartley Library Special Collections, University of Southampton Archive file MS408_ A1057 2/41, p. 111.

[15] Michelson, 1981 *I Survived Rumbuli*, p. 178. Her evidence was used to convict Arājs of murder at his trial in 1979.

[16] Ezergailis, 1996 *The Holocaust in Latvia 1941–1944*, pp. 253–5.

funeral march, as he led a group of 450 Jews dragged out of hiding to the old cemetery where they were shot.'[17]

These two massacres came close to matching Babyn Yar for the sheer number murdered in a single location in the 'Holocaust of bullets'. According to a veteran Latvian nationalist, Valentins Silamikelis, local inhabitants reached for a parallel from Christian martyrdom to mark the atrocity: 'After the war, the Latvians named the Rumbula road "Golgotha Way"—in memory of the killed Jews. That was the only memorial since the Soviet power did not allow to erect a monument.'[18]

At the time of the Rumbula killings, the strength of the Arājs Kommando was about 300—it subsequently grew to 1,200 by 1943— and it is well established that virtually the entire force was involved in transporting the Jews from the ghetto and manning the cordon to the execution pits. But, as Ezergailis points out: 'To pinpoint *by name* [authors' emphasis] the Latvian "precinct" policemen who participated in the Rumbula *Aktion* is impossible.'[19] And therein lay a problem for British lawyers in attempting to construct a murder prosecution founded on live eyewitness testimony.

The Killings in Belorussia

During the early part of 1942, a gradual transformation took place as the Kommando was moulded from a relatively fluid militia into a more disciplined fighting force capable of taking on partisans. This necessitated rigorous counter-insurgency training, which Svikeris underwent at an SS school in Fürstenberg in Germany. By June 1942, the Kommando, now renamed the Latvian Security Police and SD Auxiliary Force, had been dispatched to Minsk to launch actions against pro-Soviet partisans in the Belorussian swamps. It was responsible for the killings of men, women, and children in surrounding towns and villages which may

---

[17] Account by Benjamin Edelstein (undated) in the collection of evidence prepared for the indictment of Viktors Arājs, 141 Js 534/60, pp. 6075–97.

[18] Silamikelis, 2002 *With the Baltic Flag*, p. 44. In 2002, a memorial paid for by a number of countries as well as private donors was unveiled at Rumbula.

[19] Ezergailis, 1996 *The Holocaust in Latvia 1941–1944*, p. 247.

have exceeded the number of those murdered in its Latvian operations. Witnesses who gave evidence at the trial of Viktors Arājs alleged that 'whilst he [Svikeris] was in command, entire villages were burned to the ground and the villagers murdered'.[20]

Svikeris's assertion, when interviewed by the WCU, that he joined the Kommando in September 1941 was designed to absolve him of responsibility for any of the killings which had taken place earlier during the German occupation. But testimony from his fellow Kommando member, Eriks Parups, persuaded the two historians attached to the WCU, Martin Dean and Alisdair Macleod, that Svikeris was concealing his involvement in the mass shooting of Jews in his home town of Cēsis in August 1941, the month before he claimed to have joined up:

> There appears to be some *logic* [authors' emphasis] in Svikeris being involved in the action in Cēsis as he had just come from there and knew the situation and the local police commanders on the ground. His account of his own wartime service is subject to suspicion. Svikeris claims that he did not join the Kommando until September 1941. There seems to be sufficient evidence that he was present and associated with the Arājs Kommando as early as July 1941. Svikeris also states that he never heard about the burning of synagogues in Riga [three synagogues were burnt within days of the invasion]...he must have been aware of these activities.[21]

We have emphasized 'logic' because it explains how the uncomfortable coupling of history and law has undermined war crimes prosecutions. It is entirely consistent with the historical context to infer that Svikeris was culpable, by dint of serving as a senior officer in the Arājs Kommando, a Latvian adjunct to *Einsatzgruppe A*, whose principal purpose, when it was initially formed in 1941, was to murder Jews, gypsies, political prisoners, and suspected Communists. In the words of the historian Raul Hilberg, who testified in a deportation hearing in the United States, 'the

---

[20] Hartley Library Special Collections, Archive file MS408_A1057 2/41, pp. 25–30.
[21] Hartley Library Special Collections, University of Southampton Archive file MS408_A1057 2/41, p. 183.

Arājs Kommando had no function apart from arresting, guarding, and killing civilians.'[22] Even allowing for its role in 1942 and 1943 in confronting partisans, it would not be unreasonable to describe membership of such an outfit, with such a defined purpose, as a 'joint enterprise' in the parlance of English criminal law. But the many gaps in the historical record remained a stumbling block, as explained by Martin Dean: 'Unfortunately, we were unable to find any evidence to support this assumption [about the Cēsis killings] made on how the Arājs Kommando operated.'[23]

Indeed, there is a notable paucity of Latvian-sourced records on the Kommando, almost certainly as a result of the deliberate destruction of incriminating documents as the war turned against the Nazis and their acolytes. Initial inquiries in the Latvian state archives in 1991 and 1992 turned up no contemporaneous documents relating to the force. And, according to a meeting in September 1992, between the CPS, police, and a representative of the Canadian Justice Department—which had investigated a number of Latvian suspects—neither was there any document or witness testimony in the KGB archives implicating Svikeris in what the notes on the meeting describe as 'the smoking gun incident', believed to be a reference to the Rumbula *Aktion*.[24]

This absence of contemporary documentation, combined with Latvia's 'rediscovery' after 1990 of a national history freed from the narrative orthodoxy imposed by the Soviet Union, has inspired revisionist interpretations of the Arājs Kommando which clash with the received version accepted by most Western historians. Accounts can be found—especially on Latvian websites—which re-cast the assassinated Herberts Cukurs as a patriot and aviator-hero, a 'Latvian Lindbergh' (which is how he was seen before the war) rather than as a war criminal. Indeed, as Linda Kinstler discovered, to her astonishment, the Latvian Prosecutor-General opened an investigation in 2005 to determine whether Cukurs, though dead for fifty years at that point, might merit exoneration.[25]

---

[22] US government post-trial brief on Konrad Kalejs prepared by the OSI, February 1995.
[23] Martin Dean email, 7 October 2021.
[24] This phrase was used in an official note of the meeting, 23 September 1992. UKNA DPP 2/13571.
[25] Kinstler, 2022 *Come to This Court and Cry*, p. 120.

Perhaps she should not have been so surprised because a full fifteen years earlier, as Latvia re-emerged as an independent state in 1990, the State Prosecutor, Janis Osis, who was responsible for handling the case of another Kommando officer, Konrad Kalejs, reflected that: 'The Arājs Kommando didn't only consist of executioners but also soldiers who fought against Soviet Red Army partisans. They didn't commit any war crimes.'[26]

For the investigators of Scotland Yard's War Crimes Unit, any historical gaps in knowledge were filled by depositions provided for the trial of Arājs in Germany and the many Soviet trials of Kommando members between 1944 and 1967. On the basis of this material, primarily accumulated by the unit's historians, Detective Chief Inspector Dermot McDermott, of the WCU, interviewed Svikeris in February 1994: 'Witnesses have said that in December or January 1941, the Arājs Kommando, under your command, killed 300–400 Jews [a serious underestimate] outside Riga near Rumbula Station. The shooting went on all day.'[27]

Svikeris's response was the same as the one he had given to the Hetherington-Chalmers Inquiry five years earlier:

I joined the Arājs Kommando but distanced myself when I saw what was happening... My sole duty was to train the soldiers. I was never present when the Germans shot Jews nor was I present when they were transported. I was not a senior officer under Arājs. Arājs was not a real officer. I didn't think much of him. I spoke German and was often used as an interpreter and as a link between the Germans and Latvians. I fought in Latvia and Russia. I never went to Minsk. I heard the Germans and Arājs discussing killing mentally ill people. I was not involved.[28]

The suggestion that Arājs was not a 'real officer' echoed the line taken by the defence at the trial of Arājs in Germany, that he was a mere puppet

[26] Osis interview with author, accessed on the BBC News website, www.bbc.co.uk 'Latvia Killers Rehabilitated', 26 January 2000.
[27] Hartley Library Special Collections, Archive file MS408_A1057 2/41, p. 150.
[28] Ibid., pp. 100–1.

or conduit for German criminality. And Svikeris's claim that he 'fought' was dismissed by Eriks Parups in an interview given in June 1992:

> The Kommando was not employed at the front but behind the lines where they killed partisans and burned down villages. There was no requirement for a training officer in the Kommando...and I would have known if they required one. I would say 'Harry [i.e. Svikeris] I feel sorry for you, you have been stupid'. He's telling lies.[29]

Another former member of the Kommando, Arnis Upmalis, who spent ten years in a Soviet labour camp for war crimes and testified about the killings at Biķernieki at the trial of Victors Arājs in Germany, rubbished the claim that Svikeris never went to Minsk. In an interview with Hetherington-Chalmers in January 1989, he said that the last time he had seen Svikeris was in Minsk in August 1942. The historians Andrej Angrick and Peter Klein argue that 'Arnis Upmalis can be considered a credible witness for he was able to recall a good number of details with considerable precision...he described his various uniforms correctly; and he gave an exact description of the crime scene and the route taken'.[30] Upmalis confirmed that Svikeris was 'an important assistant aide' to Arājs.[31] One of the WCU historians told McDermott that even if Svikeris had been a training officer, he was still likely to have participated in killing. 'Even the clerk became involved in the killings'.[32]

A Priority One Killer but no Prosecution

In July 1994, Martin Dean and Detective Superintendent David Sibley conducted a review of all the 'live' cases the unit was dealing with and assessed them in order of significance. Svikeris was categorized as 'Priority One' with the CPS preparing a report for possible prosecution.[33]

[29] Ibid., p. 108.   [30] Angrick and Klein, 2009 *The "Final Solution" in Riga*, p. 222.
[31] Ibid., p. 127.
[32] Hartley Library Special Collections Archive file MS408_A1057 2/41, p. 108.
[33] Martin Dean note of case review 14 July 1994 Hartley Library Special Collections, Archive file MS408_A1057 2/35, p. 1011.

(It is worth bearing in mind that, at this point, Andrzej Sawoniuk, the sole suspect to be convicted, was only a Priority Two case.) Sibley's boss, Chief Superintendent Eddie Bathgate, had no doubts about the man they were dealing with:

> The interviews were video-taped and you could see he was guilty. One of my last remarks to the CPS was 'you are not going to be able NOT to prosecute Svikeris'. And one of the reasons we kept on with the investigation was that all the signs and hints we were getting from the CPS were positive. In fact, I believe they thought it was a runner but it was independent counsel which [sic] said 'no'.[34]

It is unclear whether Bathgate felt that he was receiving 'mixed messages' from the CPS but the archive files leave no doubt that, however compelling a case appeared on paper, it would not be prosecuted without live, legally admissible eyewitness evidence. Such was the ruthlessly efficient elimination of Latvian Jewry that no reliable survivor witnesses to the *Aktionen* in Cēsis and Rumbula could be found to identify Svikeris. And once the Kommando had been transferred to Belorussian territory, the chances of a positive identification dwindled further. As Efraim Zuroff, of the Simon Wiesenthal Center, has written:

> those who survived did not know the identity of the killers. This was particularly true of those who escaped murder by the *Einsatzgruppen* and their collaborators from local killing squads. In such cases, there was virtually no possibility that they could identify the murderers, with whom they had never had any contact either before or after the murders.[35]

For Paul Harrison, who headed the CPS Special Casework Division on war crimes, the Svikeris case foundered on insuperable obstacles:

> Eddie Bathgate is right to say that the case was extensively investigated and that we had hopes that it might go further. It was one of a handful

---

[34] Bathgate telephone interview, 4 October 1996.
[35] Zuroff, 2009 *Operation Last Chance*, p. 44.

[about six] that we identified as a possible prosecution and which we referred to Treasury Counsel and ultimately to the Attorney General. Svikeris, as I recall it, was a case that relied on documentary evidence and had no eyewitness. You perhaps would not expect a witness in a case like that. We would have had to build a case relying on documents alone.[36]

The Written Word versus Live Witnesses

The strategy pursued successfully by the Nuremberg prosecutors was to use the evidence found in captured German documents to incriminate the defendants and substantiate the charges. In setting out the rules of procedure, Charter V of the IMT gave the tribunal licence to 'admit any evidence which it deems to have probative value'.[37] This provided the court with considerably more latitude than found under the common law rules of an English murder prosecution. And it is possible to gain some instructive insights into the workings of the English legal mind by examining the confidential briefings on the Svikeris case, involving police, historians, the CPS, and Treasury Counsel. The starting point was a consideration of the American position which was heavily influenced by the opinions of the foremost Latvian authority on the Arājs Kommando, Professor Andrew Ezergailis, and the eminent historian of the Holocaust, Raul Hilberg.

A paper presented by Ezergailis at the 9th International Convention on Baltic Studies in Stockholm in June 1987 entitled 'Sonderkommando Arājs' had anatomized the structure of the Kommando—designating Svikeris as one of eight platoon leaders in the early days of the unit—and detailing its participation in the Latvian Holocaust of the Jews. For Raul Hilberg, Svikeris's role as adjutant to Arājs meant that 'he was necessarily involved in the execution actions'. On the strength of this, the American Office of Special Investigations (OSI), under its third director,

---

[36] Paul Harrison email, 12 July 2021.
[37] Charter V 'Powers of the Tribunal and Conduct of the Trial Art. 19' Agreement for the Prosecution and Punishment of the Major War Criminals of the European Axis, and Charter of the International Military Tribunal, London, 8 August 1945.

Neal Sher, believed that, had Svikeris been living in the United States, there would have been sufficient cause to instigate proceedings against him, a view later endorsed by his successor, Eli Rosenbaum.[38]

The analysis by the Crown Prosecution Service, like a counsel's strategic briefing ahead of a courtroom battle, began with a summation of the 'adversary's' position:

> Sher refers in his letter [to the Hetherington-Chalmers Inquiry] to the OSI 'prosecutions' but it should be remembered that the OSI proceedings are in respect of *immigration* [authors' emphasis] offences... the OSI case was:
>
> a) All members of the Arājs Kommando participated in some fashion in a killing action;
>
> b) That Svikeris was in charge of some of the killing operations having served as an adjutant to Viktors Arājs himself;
>
> c) That Svikeris was a Battalion Commander of the entire force of six companies of the Arājs Kommando during a series of liquidation actions;
>
> d) That documentary evidence supports Svikeris's role as Acting Commander of the Arājs Kommando;
>
> e) That reliance should be placed on Professor Hilberg's contention that Svikeris, in the senior position of adjutant to Viktors Arājs, necessarily involved Svikeris in the execution actions.[39]

The OSI assessment clearly has weight as a circumstantial indictment, but the CPS diagnosed its weak spot: that there was no direct evidence of Svikeris having served as an adjutant to Arājs nor that he was a battalion commander. Furthermore:

> An important observation to make is that the allegation put forward by the OSI against Svikeris does not contain any specific and identifiable

[38] Rosenbaum interview with authors, 18 September 2022.
[39] Legal note (unsigned) in Hartley Library Special Collections Archive file MS 408_A1057 2/41, pp. 173–4.

act of homicide…There is insufficient evidence at present to make any value judgment of the Arājs Kommando involvement in the Rumbula Forest executions…The conclusion which has to be drawn at this stage is that despite clear evidence of Arājs Kommando members being involved in the whole occupation of Latvia, there does not appear to be a specific type of activity which was compulsory and which was undertaken by all Arājs Kommando members. This being the case, there is no substance at this stage for the argument that mere membership of the Arājs Kommando is evidence of involvement in war crimes or atrocities.[40]

There are two points of interest in this confidential opinion which provide a stark illustration of the clash between history and law. The first is that, in the final sentence, the CPS appears to challenge or, at the very least, question the historiographic consensus that the Arājs Kommando was established solely for one malign purpose, namely, to assist the Germans in liquidating all the Jews of Latvia. The second is the unwillingness, 'at present to make a value judgment' about its participation in the Rumbula massacres, despite the weight of testimony proffered in numerous trials. Moreover, it is worth noting that, even had the police and lawyers been able to place Svikeris, with certainty, at Rumbula on the day of either *Aktion*, the inference is that the case would still not have reached the evidential threshold. And this despite the fact that he met the CPS-imposed 'command' criterion for culpability more conclusively than either Serafinowicz or Sawoniuk.

The transatlantic disagreement over the Svikeris case illustrates how US inquiries, because they centred around post-war immigration and naturalization law, conceived the trial process as a synergy between historian and attorney, seeing them as equal partners in the intended outcome. The historian Peter Black played an influential role in developing some of the OSI's most celebrated cases:

It is true that, in many ways, the attorneys and investigators took the lead but from fairly early on [after he joined the OSI full time in 1980],

---

[40] Ibid., pp. 173/178–9.

the historians started to gather primary documentation on individual suspects... often based on what those associated with them had said and this gave us a fairly accurate and reliable picture of what the daily life and activities of the defendant was. So, an expert witness could get up before a judge and say that... this activity [i.e. the infliction of violence etc.] was part of the standard operating procedure of this particular unit in this particular place. This enabled us to put cases together on paper when the witness testimony in court was usually not enough on its own.[41]

By contrast, the English adversarial system decreed that a case was winnable only if live witnesses could convince a jury, under cross-examination, that the defendant had committed the specific crimes with which he had been charged. This terse undated note from the CPS represents the final word on the subject: 'Insufficient evidence to prosecute Svikeris purely on the basis that he was a member of the Arājs Kommando and therefore a killer.'[42]

It can be argued persuasively that the Crown was fulfilling its function in standing foursquare behind a legal principle which was essentially the same as that expressed by the Judge Advocate General, Carl J. Sterling, during the Belsen prosecution of Irma Grese and Josef Kramer. He admonished counsel in their trial for presenting too much evidence that was 'vague' and ruled that the court should ignore witnesses who said:

> She threw people to the ground and cruelly beat them and many died... The court would have to be satisfied that a person on the staff at Auschwitz or Belsen concentration camp was guilty of deliberately committing a war crime; just being a member of the staff itself was not enough to justify conviction.[43]

[41] Peter Black Oral History Interview USHMM Collections Division Archives Branch Accession No:2000.169 RG No RG-50.030.0409.
[42] Hartley Library Special Collections Archive file MS408_A1057 2/41, p. 81.
[43] UNWCC report, p. 117.

But the historian David Fraser argues that a post-Auschwitz jurisprudence demands a different set of legal standards. Writing about suspects
who claimed exculpation on the grounds that their role was merely
to surround a ghetto or provide a cordon around a killing site while
the Germans went about their gruesome business, he refuses to see a
distinction in guilt: 'The idea that the only perpetrators who deserve
punishment or who are responsible in a legal or moral sense are those
who actually pulled the triggers... is ill-founded in law and in ethical
discourse.'[44]

The decision not to prosecute Svikeris was partly influenced by the
negative experience of Australia's Special Investigations Unit (SIU). The
three Australian prosecutions all involved crimes committed in Ukraine.
Two never made it beyond the committal stage of a trial and the third
resulted in a jury acquittal. A so-called 'fourth case' concerned a platoon
commander in the Arãjs Kommando, Karlis Ozols, who had been interrogated by the KGB at the war's end.[45] This case had been considered at
one time to be the most promising of all but after the departure from
office of Bob Hawke and Lionel Bowen, as Prime Minister and Attorney-
General, respectively, it was never prosecuted. Paul Harrison said that
the failures of the Australian war crimes process weighed heavily on
Treasury Counsel and the CPS in the UK:

> A team was sent to Australia (maybe more than once) where I think
> they had investigated an Arãjs Kommando case [in fact, several] and
> we learned a lot from them. Their cases had been document only cases
> and had failed. We decided that prosecuting a case on documents
> alone would not be attempted here as there was insufficient prospect
> of success.[46]

The police team interviewed hundreds of witnesses, some eighty of them
former members of the Arãjs Kommando scattered around the globe.
Sixteen said that they had either heard the name Svikeris in connection

[44] Fraser, 2005 Law After Auschwitz, p. 266.
[45] Ozols was interrogated at Stalinogorsk, 30 October 1945 (KGB Trial Records).
[46] Paul Harrison email, 12 July 2021.

with the unit or knew him personally as an officer in the Kommando. But, according to Martin Dean, it was felt that this testimony added very little to the *prima facie* case established by the Hetherington-Chalmers Inquiry, deriving mainly from KGB sources which the CPS would not rely on in court:

> There was some corroborating historical (non-KGB) wartime documentation but, at that time, this would never be enough to even bring a case to court let alone convict someone. The case did get stronger when we interviewed Svikeris as he admitted being present during one shooting. However, the only witness who could corroborate this became increasingly unreliable over time, which was why the CPS had not made a decision to prosecute when Svikeris died.[47]

Even allowing for the rightful primacy of due process in determining war crimes prosecutions, it is hard to argue that, in the Svikeris case and many others, the application of the War Crimes Act provided an outcome matching the enormity of the crimes. And there must be some sympathy with this rueful observation by Robert Greenwood QC, the former head of the SIU, reflecting on his country's abortive war crimes inquiries: 'Unfortunately, you see, the more civilized you get, the more obedient you get to the rule of law, the more easily we are outsmarted by devils and perhaps that is what has happened to us.'[48]

Slipping through the Net

The criticism, 'too little too late' has justifiably been applied to attempts to use the law to address Nazi-related war crimes. In many cases, it was explicable that in the post-war maelstrom of a devastated Europe, perpetrators managed to hide their identity or, if caught, benefit from the rapidly changing strategic priorities of the Allied occupiers of Germany

[47] Martin Dean email, 7 October 2021.
[48] Greenwood speech in Melbourne, 14 November 1994 reported in *Australia/Israel Review*, vol. 20(1), January 1995.

and Austria. But the fact that Svikeris avoided any judicial reckoning at all and Arājs only belatedly after many years of freedom can be laid substantially at the door of British indifference and irresolution. Both men fell into British hands at the end of the war. Svikeris, with his family, was last sighted by his fellow Latvian, Eriks Parups, in a Displaced Persons camp at Lübeck in the British occupied zone in 1946.[49] He arrived in Britain in either 1947 or 1948 as part of the European Voluntary Workers scheme to recruit workers for industry and agriculture.[50] He became a British citizen and lived in Wales before moving to Milton Keynes in 1982.

Arājs assumed a false name and for a time was interned in a general POW camp for Latvians in Schleswig. But his true identity was uncovered, or revealed by a fellow inmate, and he was sent to a transit camp for captured SS personnel at Eckenfelde and later, after a brief escape, to a British-run POW camp in Braunschweig. The Arājs Kommando men were among 50,000 Balts in the British Zone, of whom a significant portion were Latvians and according to historian David Cesarani, 'there was enormous confusion about who they were, their military history, and what should be done with them'.[51] But they had at least one influential advocate in the form of Charles Zarine, the Minister of the Latvian Legation in London, who lobbied the British authorities assiduously on behalf of Arājs and others who had been named as war criminals in the Soviet press: 'They were great national patriots, men of quite modest means; anti-Bolshevik, of course, but certainly not to be described as fascists. I should feel very relieved if His Majesty's Government would allow them to come to the safety of this country.'[52]

As one of the more egregious crimes committed by the occupation forces in the Baltic states, the liquidation of the Jews of Riga appeared to be a priority for investigation by the military authorities. What was known as the 'Riga Ghetto' case fell under the remit of the War Crimes Group of the British Army of the Rhine, and, for several months,

[49] Hartley Library Special Collections Archive file MS408_A1057 2/41, p. 108.
[50] For more information on the EVW scheme, see Cesarani, 1992 *Justice Delayed*.
[51] Cesarani, 1992 *Justice Delayed*, p. 44. .
[52] Zarine to Robert (Robin) Hankey of the Foreign Office, 21 January 1947, UKNA FO 371/65754.

Arājs was subjected to 'confrontation with witnesses and a thorough investigation'.[53] The records show that, from November 1947, the questioning took place at the Number 2 War Crimes Holding Centre.[54] In January 1948, a Major Charles Kaiser compiled a list of twenty-seven Latvians and Germans alleged to have perpetrated the Riga crimes, including both Arājs and Cukurs: 'All these people were mentioned again and again by every witness we have found up to now and they are specially accused for their bestial behaviour and their crimes...they should all be tried for mass murder, heavy ill treatment and robbery.'[55]

As Guy Walters records, there is an unexplained gap in the timeline between the middle of 1946 and November 1947, when Arājs arrived at the Holding Centre. He claimed to have been asked by British intelligence to work for them, undertaking spying missions in both Latvia and the Soviet Union: 'If such an offer was made—and it has never been denied—then the British were knowingly trying to employ one of the worst criminals of the war. Arājs was no ordinary collaborator but a man itching to participate in the slaughter of non-combatants and children.'[56]

Whatever the truth of Arājs's claim, there is no dispute that the British intelligence service, SIS (MI6) did recruit Balts during the early years of the Cold War to run missions into the Soviet Union. For example, the official historian of SIS, Keith Jeffery, notes that in October 1949 'SIS infiltrated two trained Latvian émigrés "who claimed to have the possibility of making contact...with some patriots who supported groups of Partisans living in the Latvian forests" '.[57]

The former MI6 officer Anthony Cavendish was responsible for running just such an operation and admitted to having no qualms about using collaborators, including former Waffen SS men and members of the Arājs Kommando: 'If somebody was needed to do a job and if he had committed war crimes, I would use him to do the job, ones I felt essential.'[58]

[53]   Ezergailis, 1996 *The Holocaust in Latvia 1941–1944*, p. 179.
[54]   UKNA WO 309/1819; GWDN 7237.
[55]   UKNA WO 309/1816; GWDN: 7213–7215.   [56]   Walters, 2009 *Hunting Evil*, p. 333.
[57]   Jeffery, 2010 *MI6: The History of the Secret Intelligence Service, 1909–1949*, p. 709.
[58]   Cavendish interview with Tom Bower, BBC 2 'Newsnight', 11 December 1989.

The former CIA director William Colby provided further confirmation that some Latvians were deemed useful by the agencies of the West, in a televised interview in 1986. Commenting on an accused war crimes suspect, he said: 'The man had specialized with notable success in the recruitment of Soviet Latvian defectors.'[59]

In February 1949, Arājs was released on a writ of habeas corpus secured from a judge of the British Control Commission Court, who was sympathetic to the argument that the prosecution had failed to produce sufficient evidence to justify his continued detention.[60] This despite the wealth of witness testimony about his actions in Riga, which can be seen either as a signal failure by the British military authorities, or as vindication of his claim that some sort of deal had been struck to keep him out of prison, or simply because, as Donald Bloxham speculated: 'there was no longer a court with competent jurisdiction to try him.'[61] For a period, according to Ezergailis, he even found a job as a driver for the British military in Delmhorst.[62]

In 1949, British military jurisdiction was replaced by the newly established Federal Republic of West Germany and the 'Riga Ghetto' case was handed over to the provincial court in Hamburg which issued an arrest warrant for Arājs in October of that year. But it could not be served because the suspect had disappeared and it is unclear what efforts, if any, were made to trace him. In the early 1950s, using the alias 'Viktors Zeibots' (his wife's maiden name), Arājs obtained a travel pass from the Latvian Legation in London, no doubt through the good offices of Charles Zarine. He moved to a different part of the country, settling with his family in Frankfurt, where he was finally arrested in 1975. The indictment read: 'Through the end of 1942, the extermination of the Jews in the Latvian area was the particular task of the Arājs units... These Latvians fanatically hated Jews and Communists and exploited every opportunity in order to inflict terrible vigilante justice on their opponents.'[63]

---

[59] Quoted in Feigin, 2006 *The Office of Special Investigations*, p. 125 fn. 9.

[60] PRO FO 371/77060, CG 3545/15/184.

[61] Bloxham, 2001 *Genocide on Trial*, p. 197.

[62] Ezergailis, 1996 *The Holocaust in Latvia 1941–1944*, p. 179.

[63] 'War crimes case of Viktor Bernhard Arājs', RG-06.009.03, US Department of Justice, Office of Special Investigations, USHMM, Microfiche, p. 89.

His trial in Hamburg heard witness evidence supplied by the Soviet Union, the United States, and Israel. Arājs claimed that he had been acquitted by the British at the conclusion of the 'Riga Ghetto Case'. Richard Plavnieks regards the claim as 'a clear impossibility because that case was never concluded, but instead handed over to the very court before which he was sitting'.[64]

The court took the same view and just before Christmas in 1979, Arājs was convicted of causing at least 13,000 deaths, principally on the second day, 8 December 1941, of the Rumbula *Aktion*. He was sentenced to life imprisonment and died in Kassel-Wehlheiden Prison in 1988.

The Deportable Konrad Kalejs

The mass of witness testimony gathered for the trial of Arājs threw up other names of Kommando members who had survived the war and emigrated from Europe, particularly to Australia. One was Teodors Bumanis, chief of the personnel section, whose rank was Legion *Untersturmführer*. The SIU also sought assistance from the Procurator General in Riga in locating documents and witnesses in the cases of Leo Jurka, Janis Balodis, Voldemars Balodis, Janis Inis, and Karlis Auzins, all thought to be alive in Australia in 1990.[65] But the name which provoked the greatest interest among investigators was Konrad Kalejs. He was another of the early platoon lieutenants and captains of the Arājs Kommando, who allegedly committed war crimes in Latvia. Unlike Svikeris, Kalejs did, at least, find himself arraigned in court in the United States, though facing civil rather than criminal proceedings.[66] Curiously, his post-war life was bookended by encounters with the British authorities when he found himself in a Displaced Persons Camp near Rotenburg in the British administered zone of Germany in 1946, and more than half a century later when, to the embarrassment of the British

---

[64] Plavnieks, 2013 'Nazi Collaborators on Trial during the Cold War', p. 182.

[65] File SIU 624/2 in National Records of Scotland Collection AD 43/3/12/1.

[66] Much information about the organization of Arājs Kommando killing missions emerged from his trial transcript: *In the Matter of Konrad Kalejs*, US District Court in Chicago November 1 1998, pp. 9–11.

government, he was discovered living under an alias, Viktor Kalnins (bizarrely, he'd chosen the name of another Kommando member), in a Midlands nursing home for elderly Latvians.

Kalejs had arrived in the UK in September 1999 as a visitor on a six-month tourist visa. He was not identified as a war crimes suspect and his details were not included amongst the 500,000 names in the Suspect Index held by the Immigration and Nationality Service, an omission which was subsequently the subject of an internal inquiry. Kalejs had travelled on a freshly issued passport which contained no mention of his previous deportations from the United States and Canada. Once his presence in the UK became known, he was interviewed by officers from Scotland Yard (the War Crimes Unit had, by then, been disbanded) but he was not asked about his involvement in the Arãjs Kommando. Questions were confined to his identity and when he planned to leave Britain.[67] But even if there had been a thorough investigation and sufficient evidence unearthed, it might have taken lengthy legal argument to determine whether Kalejs's 'temporary' stay at a Leicestershire nursing home counted as 'residency' in the UK, as stipulated in the terms of the War Crimes Act, thereby making him liable for prosecution.

As with the case of the former Chilean president, Augusto Pinochet, who was also temporarily marooned in a British care facility in the late 1990s, the government was faced with a barrage of human rights demands to act. The Israel Director of the Simon Wiesenthal Center, Dr Efraim Zuroff, commented: 'I believe that Britain has a historic obligation to help prosecute Kalejs. In that respect, his presence in the UK should be viewed as an opportunity to bring one of the Holocaust's terrible criminals to trial and strike a blow for justice, rather than as an annoying bureaucratic problem.'[68]

The then Home Secretary, Jack Straw, accepted that 'reasonable grounds existed to believe that Kalejs was complicit in war crimes'.[69] But because the suspect had become an Australian rather than a British citizen after the war, Straw interpreted the appeal to fulfil a 'historic obligation'

---

[67] Vikram Dodd, 'New evidence shows record of war crime suspect was not investigated', *The Guardian*, 6 January 2000.
[68] Wiesenthal Center Press Information, issued 3 January 2000.
[69] Home Secretary statement re-'Konrad Kalejs', 6 January 2000.

by signing a deportation order against Kalejs. Theorizing arguments for deploying either the civil or criminal law against Kalejs, David Fraser writes that:

> the true effect of the deportation of someone like Kalejs in this instance is the opposite of a national statement recognizing and 'nationalizing' the Holocaust. In other words, the semiotic import of deportation here is to declare the fate of Kalejs and the fate of his victims, in terms of law, to be of no concern to the government and people of Britain. If he is to be tried, that is someone else's concern.[70]

In the event, Kalejs demonstrated that he remained in control of his fate by slipping out of the country unnoticed and returning to Melbourne before legal hearings could begin. His case illustrates a truth: remarkably, some 350 Arājs Kommando members, almost a third of the total strength, survived the war and were captured and punished, the majority in Soviet courts. But a suspected killer who ended up in 'Western' hands stood a reasonable chance of escaping any kind of justice at all. For example, in the 1990s, the Canadian government failed in its attempt to deport a former Latvian police and Waffen SS member, Peter Vitols, accused of collaboration with the Nazis. A court ruled that it had not met the threshold of evidence to establish that he had lied on his immigration entry form.[71]

Much of the information about the wartime activities of Konrad Kalejs was unearthed by Australia's SIU and the American OSI. Both of these bodies believed in discharging a duty to the historical record and the following information comes from a US Department of Justice Post-Trial Brief submitted for denaturalization hearings against Kalejs between 1985 and 1994.[72]

Like Svikeris, Kalejs joined the Arājs Kommando almost at its inception in July 1941. The historian Raul Hilberg testified that 'those

---

[70] Fraser, 2005 *Law After Auschwitz*, p. 300.

[71] *Minister of Citizenship and Immigration v. Vitols* Part IV, paras. 89 et seq.

[72] Details from the Brief were published in a Special Report for the *Australia/Israel Review*, 15 February–7 March 1995, pp. 6–11. Two caveats should be borne in mind. This publication was a strong supporter of war crimes trials and the quoted sections are described as 'excerpts'.

individuals, such as Konrad Kalejs, who joined after the first few weeks, could not have been in any doubt as to the nature of the duties that they would be expected to carry out, since the unit had already been involved in arrests of civilians as well as shootings totalling in the thousands'.[73]

The standard defence put forward by those suspects who admitted to membership of the Kommando was that their assigned tasks did not include hands-on participation in *Aktionen*. Hilberg's research suggested otherwise:

> Because the unit had so few members who were available to be assigned to any particular shooting operation, and because the shooting actions took place so frequently, all Latvian Auxiliary Security Police personnel were personally involved in the killings, even the staff of the supply department and the motor-pool mechanics. These executions were supervised by officers *such as Kalejs* [authors' emphasis] who were present at the shooting sites.[74]

The Horror of Salaspils

The point has already been made that Raul Hilberg's assessment was regarded as no more than circumstantial by common law criminal jurisdictions which would not rely on it without supporting eyewitness testimony. But the case against Kalejs was bolstered by the fact that he was known to have commanded an Arājs Kommando detachment which guarded the Salaspils slave labour camp (officially designated as a Police Prison and Work Education Camp) south-east of Riga. Thousands of Jews from many parts of Europe, including Poland, Czechoslovakia, and Austria, as well as Soviet citizens, were held there in inhuman conditions.[75]

---

[73] Special Report of the *Australia/Israel Review*, p. 6.   [74] Ibid., p. 6.
[75] The former head of the investigation department of the KGB of the Latvian SSR, Vladimir Izvestnyi, carried out a war crimes investigation into the head of construction at Salaspils and gave a vivid description of conditions at the camp in an oral history interview recorded in March 2004, to be found in the USHMM Collections Division Archives Branch. Oral History Accession No. 2003.456.29 RG No. RG-50.568.0029.

Alfred Winter, who became a US citizen after the war, was assigned to the burial detail with his brother between December 1941 and May 1942. His job was to retrieve corpses from the barracks and bury them. In evidence given to the US Department of Justice, he said: 'Since the ground was frozen, the bodies collected were left out in a field until a mass grave could be dynamited open. During the three months that this dynamiting was going on, crows fed on the corpses in the field. Eight hundred and fifty bodies were put into the grave, filling it only two-thirds full.'[76]

Kalejs was said to have had responsibility for assigning guards to specific duties and exercising disciplinary authority over the guards company, one of whom was Arnis Upmalis, later convicted of war crimes. In 2000, Upmalis told one of the authors that his job was 'just to stop trespassers' and that he was not directly involved in killings. But he admitted that 'There was a special execution unit and yes, it was a crime against humanity.'[77]

One of the denaturalization hearings in the US heard testimony from a former Arājs Kommando member, Karlis Strazds, who had been sent to join the guard detachment at Salaspils in November 1942 under the command of Kalejs. He described the prisoners' living conditions as 'very hard, very crowded, with inedible food in meagre portions and much disease. They [the prisoners] were also subject to beatings. Many people died as a result of the living conditions, disease and overwork.'[78]

Prisoners too weak to work were taken to a secluded spot and shot. It was also alleged that German doctors visited Salaspils to perform involuntary quasi-medical experiments on inmates. Two former Arājs Kommando members, Rudolf Soms and Karlis Rozkalns, testified about battles in which they had participated with Kalejs in February 1942 at Zabolotye and Sanniki in Belorussia when the force had been sent to join Einsatzcommando units attempting to quell partisan resistance.

---

[76] Quoted in US Department of Justice brief, excerpts of which were published in a Special Report for the *Australia/Israel Review*, 15 February–7 March 1995, pp. 6–7.

[77] Upmalis interview with Jon Silverman, accessed on the BBC News website, www.bbc.co.uk, 'Latvia Killers Rehabilitated', 26 January 2000.

[78] Special Report of the *Australia/Israel Review*, 15 February–7 March 1995: *The Evidence Against Konrad Kalejs*, p. 11.

The latter engagement, in which Harijs Svikeris also took part, was notable for the death in action of the overall commander of *Einsatzgruppe A*, SS General Franz Stahlecker. The witnesses said that: 'In retaliation for Stahlecker's [fatal] injury, Kalej's company annihilated the villagers and burned the village to the ground. In one village, the villagers were all driven into one building and the building was then burned down with them inside.'[79]

The Post-War Journey of Kalejs

There are conflicting accounts of exactly when Kalejs arrived in Australia from Europe as a Displaced Person (DP) but the consensus seems to be 1950. The UK had encouraged Australia's Minister of Immigration to sign an agreement with the International Refugee Organization in July 1947 to resettle DPs and, under its terms, more than 170,000 immigrated to Australia.[80] It is known that for three years in the early 1950s Kalejs worked at the Bonegilla migrant camp in the state of Victoria. The investigative journalist Mark Aarons wrote that: 'Kalejs occupied the important position of documentation and processing clerk at the Bonegilla camp. In this position, he was well placed to help other ex-Nazis, handling many sensitive documents, especially the issuing of identity cards to other migrants who had no papers.'[81]

This has led to speculation that he may have been co-opted by the Australian Security Intelligence Organization (ASIO) to vet other European refugees of interest.[82] There is no firm evidence for this suggestion though the former head of the SIU, Robert Greenwood, confirmed that amongst the voluminous files on the Arājs Kommando cases which his team had collected, were a number of ASIO 'activity files'.[83]

Kalejs became an Australian citizen in 1957, having claimed on his application that he had spent the war years as a farm labourer (pre-war,

[79] Ibid., p. 7.
[80] *Review of Material Relating to the Entry of Suspected War Criminals into Australia* (known as the Menzies Report), submitted to the Australian government, 28 November 1986, p. 34.
[81] Aarons, 1989 *Sanctuary*, p. 98.   [82] Ibid., p. 98.
[83] *Sydney Morning Herald* online, http://www.smh.com.au (accessed 4 January 2000).

he had actually been a farmhand before joining the Latvian army and then the Arājs Kommando). But within two years, he had moved to the United States, where over time, he became a wealthy property developer, so wealthy that he was reported to have posted a bond of $750,000 when his deportation case was pending, to keep him out of custody.[84] Kalejs did not petition for US citizenship and lived openly under his own name.

It is surprising that despite the number of Arājs Kommando cases disposed of by Soviet courts in the quarter century after the war, and the growing amount of information about the Latvian Holocaust, that Kalejs's name did not appear on any war crimes list nor was he the subject of an extradition request until the very end of his life. It was only in 1984, when he was living in St. Petersburg, Florida, that he came to the attention of the OSI which filed a suit for removal on the grounds that he had made a 'wilful misrepresentation or concealment' about his wartime activities when applying for a visa to enter the US. In 1985, he was arrested.

The background information which could have accelerated the proceedings in the United States was held by Australia but the authorities there, perhaps under pressure from Latvian emigrant organizations, were reluctant to hand it over. In response, a highly placed OSI source dismissed Australian interlocutors as 'incompetent buffoons'.[85] Mark Aarons, whose revelations galvanized the Canberra government into examining its post-war immigration record on Nazi collaborators, concluding that a war crimes act was needed, wrote: 'The Kalejs case takes on a special irony because...the US authorities made repeated approaches to the Australian government for assistance in preparing their case against him. But the Aussies did nothing until 1986 [when the Menzies Inquiry recommended a law change].'[86]

It took nine years of hearings by US immigration judges and adjudications through the labyrinthine Federal appellate system before a final deportation ruling was made. At one point, Kalejs produced documents purporting to be 'certificates of good conduct' from both the US and

---

[84] Andrew Buncombe, *The Independent*, 4 January 2000, p. 3.
[85] Off-the-record conversation with Jon Silverman, 5 January 2000.
[86] Aarons, 1989 *Sanctuary*, p. 99.

British military dating from the 1940s and early 1950s to support his case. One of the four primary grounds for removal from the US is membership in a 'hostile movement', i.e., one that was hostile to the United States during the war. Unlike the test applied by the CPS in the UK, the administration does not need to prove that the defendant/respondent engaged in any specific conduct.[87] Testimony from Arājs Kommando members who had been imprisoned by the Soviet Union left no room for doubt that Kalejs had been a prominent officer in the force. And in 1988 a Federal appellate judge ruled that he had been in command of guard units not only at Salaspils but also two other concentration camps, Porkhov and Sauriesi. By 1994, with all legal options exhausted, Kalejs was finally deported to Australia.

Kalejs was then in his eighties but determined to return to North America and he made two attempts to enter Canada. This resulted in a number of legal hearings as he contested the clear evidence of his involvement with the Arājs Kommando, claiming that documents incriminating him were forgeries. When the deportation proceedings went against him, he again returned to Australia. The last dramatic act of his post-war odyssey was his clandestine entry to the UK in 1999 and concealment in a nursing/retirement home run by the Latvian Welfare Association. His stay lasted only four months and before a deportation order could be progressed with a hearing in person, he returned surreptitiously to Australia, labelled by the former war crimes investigator, Lord (Greville) Janner, 'the most unwanted wanted man in the world'.[88]

Given the global publicity, the presence of Kalejs was as much an embarrassment to the Australian government as it had been to the British, the more so since questions were asked about why he hadn't been prosecuted when the Special Investigation Unit was functioning. Indeed, the decision to close down the SIU from June 1992, and not pursue any more indictments, was taken even before the three cases already prosecuted had finished their journey through the courts. Historian Martin Dean later expressed his chagrin:

[87] See e.g. *United States v. Wittje*, 333 F.Supp.2d 737,748(N.D.Ill.2004)aff'd,422 F.3d 479 (7th Cir.2005).
[88] *Daily Telegraph*, 4 January 2000, p. 6.

it was clearly frustrating for me to see many of them closed down before even an effective preliminary historical analysis had been conducted. Access to search files (or summaries thereof) in these cases would have helped in identifying those that were most promising and in shifting resources in a timely fashion to pursue those leads.[89]

Unlike the UK, where a change of government in 1997 did not have an influence on the war crimes investigations, party politics impacted heavily on the Australian SIU. After it was disbanded, its former head, Robert Greenwood, said that when the newly appointed Attorney-General, Michael Duffy, assumed responsibility for prosecuting policy in 1990:

> my task immediately became not only difficult, not only incredibly frustrating, not only incredibly exhausting, but nigh on impossible.... The politicians of this country have let down the Jewish people who survived, the Jewish people who did not survive.[90]

Duffy rejected Greenwood's assertions but despite continuing pressure from the Australian Jewish community, the government refused to back down on its decision.[91]

Conclusion

Australia was not the only jurisdiction on which the Kalejs case had focused a legal spotlight. Latvia, since gaining its independence from the Soviet Union in 1991, had not prosecuted a single Nazi collaborator despite investigations into former Communist officials and the payment of extra pensions and welfare benefits to convicted war criminals. Under

[89] Dean, 2005 'Soviet War Crimes Lists and Their Role in the Investigation of Nazi War Criminals in the West, 1987–2000', in *NS-Gewaltherrschaft: Beiträge zur historischen Forschung und juristischen Aufarbeitung*, ed. Gottwaldt et al., p. 641.

[90] Greenwood speech in Melbourne, 14 November 1994 reported in *Australia/Israel Review*, vol. 20(1) January 1995.

[91] Fraser, 2010 *Daviborshch's Cart*, p. 308.

pressure, the Latvian government made a formal extradition request to Australia, the prosecutor's case restricted to charges that Kalejs had ordered the shooting of six prisoners at Salaspils. In May 2001, a magistrate in Melbourne approved the extradition request but Kalejs, though 88 and ailing, continued to appeal and died in November that year without ever appearing before a criminal court in any jurisdiction.

As a coda to this chapter, we return briefly to the UK's own 'failure'— to prosecute Harijs Svikeris. In 1997, the Australian Broadcasting Corporation reported that in one of his police interviews in 1993, Svikeris was asked about fellow Arājs Kommando officers. The only one he named was Konrad Kalejs.[92] Although neither was ever prosecuted, Svikeris may have been the more concerned that he would be. In the summer of 1995, he was told via his solicitor that he would not be charged, but warned that that could change if more evidence was found.[93] In July, shortly after the UK announced its first prosecution, of Szymon Serafinowicz, Svikeris had a fatal heart attack at home in Milton Keynes. It was reported that he died clutching a newspaper open at a page which carried the headline 'First man to be charged with Nazi war crimes arrested in Surrey.'[94]

[92] *The Herald Scotland*, 14 October 1997. https://www.heraldscotland.com/news/12286078. war-crime-suspect-found-out-by-british/ (accessed 5 November 2021).
[93] Paul Harrison interview with author, 13 September 1995.
[94] *The Independent*, 'War Crimes Suspect Dies During Inquiry', 5 August 1995.

4

Gecas and the Failure of Law

Scotland's War Crimes Trial

> We think this is a great victory...it is a crucial and historic
> decision. We have every expectation it will now clear the way
> quickly for the first Nazi war crimes trial in the United
> Kingdom. We are thankful to the system in Scotland and for
> having reached this conclusion.[1]

In 1992, the optimism expressed by Rabbi Abraham Cooper of the
Simon Wiesenthal Center in Los Angeles was shared by many who had
been troubled by the case of the Lithuanian Anton Gecas, since the
mid-1980s. Gecas, born Antanas Gecevicius in 1916 (Fig. 4.1), was the
most prominent and senior of the seventeen names on the list of alleged
war criminals living in the UK handed by the Wiesenthal Center to the
British government in 1986. This list, of eleven Latvians and six
Lithuanians, was the catalyst for the law change which brought in the
War Crimes Act in 1991. Alone of those in the late modern period suspected of war crimes, Gecas had unwisely chosen to launch an action for
defamation against Scottish Television which had exposed his culpability in a documentary, *Crimes of War*.[2] In a crushing judgement delivered
at the Court of Session in Edinburgh in July 1992, Lord Milligan said:

[1] Rabbi Abraham Cooper, Associate Dean of the Simon Wiesenthal Center in Los Angeles,
18 July 1992. Reported in *The Herald*, https://www.heraldscotland.com/news/12641016.tv-
company-cleared-of-libel-judge-brands-gecas-mass-murderer-and-war-criminal/ (accessed
5 May 2022).

[2] The only other person in the post-war period to take court action in the UK to defend
their reputation was Dr Wladyslaw Dering who sued the author of *Exodus*, Leon Uris, over a
section in the book describing medical experiments at Auschwitz. He too could be said to have
'lost' since he was awarded a derisory halfpenny in damages.

Safe Haven: The United Kingdom's Investigations into Nazi Collaborators and the Failure of Justice.
Jon Silverman and Robert Sherwood, Oxford University Press. © Jon Silverman and Robert Sherwood 2023.
DOI: 10.1093/oso/9780192855176.003.0005

Fig. 4.1 Anton Gecas pictured in Edinburgh in 1990 before being branded a war criminal by a Court of Sessions judge. News UK/News Licensing.

I am clearly satisfied...that the pursuer [i.e. Gecas] participated in many operations involving the killing of innocent Soviet citizens, including Jews in particular, in Byelorussia during the last three months of 1941, and in so doing, committed war crimes against Soviet citizens who included old men, women and children.[3]

---

[3] Opinion of Lord Milligan *in causa* Antony Gecas, Pursuer, against Scottish Television PLC (Defenders), 17 July 1992, pp. 180–1.

Gecas's action to salvage his reputation was decided on the civil standard of proof, the 'balance of probabilities', which fell short of the threshold of 'beyond reasonable doubt', required to secure a criminal conviction. Nevertheless, many interested parties, certainly those outside the legal establishment, hoped that it might, and believed that it should, be a spur to a criminal prosecution. They were wrong. In 1993, the Lord Advocate, the equivalent in Scotland of the Attorney-General in England, examined the file submitted by the Scottish Crown Office and decided that there was insufficient evidence to prosecute, despite over a thousand inquiries made in Germany, Lithuania, Russia, Belorussia, Israel, Canada, the United States, Australia, and New Zealand.

Gecas was one of seventeen Scottish 'suspects'. Detective Inspector John Montgomery who examined them, said: 'Sixteen were dismissed in about four weeks. They were "Hitler lives next door" types. None was even close to being a good case.'[4] Gecas was in an entirely different category and the decision not to put him before a jury was the first of many occasions when the application of the 1991 War Crimes Act proved hopelessly inadequate to tackle the iniquities of the Holocaust. Gavin Ruxton, the Procurator-Fiscal, who headed the Crown Office war crimes team, laid bare the problem in a short closing report sent to the Lord Advocate:

> Having undertaken some fifteen months of active investigation, I have little doubt that Antanas Gecevicius, now Anthony Gecas, is a war criminal but I am afraid that I am equally convinced that we cannot prove a relevant charge against him in a criminal court. While it may be possible to establish his wartime activities *to the satisfaction of historians* [authors' emphasis], or indeed to the standard required by a civil court dealing with broad and general allegations, there is, in my view, too great a gulf between what we know and what we can prove for any prosecution to succeed.[5]

The decision that there was insufficient *available* (authors' emphasis) evidence to prosecute Gecas created more controversy and unsubstantiated speculation than any other war crimes case. There are many examples

[4] Montgomery interview with author, 26 February 2018.
[5] National Records of Scotland AD 43/1/1/4.

discussed in this chapter. Bob Tomlinson, the maker of *Crimes of War*, which provoked Gecas's defamation action, put forward his own theory:

> I know from contacts that there was no intention to prosecute Gecas. We offered to hold back on broadcasting *Crimes of War* if there was a declared intention to bring charges but they declined to make that commitment. The fact is that the UK government has always been reluctant to bring war crimes prosecutions going right back to the 1940s.[6]

Others have stated with equal certainty that Gecas was not tried because he had been protected by the security and intelligence agencies, MI5 and MI6. Some of these claims may have shared the same source. An article in the Jewish Virtual Library asserted that 'Gecas had worked for British intelligence following his arrival in the UK, a factor that apparently influenced the authorities.'[7] In 1994, the Jerusalem director of the Wiesenthal Center, Efraim Zuroff, wrote, citing an (unnamed) newspaper article:

> Gecas, it was recently revealed, worked, following his arrival in Great Britain in 1948 [the date is incorrect] for British intelligence, which perhaps explains his admission of wartime service in the 12th Lithuanian Auxiliary Police Battalion and may have had an effect on the decision not to prosecute him.[8]

And in September 2001, a member of the Scottish Parliament, Lloyd Quinan, claimed that Gecas had been protected because he had been recruited by the Secret Intelligence Service (MI6) to provide low level intelligence during the Cold War.[9] An alternative theory propounded was that Gecas had been an 'agent' for the security service, MI5, and had

---

[6] Bob Tomlinson interview with authors, 13 August 2021.
[7] Jewish Virtual Library, https://www.jewishvirtuallibrary.org/war-crimes-trials (accessed 20 June 2022).
[8] Zuroff, 1994 *Occupation: Nazi Hunter*, p. 306. The article cited is Ian McKerron and Stephen Grey, 'Nazi Mass Killer Was a British Spy', *Daily Express*, 3 February 1994.
[9] https://www.belfasttelegraph.co.uk/news/northern-ireland/fermanagh-war-hero-who-captured-suspected-ss-butcher-dies-at-age-98-37314604.html (accessed 23 June 2022).

passed on valuable information, especially during the miners' strike of 1984–5 when he was a manager at the National Coal Board. Gavin Ruxton said he had no knowledge of MI5 involvement and that, even if it were true, it would have had no bearing on the decision not to prosecute: 'We were driven only by finding available evidence to take to court. I can assure you that there was no pressure on anyone involved in the inquiry not to prosecute. That's not who we were.'[10]

DI Montgomery, of the Lothian and Borders police, who interviewed Gecas, said:

> My background was Special Branch and I would have known if he was working for MI5. I found nothing to establish that Gecas had had specific contact with the Security Service. I did speak to one or two of my former colleagues in the Branch who said they knew of him, in the sense that they had heard his name, but nothing more than that.[11]

In view of MI6's known recruitment of anti-Communist Balts it is tempting to give credence to claims of an 'establishment' cover-up to shelter Gecas. But none contain any verifying evidence and until such time as the Secret Intelligence Service and/or Security Service are persuaded to open their files on this issue to scrutiny such claims remain unsubstantiated.

Gecevicius the Suspect

By the time the decision was taken not to prosecute Gecas, he had been on the radar of war crimes investigators in the United States for more than a decade and one of the hitherto unexplored fault lines which distinguishes the Gecas case from many others is the souring of the relationship between Washington's Office of Special Investigations and Edinburgh's Crown Office as the Gecas inquiry unfolded. We examine the roots of this rancour later in the chapter.

[10]   Ruxton interview with authors, 16 November 2022.
[11]   Montgomery interview with authors, 16 November 2022.

Gecas's name first came to the attention of the US authorities in October 1981 in connection with an investigation into a man called Jurgis Juodis, who had served in the notorious 12th Lithuanian Auxiliary Police Battalion and who had immigrated to Florida after the war.[12] Juodis was accused in a publication of the Novosti news agency of being one of the perpetrators of a massacre in the town of Slutsk in Belorussia in 1941. The Jews of Slutsk were murdered over two days in a wanton excess of savagery which shocked even some of those charged with administering the occupation. The manner of the killings was the subject of a *cri de coeur* by the civilian administrator, *Gebeitskommissar* Carl, cited at the Nuremberg International Military Tribunal, and subsequently in many histories of the Holocaust. He complained that:

The whole picture was generally worse than disgusting .... With indescribable brutality...bordering on sadism on the part of both the German police officers and particularly the Lithuanian partisans [i.e. the auxiliaries of the 12th Battalion] who herded the Jews out of their houses ....To have buried alive seriously wounded people, who then worked their way out of their graves again, is such extreme beastliness that this incident as such must be reported to the Führer and the Reich Marshal. Only I beg of you to grant me one request: in the future, keep this Police Battalion away from me by all means.[13]

The Soviets had identified the battalion which had carried out the massacre as the 12th (previously called the 2nd battalion) but as far as Western investigators were concerned there was no independent verification of this claim until the discovery of Juodis, who had been commissioned as an *Oberleutnant* in the battalion. Testimony (unsourced) that triggered the OSI investigation (now lodged with the United States Holocaust Memorial Museum) alleged that: 'the defendant personally commanded and participated in the assault, arrest, detention and murder of unarmed Jews and other civilians in Lithuania and Byelorussia.'[14]

---

[12] Gecas deposition in Juodis case, 12 August 1982, C.A. No.81-1013-CIV-T-H., p. 27.
[13] Report written by Carl to the *Generalkommissar* Minsk, Wilhelm Kube, 30 October 1941; International Military Tribunal Nuremberg, document PS-1104.
[14] From the Erlean McCarrick Collection Accession no. 1997.A.0189 USHMM Shapell Center.

Juodis refused to divulge any information about his wartime role when questioned, but the search for cohort testimony to build a case against him was revivified when further information from a Soviet publication named Antanas Gecevicius as one of the killers and disclosed his address in Edinburgh. The then head of the OSI, Neal Sher, flew to Edinburgh and secured from Gecas an admission that he had served in the 12th Battalion. For the OSI, this was groundbreaking, as Sher's successor, Eli Rosenbaum, explained:

> I can't tell you how excited we were. This was huge. It was the first time anywhere in the West that we had found someone who could verify that it was the 12th which had perpetrated this appalling crime at Slutsk. It was there in a handwritten statement from Gecas, which he had signed in front of Sher. It was a brilliant breakthrough.[15]

However, Gecas was fully alive to the implications of the 2nd/12th Battalion's record of atrocities and the information he offered was designed to distance him from personal culpability: 'Shortly after the 2nd Battalion went to Minsk we went to the village of Dukara. At that time, the Jews and suspected communists in Dukara were taken to the forest and shot by members of the 2nd Battalion; I witnessed this shooting but I did not participate. There were approximately 150 people shot.'[16]

Gecas had enrolled as an officer cadet in the Lithuania Military Academy in Kaunas (Kovno) in 1937 (where he met Jurgis Juodis). He said that at the age of twenty-two, in November 1938, he had been made a Lance Corporal in the Air Force and completed his officer probation in July 1939. For a brief two-month period after the Soviet occupation of Lithuania, in June 1940, he had served in the police.[17] He did not deny joining what was then the 2nd Lithuanian Auxiliary Police Battalion in the city of Kaunas shortly after the German invasion in June 1941. A Kaunas resident, Leonas Mickevicius, cross-examined by the Lithuanian Assistant Procurator in March 1987, offered confirmation: 'Gecevicius

---

[15] Rosenbaum interview with authors, 18 September 2022.
[16] Gecas deposition in Juodis case.
[17] Notes on Gecas, 011/02 National Records of Scotland AD43/3/12/9.

I knew by sight. He would have been, at that time, about thirty [in fact, he was several years younger], tall, dressed in a Lithuanian Air Force uniform, holding the rank of sub-lieutenant.'[18]

At his interview with Gecas, Sher was accompanied by an Edinburgh police constable, Gordon McBain, from the Lothian and Borders force and although Gecas was being questioned as a witness in a US-led inquiry rather than as a suspect in his own right, the Americans were astonished that there was no follow-up to the admissions. Eli Rosenbaum, who succeeded Sher as head of the OSI, later made an unsuccessful attempt to speak to Gecas on a visit to Edinburgh:

> Frankly what shocked us was not just the fact that he was living here [i.e. in Scotland] but that our interview with him was conducted in the presence of the Lothian and Borders police. The evidence against Gecas was overwhelming yet it did not lead to any kind of investigation nor to any kind of action on the part of the UK authorities.[19]

Neal Sher, rather gilding the lily, commented in the 1990s: 'We handed all the information we had on Gecas to the Hetherington-Chalmers Inquiry. We gave him on a silver platter to the Brits. It's scandalous they didn't prosecute him.'[20]

As ever, the truth is more complicated and laced with some irony. In the 1980s, the witnesses were available to inculpate Gecas but the criminal law did not provide a route to prosecution. And, as we shall show, in the 1990s, when the law had been changed, the evidence of cohort witnesses, that is, surviving members of his battalion, proved frustratingly elusive to capture.

The 12th Lithuanian Police Battalion and Its Crimes

What began life as the 2nd Lithuanian *Schutzmannschaft* Battalion was formed in Kaunas shortly after the German invasion of June 1941.

---

[18] From SIU file 3443/WCP 11/8 National Records of Scotland AD43/3/12/5.
[19] Cited in Hutchinson, 1994 *Crimes of War*, p. 51.
[20] Sher conversation with author, 25 June 1996.

Before entering the city, the Germans had encouraged so-called Lithuanian 'partisans' to launch pogroms. Gecas's excellent German made him a valuable liaison between the *Schutzmänner* and the occupying forces. Kaunas—Kovno to its Jewish citizens—then the capital of independent Lithuania, was a historic centre of Yiddish learning and culture and was home to about 32,000 Jews, a quarter of its population. Within days, *Einsatzgruppen* detachments and their Lithuanian auxiliaries began the killings. Between June 25 and June 27, 3,800 Jews were killed and an entire Jewish residential quarter and its synagogues burned down. Victims—men, women, and children—were taken to one of several numbered Czarist-era forts which ringed the city and shot. The leader of *Einsatzgruppe A*, Walter Stahlecker, reported that within one week of the invasion, some 5,000 Jews had been killed.[21]

At its peak, the 12th Battalion had no more than five hundred men but its importance to the Nazi programme of liquidation lay in the local knowledge of the police auxiliaries, as emphasized by SS Colonel Carl Jaeger, head of *Einsatzkommando 3*: 'The decision to free each district of Jews necessitated thorough preparation of each action as well as *acquisition of information about local conditions* [authors' emphasis].'

Jaeger reported that 'trained' Lithuanians were available 'in sufficient number'. As a result, the city was 'comparatively speaking, a shooting paradise'.[22] The meticulousness of German record-keeping leaves no doubt that junior Lieutenant Antanas Gecevicius was present at these massacres, according to the archive researcher in Vilnius, Alicia Zukauskaite: 'The files show us that he participated in all the shooting actions of the 2nd/12th Battalion, starting from the 7th Fort in Kaunas.... He was an important man, very cruel, it's why people remember him. I think they [the auxiliaries] enjoyed killing.'[23]

The battalion took part in the murder of more than 20,000 Jews and others in Forts IV, VII, and IX between July and November 1941, by which time the drive to make the entirety of Lithuania *judenrein*

[21] USHMM Holocaust Encyclopedia.

[22] Report by Jaeger, 1 December 1941, cited in Hilberg, 1961 *The Destruction of the European Jews*, pp. 56–7.

[23] Alicia Zukauskaite, Archive Researcher in Vilnius, interviewed in the Frontline Scotland television documentary *Forgotten Nazi*, broadcast 10 April 2001.

(Jew free) was complete. Forty-five years later, when he became a prime suspect for the Hetherington-Chalmers Inquiry investigating war crimes, Gecas was at pains to conceal the fact that he had joined the auxiliary police at the very outset of the Nazi occupation. The former Crown Agent, William Chalmers, interviewed him in Edinburgh on 15 May 1989:

> Q. You joined the police defence battalion and you say you joined at the beginning of September 1941, that's what you say in your statement?
>
> A. Something like that, I can't remember.
>
> Q. I have recovered some of the documents from your battalion … and in the order of your battalion, at no. 14, [it says] 'Lt. Gecevicius Antanas is appointed, from July 21 1941, commander of the 1st Company Platoon.' Now, does that not indicate that you joined on July 21?
>
> A. Can't remember sir, can't remember.
>
> Q. Do you appreciate the significance of the question? If you were there on July 21 you were in the army [sic] of Kaunas at a time when Jews were being massacred at the fort.
>
> A. I can't remember when I joined but I was never [indistinct] … I was in barracks because I was youngest officer in the barracks, training the recruits.[24]

In Lithuania, Chalmers had interviewed cohort witnesses from the battalion and was well prepared for the confrontation with Gecas. He challenged his earlier response with a statement made by a former member of the battalion, Moteyusa Migonis, about the killings at the 9th Fort in Kaunas:

> I also saw Lt. Gecevicius there because I was on guard duty. The officers ordered the soldiers to shoot the prisoners. I saw Gecevicius giving orders. At any one time, the shooting continued for three, four or five hours, maybe 300–400 were shot but I did not count them, there

---

[24] National Records of Scotland AD43/3/11 Incident I05 OP1975.

were certainly more than a hundred ....I went there for four or five days. Although the same officers were not always present, Gecevicius was most often present there, giving orders, as he was in command of the *Jagdkommand*.[25]

Q. (from Chalmers). Now that's a man who was charged with treason after the war, sentenced to capital punishment but that was reduced to twenty-five years imprisonment in Siberia. Why would such a person say that to me?

A. This poor man had no alternative, they shove gun in his neck and he had to say whatever NKVD told him to say.

Q. Well, he's a man in his seventies now and he served his sentence in Siberia. What has he to gain?[26]

In all his interviews, Gecas maintained the fiction that, despite his presence at massacres between 1941 and 1944, he never killed anyone. He said it was because, as a devout Catholic, killing was against his religious convictions. In a statement to the Hetherington-Chalmers Inquiry, drafted by his lawyers in March 1988, he said: 'I wish to assert unequivocally that, at no time, did I take part or assist in any way at the execution of civilians, though on two occasions I witnessed what I *now know* [authors' emphasis] may well have been such executions.'[27]

The author of *Law After Auschwitz*, David Fraser, argues that Gecas's denial of active participation in killing:

serves another set of discursive constructions of the Holocaust and various levels and degrees of responsibility.... Here, for Gecas, it is the Germans who are primarily, if not solely responsible. It is the Germans who collect those destined for extermination and who pull the trigger while the subordinate Lithuanians simply stand by and obey orders. We know from eyewitness and documentary evidence that this is not a true account of the level of active and often independent action taken by Lithuanian police auxiliaries and other forces in the Holocaust in

[25]   National Records of Scotland AD43/3/11.
[26]   National Records of Scotland AD43/3/11.
[27]   National Records of Scotland AD 43/3/12/10.

the Soviet Union. Yet the construction of the Balts as double victims, of the Russians and of the Germans, is a constant and common refrain throughout the construction of the Shoah in the legal arena.[28]

Certainly, Gecas had no qualms about admitting that the Soviet occupation of Lithuania between 1939 and 1941 had left him with a legacy of hatred for Russians and Communism:

> Yes, because I was born in a free Lithuania and what they [i.e. the Soviets] have done first of all, it was against what we worshipped, our Gods. The churches were converted to granaries and anti-religious meetings, every Christmas, every religious function was always anti-religious and what we seen were told what they have done with our history. We were anti-communist.

Gecas's fear and loathing of the Soviets was such that he objected to his interview with Chalmers being video-taped because, as a letter from his legal team expressed it: 'of a concern that such tapes could be seen by persons in Russia who might be called as witnesses should there be any subsequent criminal proceedings.'[29]

Despite an assurance that the video-recording would not be shown to anyone in the Soviet Union, Gecas was insistent that he would not appear before the inquiry unless his condition was met. Reading the files, it is clear that Gecas presented himself as a man of some substance, who would contest every adverse assertion.[30] At his first interview with William Chalmers in May 1989, he was accompanied by no fewer than two counsel, two solicitors, and an investigator. Chalmers, who had won the Military Cross during the Second World War, was a formidable advocate and not likely to be overawed facing a battalion of lawyers. However, he reluctantly conceded to Gecas's demand: 'I note that your client does not wish the proceedings to be video-taped. I do not understand the reasoning behind it because I will be able to identify

---

[28] Fraser, 2005 *Law After Auschwitz*, p. 266.
[29] Letter from his lawyers, Wilson, Terris & Co., to the secretary of the Hetherington-Chalmers Inquiry, David Ackland, 10 March 1989, Ref: NRD/CJP National Records of Scotland AD43/3/12/12.
[30] National Records of Scotland AD 43/3/11 Incident I05 OP1975.

your client as the person who made the statement but if he is still of that opinion, the proceedings will be audio-taped only.'[31]

This concession only partially defused the tension with Gecas's lawyers who then accused the team at the Hetherington-Chalmers Inquiry of leaking damaging information to the press. In May 1989, as Chalmers prepared for the first interview, stories in two national newspapers, the *Mail on Sunday* and *The Observer*, suggested that, if the law was changed, Gecas would be prosecuted. Chalmers received an irate letter from the solicitors:

> You will appreciate our client's concern about his appearance before the Inquiry in the light of these publications. We come now to the point of this letter. As we see it, either these articles were deliberately leaked by a member of the Inquiry or they are inspired speculation by the press. There is no third option as far as we can see... More sinister, are they attempts to put pressure on the Inquiry or yourself? Our client cannot be blamed for wondering whether it is worth his while appearing before an inquiry that has already decided that his version of events is untrue and that prosecution will be recommended.[32]

The Inquiry secretary, David Ackland, replied on Chalmers's behalf:

> We have no knowledge of the sources used in writing either article. We note however that the name of your client, together with the names of fifty other persons on the lists supplied to the Home Office by the Simon Wiesenthal Center and Scottish Television were published in the press before the establishment of the Inquiry, having been released by non-governmental sources.[33]

Nevertheless, the continued focus on Gecas in both the Scottish and national media, both before and after 1991–2, was a matter of concern to the investigators, as John Montgomery explained:

---

[31]   Letter from Chalmers, 29 March 1989.

[32]   Letter from Wilson, Terris & Co. to William Chalmers, 8 May 1989, Ref: NRD/PR National Records of Scotland AD 43/3/12/12.

[33]   Ackland letter, 10 May 1989.

After the failure of his defamation action against Scottish Television, I remember at least one newspaper headline describing Gecas as a 'Nazi'. That kind of commentary didn't help us at all because if we had succeeded in bringing a prosecution, his lawyers were bound to have argued that he couldn't get a fair trial because of the adverse publicity.[34]

Gecas in Belorussia

Having completed its task in Lithuania, the 12th Battalion was issued with Order no. 42 on 6 October 1941 to move to Belorussia under the control of German Reserve Police Battalion 11. Here, the Nazi-led slaughter of civilians was even more intense. In under two months, in the centres of Minsk, Slutsk, and Borisov, 46,000 civilians, mainly Jews, and 9,000 Russian prisoners of war were put to death. The rate of killing was relentless. On the 9th/10th of November (the anniversary of *Kristallnacht*), 8,000 people were shot in Borisov. Four days later, on the 13th, a further 4,000 were murdered in the township of Kletsk in the region of the capital, Minsk. The battalion was led by Major Antanas Impulevicius (who fled to Germany in 1944 and was sentenced to death *in absentia* in 1962 at a Soviet trial in Vilnius) and Gecas was in command of 1st Company, 3rd Platoon.[35]

In Slutsk, sixty miles south of Minsk on the edge of the Pripyat marshes, the killings were witnessed by a former (non-Jewish) partisan, Mrs Nadezhda Dmitrievna Roshtchenko, who told Chalmers in an interview what she had seen:

> The pogroms were mainly carried out by the Lithuanian execution squad... The Jews were shot on the spot and dead bodies thrown on to the trucks amongst the living. It was an especially terrible sight to see the children driven on to the vehicles...there were probably six to

---

[34] Montgomery interview with authors.
[35] SIU file 5509, p. 110 in National Records of Scotland AD43/3/12/2.

seven thousand Jews killed in Slutsk...I would come to Great Britain to testify in a case of a Lithuanian officer even if I had to walk there.[36]

A member of Gecas's platoon, Juozas Aleksynas, was interviewed by the Hetherington-Chalmers Inquiry and by Scottish Television about the killings in Slutsk, naming his direct commander as Gecevicius: 'he stood on the edge of the pit and gave the order to fire.... After executions, he would check the pits and finish off anyone still alive with his pistol. The corpses were one and a half metres deep.'[37]

Aleksynas repeated that assertion in the defamation action brought by Gecas and remarkably, at the age of eighty-four in 1998, he consented to an interview, recorded in Lithuania, for the United States Holocaust Memorial Museum. As a rare testimony of a perpetrator, given voluntarily, it is an invaluable historical record. He estimated that he was present at the site of ten massacres in Belorussia and explained in great detail the method of killing:

> The Jews were rounded up and first massed together before being split into groups of four. They were taken to a grave, which had been pre-dug, forced to lie down in it and shot, either in the chest or sometimes in the back of the head. The victims would have to lie on top of one another. At the very end (of the *Aktion*), the Germans would pour bleach on the grave. The entire scene was despicable. A person who has not seen this could not imagine it. The soldiers were issued with Russian weapons and ammunition which were exploding or incendiary bullets. The clothes of the victims lit on fire in the pits. The victims had to climb on top of burning corpses, the odour of burning bodies was unbearable.[38]

Tellingly, Aleksynas stated that the Germans rarely shot victims, assigning that task to members of the Auxiliary Battalion. When confronted with this testimony, Gecas said he had no recollection of Aleksynas. Another former member of the battalion, Leonas Mickevicius, described

---

[36] Interview conducted in Lithuania by Chalmers, 4 October 1988 in National Records of Scotland AD 43/3/12/10 011/1.

[37] *Forgotten Nazi* documentary, 10 April 2001.

[38] USHMM Collections Division, Archives Branch Accession no. 1998.A.0221.10. RG No RG-50.473.0010.

a similar pattern of killing when Gecas's company began clearing the Jewish ghettoes in Minsk and Kletsk. In Minsk: 'Gecevicius ordered us to take them [i.e. the Jews] out of the town...Outside the town, a pit had been dug in a field...I was standing on guard nearby and saw that sub-Lieutenant Gecevicius, together with troops from our battalion and Germans, were machine-gunning the Jews.'[39]

A member of the company, Juozas Knyrimas, testified at a 1961 trial about the slaughter:

> I saw how the wounded were buried alive and moans could be heard coming from under the earth .... The shooting lasted from morning to night. The clothes were taken by the Germans. The kitchen cart was also at the site of execution and dinner was served on the spot...Then we returned to Minsk.[40]

In Kletsk, some 4,000 Jews were murdered on 6 October 1941. Leonas Mickevicius said:

> I saw how the Jews, several people at a time, were made to lie down in the pit and were then shot by soldiers with rifles at Gecevicius's command. When the shooting was over, Gecevicius and several soldiers checked to see if there was anyone in the pit still alive and if there was, they were finished off.[41]

Amidst the litany of atrocities in which Gecas and his men participated was a reprisal action against suspected partisans on 26 October 1941 remembered vividly by cohort witnesses interviewed by the Hetherington-Chalmers Inquiry. The incident has been frozen in time in a collection of stark black and white images which arrest the gaze of visitors to the Central Museum of Minsk. The photographs depict the public hanging of six men and one woman, 17-year-old Maria (Masha) Bruskina,

[39] Mickevicius interview with Lithuanian Assistant Procurator, A. Kirijenka, 11 March 1987 in National Records of Scotland AD 43/3/12/5.
[40] Knyrimas affidavit sworn on 6 October 1961, SIU 572.
[41] Mickevicius interview with Lithuanian Assistant Procurator, A. Kirijenka, 11 March 1987 in National Records of Scotland AD 43/3/12/5.

from a crossbeam slung between two telegraph poles. Around their necks each wore a handwritten placard proclaiming: 'We are partisans who shot at German soldiers.' The officer shown adjusting the noose around the neck of Bruskina was Major Impulevicius, the battalion commander, but, according to a witness, Leonas Potsevicius, three of his fellow platoon members carried out the punishment on the orders of Antanas Gecevicius.[42]

One of those who implemented the order was Juozas Knyrimas, who was interrogated by the KGB in Vilnius for the trial *in absentia* of Impulevicius in October 1961:

> We were to hang a man and a woman. They were hanged from the beams of two telegraph poles. Before the executions, Gecevicius gave me some alcohol. It was obvious Gecevicius received alcohol specially for this purpose.... He told us they were Soviet partisans... The executed were left on the gallows for three days.[43]

Gecas, when interviewed, did not deny being present but claimed that the hangings were ordered by German officers and not him.

However, Gecas was known to have been given, or perhaps, in view of his virulent anti-Communism, willingly taken, responsibility for anti-partisan activity, according to other members of the battalion. Moteyusa Migonis told Scottish Television that: 'Gecevicius always carried a pistol and when hunting partisans he would carry an automatic rifle, a special German rifle that could be carried on the shoulder but had to be fired from the hip.'[44]

Jonas Kleinauskas, who was interviewed by William Chalmers in the State Procurator's office in Vilnius in September 1988, said: 'in Minsk, Lieutenant Gecevicius had a special group of men—the *Jagdkommand*—which hunted parachutists and partisans. It was a very small group.... I have heard that the *Jagdkommand* encircled people and caught a parachutist.'[45]

[42] Potsevicius interviewed by Chalmers, 1 October 1988, National Records of Scotland AD 43/3/11, pp. 27–8.
[43] Criminal case no. 60 of the defendant Impulevicius Antanas file, vol. 1, p. 270.
[44] *Forgotten Nazi* documentary, 10 April 2001.
[45] Chalmers interview, 30 September 1988.

Chalmers put it to Gecas that some people deserted from the battalion 'because they were horrified by the brutality towards the Jews and the local people'. Gecas's response was: 'No, when deserted we had to, we didn't fight against any Jews, we were mostly fighting partisans.'[46]

The word 'mostly' carries a weight of significance. The liquidation of Lithuania's Jews was not fighting but counted as 'any other business'.

Gecas Post-War and Under Investigation

As the Nazi dominion over Eastern Europe began to crumble in the summer of 1944, Gecas and an entire company of the 12th Battalion—about 160 men—withdrew with the retreating German forces to Stettin. Their 'war', most of which involved killing civilians, ended in Italy with surrender to the US 5th Army. Despite being awarded the Iron Cross by the Germans—for his anti-partisan 'work' on the Russian front—Gecas, like so many of the *Schutzmannschaften*, had little trouble reinventing himself as a patriotic Pole and was incorporated seamlessly into the Polish 8th Army and later the Polish Resettlement Corps (PRC). The swiftness of the transformation from war criminal to putative British citizen of exemplary qualities is evidenced by this testimonial written on behalf of his commanding officer in June 1946:

(Doct). British Control of Polish Repatriation Camp, C.M.F

To Whom It May Concern

249/LII Lieut. Gecas Anthony

This officer is of Lithuanian origin. He does not wish to return to his own country. He served with the Polish Commando Forces in Italy from 2.11.44 until 30.9.45 and was awarded the Polish Military Cross, joining this Repatriation Camp on 1.10.45.

He is anxious to become a British citizen and to join the British Army. His work whilst in this Camp has been invaluable, he is a fine officer with *outstanding character* [authors' emphasis], is respected immensely

---

[46] National Records of Scotland AD 43/3/11, p. 74.

by British and Polish officers and ORs [other ranks]. He has learnt to speak English fluently whilst in this Camp.

I, on behalf of the Commandant, have no hesitation whatever in recommending him to the appropriate authorities in the United Kingdom.

NE Brayne, Capt. Adjutant.[47]

The following year, Gecas earned an equally glowing endorsement from the commanding officer of a Polish Resettlement Corps camp in Scotland:

Pennylands Camp, Cumnock, Ayrshire 28.7.47 Lieut. Antoni Gecas

This officer has served under my command for the past year as Company Commander and as Mess President for some time. He is reliable and trustworthy and has carried out all his duties in a very satisfactory manner. He is active, cheerful and intelligent and I know he had *an excellent record as a Commando during the war* [authors' emphasis].

He has decided to undergo training for Coal Mining and I am sure that he will prove himself to be thoroughly worth the training. I can confidently recommend him to any employer.

Lt. Col. Commanding, 98 Polish Repatriation Camp

[Signature illegible].[48]

Gecas could almost be described as a 'poster boy' for the PRC which was formed after a policy announcement by the Foreign Secretary, Ernest Bevin, in May 1946 that ex-servicemen who wished to integrate into civilian life in the UK should be assisted to do so. When he was demobbed, Gecas had little trouble finding a job with the newly created National Coal Board, where he worked as a mining engineer until his retirement in 1981. In 1952, he was interviewed by the MI5-led screening operation, Post Report, which raised no 'red flags' about his wartime past and in 1955, he was interviewed again, this time by the Edinburgh

---

[47] From the files of the Polish Resettlement Corps, Hayes.
[48] From the files of the Polish Resettlement Corps.

police, when he applied for naturalization as a British citizen. He obtained citizenship in 1956. Gecas married a 19-year-old nurse, Astrid, in 1959 when he was 43.

Like many of the Nazi collaborators who fled to the West, Gecas lived with a residual fear of being exposed and returned to the Soviet Union to face his accusers and quite possibly, the death penalty. This necessitated maintaining a low profile and keeping the number of contacts with government 'officialdom' to a minimum. For example, he did not apply for a passport. But when it became known that his name was on the Wiesenthal Center list handed to the British government in 1986, he suddenly lost the protection of anonymity and felt obliged to give one or two newspaper interviews denying the allegations. In 1987, the pressure on Gecas appeared to increase, with a Soviet Union request for his extradition which was rejected, followed in 1988, by the setting up the Hetherington-Chalmers Inquiry to examine the whole issue of alleged war criminals in the UK. A letter in the Gecas files from a senior Home Office civil servant to the UK Passport Office, sent in August 1987, reveals that the government wanted to prevent Gecas obtaining a passport, as the official, Neville Nagler, recalled:

At the time I was the head of C5 division, which was the division in the Criminal Department that *inter alia* dealt with extradition and judicial cooperation abroad ....I would have known that Gecas could not be extradited to the USSR or Israel or indeed to any of the Eastern Bloc countries where he was alleged to have been engaged in war crimes. Our concern would have been to try to ensure that Gecas could not leave the UK if the law was changed so that he could be prosecuted: I think we had already ascertained that he did not possess a UK passport.[49]

R. I. Henderson, of the Passport Office, replied to Nagler that the Home Secretary alone had the authority to refuse someone a passport, on one limited ground:

---

[49] Nagler email to author, 22 March 2022.

In very rare cases where a person whose past or proposed activities are so demonstrably undesirable that the grant or continued enjoyment of passport facilities would be contrary to the public interest. This power would be used where national security or major foreign policy considerations are involved – and it is very rarely used in practice. The last occasion was in 1976 when the passports of a number of British mercenaries were impounded at Heathrow to prevent them travelling to Angola. It would not be practicable to prevent him [i.e. Gecas] obtaining a British Visitors passport though.[50]

In the event, there is no evidence that Gecas applied for a passport, of any kind, mainly it seems, because he remained confident that he would not face a trial. After his arrest in March 1993, he stonewalled his police interviewer, Detective Inspector John Montgomery, with a series of 'No comment' answers:

It sounds terrible to say but we knew that the interview was really just going through the motions. We had to do it but there was no expectation that we would get anything out of him. He sat there accompanied by his lawyer and gave nothing away. He was an old man [he was 77] and very clever at playing the age card. Frankly, I think he would have used the same tactic in court if he had been charged, that he was an old man being unfairly persecuted.[51]

It was rapidly becoming clear by this point that earlier hopes that a criminal case could be put together hinged on whether the standard requirement for live eyewitnesses prepared to testify in court could be met. With hindsight, a document in the file compiled during William Chalmers's investigation looks somewhat over-optimistic:

There appears to be a prima facie case against him. Some of the witnesses could give oral evidence in courts here...Gecas was interviewed in Edinburgh on May 15 1989...He claims that the witnesses who speak

[50] Henderson letter, Ref: WCP011/02, 11 August 1987, National Records of Scotland AD 43/3/12/11.
[51] Montgomery interview with authors, 16 November 2022.

to his guilt have been intimidated by the Soviet authorities and the allegations against him are part of a Soviet plot to discredit Balts who did not go home after the war. He is plausible. If he is prosecuted and all the evidence is led in court, it will at the end of the day be a jury question. Who is to be believed – Gecas or the prosecution witnesses?[52]

In Ruxton's opinion, Gecas's defence was so weak that the answer to that question would not have tilted in his favour.

Where Were the Witnesses?

Into the 1990s, there were at least a dozen surviving members of Gecas's platoon living in England and had only a small number been persuaded to testify against him, there might well have been a trial. In the search for reasons why the case did not reach a criminal court, commentators have suggested that the Scottish war crimes team wanted these men to be offered immunity from prosecution in return for giving evidence but that the English authorities would not agree. David Cesarani wrote in 2001:

The Scottish unit failed to interview any of a dozen men living in England who had served with Gecas. Since they risked self-incrimination, it was essential to give the men immunity but the Met [police] refused to exempt them from prosecution, claiming that it had them in its sights. Without a guarantee the men would never tell what they knew and the Scottish investigation bypassed them. But the Met never acted against any of the former collaborators and it later transpired that there was no intention to do so.[53]

This assertion was disputed by Paul Harrison, who headed the Crown Prosecution Service Special Casework team south of the border:

I did know of the Gecas case, of course. In fact I went to Edinburgh to watch some of the libel case and speak to the Scottish team, including

[52] Notes on Gecas 011/02 National Records of Scotland AD 43/3/12/9.
[53] Cesarani, 2001 'Getting Away with Murder', *The Guardian*, 25 April.

Gavin Ruxton. I knew Gavin quite well and this point was never mentioned to me, either then or later when we met in, I think Moscow and Ottawa. Of course, any question of immunity would be for the Attorney but nothing came through me or was mentioned to me.[54]

Former Detective Inspector David Drinkald of the Metropolitan Police WCU, said: 'I worked both sides of the border with the Scottish officers but don't recall anything about this.'[55] In fact, one or two witnesses in England were seen by investigators at a late stage. Ruxton pointed out in his closing report: 'Interviews conducted last week in England…show that not all battalion members refuse to speak up at all. The interview with Bronius Benevicius shows how close investigators have come to finding a key witness willing to cooperate and able to give the necessary amount of detail in his evidence.'[56] As Ruxton admitted: 'We did get close but we fell short of the evidence we needed.'[57]

The other potential source of testimony was to be found in Lithuania where some surviving members of Gecas's platoon had testified in the defamation trial which inflicted such a blow to his reputation. This was, of course, a tumultuous period in Lithuanian history. The investigators from the Scottish Crown Office arrived in the country within months of the independence 'revolution' in 1991. Various theories have been floated about the significance of the timing. For example, the historian for the English War Crimes Unit, Martin Dean, argued that this might have had a bearing on the willingness of the cohort members to incriminate the staunchly anti-Communist Gecas in a criminal prosecution:

All the witnesses who had previously given evidence about Gecas [to Hetherington-Chalmers and Scottish Television] turned turtle after Lithuania gained independence in 1991 probably because they were no longer afraid of the Soviet Union and didn't want to besmirch their homeland.[58]

[54] Harrison email to author, 21 June 2022.
[55] Drinkald email to authors, 21 June 2022.
[56] National Records of Scotland AD43/1/1 Ruxton report, p. 2.
[57] Ruxton interview with authors, 16 November 2022.
[58] Dean interview with authors, 20 September 2022.

But Gavin Ruxton believes that the real reason was personal rather than political:

> By the time we got to the witnesses, they had been interviewed on several occasions over a number of years and they simply had no interest in travelling to Scotland to testify. I remember one man saying to me 'but who will look after my pigs while I'm away?' Faced with their refusal, what could we do? We had no way of compelling them.[59]

Neither was the cause helped by an admission by two of the cohort witnesses that they had been put under duress by the KGB to embellish the evidence they had given in post-war trials. Ruxton set out the dilemma in his closing report to the Lord Advocate:

> You will see from the volumes of statements that those in a position to identify Gecevicius (the former battalion members) are mostly either unwilling to speak up or to travel, or give vague details; while those willing to speak of atrocities (the survivors) are only able to say that "Lithuanians" in general were responsible. The former battalion members who do mention killings cannot be exact about when or where they occurred. For this reason, it has not been possible to combine the accounts of the battalion members and those of the survivors in such a way as to make a coherent case. *It is ironic that we cannot prove the necessary specific murders because so much mass killing was taking place* [authors' emphasis].[60]

Friction with the OSI

Ruxton's report to the Lord Advocate is a summary, barely three pages, of the eight or nine volumes of material detailing the work of the unit during the course of the Gecas inquiry. The report was not intended for publication and it took a request from the authors to the National

---

[59] Ruxton interview with authors, 16 November 2022.
[60] National Records of Scotland AD43/1/1 Ruxton report, p. 2.

Archives of Scotland, where it is lodged, to obtain a copy, some of which has been redacted. Ruxton said:

> It wasn't published because at that time, 1994, it remained an ongoing criminal case. Gecas was still alive, of course, and so were witnesses, and if we had put anything in the public domain, it could have prejudiced a possible trial. I don't know why the redactions have been made.[61]

Even in such a truncated form, Ruxton's 'confidential' observations to the Lord Advocate illuminate an issue which had soured relations between the Scottish team and the American OSI. This tension had been festering since the early 1980s when the OSI first encountered Gecas in Edinburgh. Ruxton wrote:

> I am concerned that...we have not taken any evidence from witnesses in the United States and that the OSI in Washington, with whom relations have been strained, will be quick to criticise any decision to discontinue the investigation ....As you know, the OSI for many months blocked our attempts to interview battalion members in the USA, as we have done in other western countries which have 12th Battalion suspects.[62]

This claim is not supported by an examination of OSI archive files. According to an undated planning memo, written in either late 1992 or early 1993, the OSI arranged for unannounced (aka 'knock-and-talk') interviews with four 12th Battalion members living in the US in February 1993 to *assist Ruxton's office*. According to Eli Rosenbaum:

> We would have sought to interview these men anyway for our own program but our small and overwhelmed office probably moved the interviews up the schedule and prioritized completion of the fairly elaborate investigative research needed to properly prepare for those attempts, specifically in order to accommodate Scottish authorities'

[61] Ruxton interview with authors, 16 November 2022.
[62] National Records of Scotland archive file AD43/1/1 Ruxton report, p. 3.

needs. Scottish authorities were permitted to join and agreement was reached that they would do so. (That was an exceptional permission that OSI granted and I am aware of only one other instance in which such permission was granted to any foreign law enforcement authority.)[63]

In the event, the OSI did not prosecute any of the four men, leading to the inference that none admitted membership in the battalion and would therefore have been of little help to the Scottish inquiry. Eli Rosenbaum believes Gavin Ruxton's complaint to be disingenuous, serving, in his view, to distract from the criticism directed at the Scottish Crown Office over its 'failure' to bring Gecas to trial:

> I could imagine a delay, sure, while we were conducting our own investigations of certain individuals...but what does 'many' months mean? And how did any such delay impact his office's decision? Answer: surely not at all. Battalion vets in the US never (or, at least hardly ever)...identified other battalion members.... For what it's worth, Gecas himself had already admitted serving in the battalion, as you know, and the absolute most I could have imagined any of the battalion members in the US having done (if they agreed to speak at all) was confirm that Gecas too was in the battalion—not very helpful to Scottish authorities under the circumstances.... Ruxton's insinuation is absurd.[64]

Ruxton maintained that the Scottish team provided as much information as it received from the OSI:

> We presented them with the names of various members of the 12th Battalion living in the States, which we'd come across in the Sikorski Institute in London. It held files on those claiming army pensions, as well as identifying information such as photographs, fingerprints and so on. The truth is that, whereas we worked closely with war crimes colleagues in Canada and Australia, the American legal process kept us at a distance.[65]

---

[63] Rosenbaum email to authors, 8 October 2022.
[64] Rosenbaum email to authors, 7 October 2022.
[65] Ruxton interview with authors, 16 November 2022.

Further evidence of the breakdown in relations between the Scottish and US agencies can be found in a line in the Crown Office report which comes perilously close to reading as an anti-Semitic trope. Ruxton deepened his criticism of the OSI by bracketing it with the campaigners of the Simon Wiesenthal Center:

> Although they have privately said that they think our case [the 'evidence' amassed against Gecas] is worthless, they may publicly attempt to play to the *powerful Jewish lobby* [authors' emphasis]....Once the fact of the unit's closure becomes known, (Efraim) Zuroff will condemn the move and it would be unfortunate if the OSI, playing the part of the established professionals in the sphere, were to seek to lend weight to his protests.[66]

At the outset of the Gecas inquiry, the Wiesenthal Center had handed over a dossier of a thousand pages to the Scottish war crimes team. In Ruxton's view, 'they were for going ahead with all guns blazing to prosecute Gecas'. This touches on a core conceptual point about approaches to war crimes justice. It is no surprise that, in its annual assessment of legal actions taken by states against former Nazis, the Wiesenthal Center has consistently placed the United States at the head of the table of 'successes'.[67] The Center's director, Dr. Efraim Zuroff worked for a short time at the OSI and the ethos of both organizations is victim focused. The Anglo-Saxon criminal jurisdictions have a different mandate, as Ruxton explained:

> I can well understand Zuroff's attitude but we in the Fiscal Service were never the victims' lawyers. We were there to put forward a case in the public interest. But bear in mind that this was thirty years ago and since then, the case for prosecutors foregrounding the victim seems to have become stronger.[68]

---

[66] National Records of Scotland AD43/1/1 Ruxton report, p. 5.

[67] See various Annual Status Reports titled *Worldwide Investigation and Prosecution of Nazi War Criminals* published by the Simon Wiesenthal Center Israel Office/Snider Social Action Institute.

[68] Ruxton interview with authors.

The Final Act

When Gecas was informed in 1994 that he would not be prosecuted in Scotland on the evidence then available, it appeared that he had successfully outlasted jurisprudential attempts to hold him accountable for war crimes. His country of origin, Lithuania, showed little sign of being interested in extraditing him and indeed, in the mid-to-late 1990s, was more active in rehabilitating hundreds of Lithuanians who had been convicted during the era of Soviet domination. Ironically, 'rehabilitation' was a concept which had originated in the Soviet Union, following the death of Stalin, as a formal legal process by which citizens could petition the state to have their (or their relatives') criminal records wiped clean by a decision of the Prosecutor's office and their reputations restored. In the Baltic states, many beneficiaries of the process had committed crimes as collaborators of the Nazis. According to Efraim Zuroff:

> Tens of thousands of Lithuanians were granted pardons, monetary compensation for time in jail and special financial benefits. Even though 'those who had participated in genocide' [in the words of the law under which they had been convicted] were officially ineligible for this program, at least several dozen Nazi war criminals were rehabilitated.[69]

However, as Zuroff points out, in the new post-Soviet era, wider diplomatic considerations began to impinge on Lithuania, namely the goals of gaining membership of the European Union and of NATO. To this end, successive administrations in Vilnius recognized the truth of the mantra 'the road to Brussels and Washington goes through Jerusalem', i.e. that dealing with unresolved Holocaust issues was a prerequisite for being embraced by the Western community. The opportunity arose with the deportation from the United States of two high-ranking collaborators, one of whom, Kazys Gimzauskas, was eventually convicted in Lithuania at the age of 93, and a number of officers from Gecas's

---

[69] Zuroff, 2017 'The Prosecution of Local Nazi Collaborators in Post-Communist Eastern Europe: A Squandered Opportunity to Confront Holocaust Crimes', p. 296.

12th Auxiliary Police Battalion. And though there was patently little enthusiasm, either amongst the Lithuanian public or political class for holding trials, the Prosecutor's office opened a number of pre-trial investigations and began a serious search in the Vilnius archives for incriminating evidence which had been readily available for years, had the will existed to seek it out.

In 2000, the Prosecutor's office opened a formal investigation into Gecas on the basis that 'new evidence' had come to light, though, in reality, this was information, available for almost two decades, supplied by the OSI in Washington, as Eli Rosenbaum explained:

> OSI was asked by the Lithuanian authorities to help out in the Gecas matter. We sent two of our best people to Vilnius and helped them understand the case (which they initially felt could not be prosecuted – sound familiar?). They didn't even have Lord Milligan's judgment in the libel action to consult. So yes, we did bring new evidence to them – new in the sense that they weren't aware of it.[70]

In February 2001, a district court in Vilnius granted a warrant for the arrest of Gecas, who, by this time, was eighty-five and in poor health. He was accused of involvement in the murder of 32,000 civilians and charged with thirteen specific crimes, eleven of which were described as 'especially dangerous to the state'. The indictment read at court by prosecutors, couched in Soviet era circumlocution, stated that: 'Antanas Gecevicius (currently named Anton Gecas) is charged with genocide in the physical extinction of peaceful civil citizens belonging to the ethnic Jewish group.'[71]

The Chief Prosecutor, Rymvydas Valentukevicius, was confident that, with thirteen written statements from former members of Gecas's platoon and five living witnesses prepared to testify, he had a robust case to present:

> After analyzing this material, I and my colleagues have no doubts about the case. I can say from experience of similar cases that the

[70] Rosenbaum email to authors, 5 March 2001.
[71] Reported in Seenan, 2001 'Lithuania demands extradition of Nazi war crime suspect from UK', *The Guardian*, 20 February.

evidence is strong enough to be acted upon and to get a verdict. I hope
there will be a criminal punishment. It is especially important to bear
in mind that however some might try to deny the past, the facts are
impossible to deny. One can't contradict history.[72]

As he had done for fifteen years or more, Gecas continued to deny the
charges and relied on the somnolent pace of legal bureaucracy and
infirmity to stave off extradition. By the time that the Edinburgh
Sheriff's Court issued a warrant for his arrest in July 2001, he had suffered a stroke and the police were unable to execute the warrant. Efraim
Zuroff of the Simon Wiesenthal Center responded with a letter to the
Scottish Justice Minister, Jim Wallace, urging him to appoint an independent medical expert to assess Gecas's health: 'Extensive experience
with such cases has shown that suspected Nazi war criminals often make
every effort to appear as ill as possible in order to avoid prosecution and
punishment and therefore every precaution must be taken to carefully
determine Mr Gecas's condition.'[73]

An independent medical assessment was commissioned and concluded that Gecas was not faking his condition and it came as little surprise when the Scottish Executive ordered the proceedings to be
discontinued in September 2001. Gecas died on 12 September, his passing barely registering in the wake of the 9/11 attacks a day earlier. He
was cremated at Edinburgh's Mortonhall Crematorium where he was
identified as 'A. Smith' to avoid the attention of protesters or neo-Nazi
supporters. At no time during the decades-long saga had Gecas publicly
expressed any remorse for the number of innocent victims of the 12th
Lithuanian Auxiliary Police Battalion.

Conclusion

Given the longevity of the OSI's involvement with the Gecas case, it is
perhaps unsurprising that Eli Rosenbaum continues (at the time of

---

[72] *Forgotten Nazi* documentary, 10 April 2001.
[73] Zuroff letter Ref: W1501, 14 August 2001.

writing in 2022) 'to be incredulous that the Scots didn't prosecute Gecas'.[74] But that view is also reflective of the institutional 'stamina' of the OSI which is still actively engaged in tracking down Nazi collaborators more than four decades after it was founded.[75]

The elements of the Gecas case have a depressing familiarity: the ease with which a war criminal could launder his past on entering the UK in the 1940s, the mistrust by the legal authorities of Soviet-sourced evidence, the weary acceptance at the end that age and illness would replace a judicial forum for a verdict on man's criminality. But somehow, the Gecas story carries a significance greater than the sum of its parts because of the frustrated hopes in the early 1990s that his would be the first UK war crimes trial and thus an encouragement to the prosecutors in England and Wales to pursue their own suspects with vigour.

Efraim Zuroff, who travelled to Gecas's home in Edinburgh in July 1987 with the intention of confronting him, argues that although the failure to prosecute stands as an indictment of Anglo-Saxon jurisprudence, at least the pressure from the Wiesenthal Center catalysed a law change:

> When we began our campaign to convince countries to take action about the Nazis in their midst, we did so in the belief that if we could trust the judicial system of a country, such as Scotland, Canada or Australia, we could hand the problem over to their authorities. This is why we invested such time and effort in lobbying some of these key Western democracies. It is very disappointing that Gecas wasn't prosecuted but imagine if the War Crimes Act hadn't been passed. What would that have said about the UK's attitude to the Nazis living openly and the issue of impunity?[76]

But in summation, the only unqualified credit goes to Scottish Television for their exposure of the crimes and having the bravery to defend Gecas's action for defamation: the one trial he was subjected to.

---

[74] Rosenbaum interview with authors, 18 September 2022. The secretary of the Hetherington-Chalmers Inquiry, David Ackland, had also been puzzled by the failure to prosecute Gecas when interviewed by one of the authors in June 1996.

[75] The OSI tried a case as late as 2020 against an SS guard, Friedrich Berger, living in Tennessee.

[76] Zuroff interview with author, 29 August 2022.

5

Serafinowicz, the Belorussian Nationalist from Mir

Introduction

Szymon Serafinowicz, a *Schutzmannschaft* from Belorussia, had the
unwanted distinction of being the first person prosecuted under the
War Crimes Act 1991. When the War Crimes Unit began their investigations, they were unaware of his significance and, more surprisingly, so
was the Hetherington-Chalmers Inquiry, even though a team had been
to Minsk in Belorussia to interview witnesses to massacres carried out
by the auxiliary police from Mir and Turets, which he commanded.
They either missed or were never shown statements in the KGB archives
from 1949 and 1951 by a member of the Mir *Schutzmannschaften* called
Ivan Grigorevich describing Serafinowicz as 'the most terrible of all... he
was the most important of all the Belorussians over us, apart from the
Germans.'[1]

In addition, consistently strong witness testimony against Serafinowicz
had already emerged from war crimes inquiries or trials in West Germany,
the United States, Israel, and Australia. And far closer to home, in the
archives of the Home Office and MI5, lay evidence of allegations which
had been brought to the attention of the UK authorities in 1947 and
1948. Had they been investigated thoroughly, his entry could have been
barred to the country which became his 'safe haven'.

---

[1] Unused prosecution material in Serafinowicz case 380–841 Hartley Library Special
Collections, University of Southampton Archive file MS 408_A1057.

Safe Haven: The United Kingdom's Investigations into Nazi Collaborators and the Failure of Justice.
Jon Silverman and Robert Sherwood, Oxford University Press. © Jon Silverman and Robert Sherwood 2023.
DOI: 10.1093/oso/9780192855176.003.0006

The next missed opportunity to identify him came in 1982 when the American OSI was investigating a former *Schuma* from Mir, Volodimir Wolczek. Eli Rosenbaum was then in his early career at the OSI:

> As part of our inquiry, I came across the name Serafimowicz, spelled in three different ways, in an émigré newspaper account of a conference of Belorussian nationalists which had taken place in London years before. So, on 19 July 1982, I sent a cable via the State Department to the Foreign Office in London, asking whether he could be found as a potential witness in the Wolczek case. There was a considerable delay in getting a response. And the answer, when it eventually came, was that the police could not find anyone of that name in the UK.[2]

After decades of deflecting Soviet inquiries about war criminals, the Foreign Office had no institutional impulse to mount its own searches so it is doubtful that the request from Washington was given anything but the lowest priority. The fact that eleven years later, an 'unknown' figure became the principal focus for the WCU shows that it was an error of some consequence. It also illustrates how closely the Australian inquiries of the Special Investigation Unit intertwined with those of their British counterparts. The bridge between the two was provided by the historian Martin Dean, who joined the British team in the autumn of 1992 after doing the same research task for the Australians.

The 'Treasure' in the Archives

In November 1991, Martin Dean wrote a briefing note about his searches in the Belorussian archives for the SIU headed: 'Re-Case of Serafimowicz [still the earlier spelling of his name with an 'm']: A most interesting discovery was that one witness, Dov Resnik, claims that Serafimowicz, then head of the Turets police, who moved to Mir after the first *Aktion*, was believed to be living in England after the war.'[3]

---

[2] Rosenbaum interview with authors, 18 September 2022. The cable is headed 'Outgoing Telegram, Unclassified Department of State'.
[3] Dean briefing, 26 November 1991 in Hartley Library Special Collections, Archive file MS 408_A1057 2/5, p. 342.

Resnik, who was interviewed by the Israeli police, had testified in the 1967 trial in West Germany of Captain Max Eibner, who had been a regional commander (described in the files as district lieutenant) of the German gendarmerie based in Baranovichi. Resnik had good cause to remember Serafinowicz. He lived in Mir, the principal town of the *rayon* (administrative region), which had a population of about 6,000, half of whom were Jews, many of them merchants and craftsmen. There was a thriving orthodox seminary or yeshiva, attended by up to 500 seminar-ians from many parts of Europe. In addition, Mir had five synagogues. A week after the German invasion in June 1941 the Jews were forcibly confined within a number of streets which effectively became the ghetto. Resnik recalled that during the main *Aktion* in Mir, on 9 November 1941, when between 1,500 and 1,800 Jews were killed, Serafinowicz had shot Resnik's 16-year-old son and a friend, Aron Rudicki, with his wife and two children. The murders had been part of an *Aktion* carried out by the 'Stolbsty Ortskommandantur with the support of the Russian volunteer force [i.e. the *Schutzmannschaft*] under the command of a certain Serafimovich. Everyone was murdered, from babies in arms to old people. Only 800 Jews managed to save themselves [but only until the next massacre].'[4]

Resnik's information that Serafinowicz was living in England needed to be treated with caution but from what Dean knew about the post-war exodus westwards of former *Schutzmannschaften*, it was plausible: 'This is as yet no more than rumour but it makes sense from the subsequent history of the Byelorussian Police in the Baranovichi area, which also explains why so many of the British allegations refer to Byelorussians.'[5]

The original source of the allegations relating to the Turets *Schutz-mannschaften* was an investigation conducted by an NKVD team for the Soviet Extraordinary State Commission (ESC) in April 1945 into crimes committed by 'German-fascist cannibals and their accomplices in Mir district, Baranovichi'. It was an audit of atrocity:

[4] Report 11 202 AR-Z 16/67 in connection with the trial of Max Eibner. Hartley Library Special Collections, Archive file MS 408_A1057 2/10, p. 828.
[5] Dean briefing, 26 November 1991 in Hartley Library Special Collections.

...2,754 people from Mir district killed, tortured, or burnt alive listed – 1,750 in Mir, 450 in Turets. The main criminals in the area were: Serafimovitch Semion [the Russian spelling of his first name] and Pankevitch – commandants of district police [a number of other names are also listed]. This gang of German accomplices burned down the village of Lyadki (130 homesteads), killed and burned alive, children, women, old people.... Serafimovitch, Mazurek and Lenkovich set up a den at a house in Zavalnaya Street, Mir, where they brought by force young women, raped and abused them and then shot them.[6]

The Lyadki massacre in 1943 had come up during the Hetherington-Chalmers Inquiry—though not the name, Serafinowicz—because one of the alleged perpetrators, Konstantin Okun, had been on a 1988 list of suspects, believed to be living in England, supplied by the Soviet embassy. When Okun was interviewed by Detective Inspector Howard Chapman of the WCU at an East London police station on 7 October 1993, he admitted that he had served in the *Schutzmannschaft* but claimed that during the Lyadki *Aktion*, he had 'merely' served as a guard: 'I just stood, I kept watch, that's all I did. I stood on watch. I didn't even fire one single shot.'[7]

Okun also denied any knowledge about, or complicity in, the killing of ninety-seven Jews by the River Nieman at Yeremichi, in which the Turets cohort was deeply implicated.

Q. If you didn't harm anybody...why was it that you fled with the Germans?

A. Because I was afraid to leave my family behind with the partisans. I didn't run away.[8]

Okun was conspicuously uncooperative during his police interview, providing little information about Serafinowicz, but a fellow member

---

[6] Mir District Commission report for the ESC, 25 April 1945, Hartley Library Special Collections, Archive file MS 408_A1057 2/5, p. 342.

[7] HC/190 Hartley Library Special Collections, Archive file MS 408_A1057 2/6.

[8] Ibid.

of the Turets cohort, Jan Mazurek, named by witnesses as one of the executioners at Lyadki, was more forthcoming. When interviewed at Gloucester police station on 3 August 1993, he provided useful confirmatory information about the Mir/Turets personnel, including that Serafinowicz was commander and that the uniform the police wore was black, with grey sleeves and collars to distinguish them from the SS.[9]

The Investigation Gathers Pace

The WCU's interest in Serafinowicz grew with each piece of evidence that he had been in a position of authority amongst the *Schutzmannschaften*. In October and November 1941, 600 Jews were murdered in Turets in two separate *Aktionen*. On the second occasion, the victims were taken to the cemetery and shot with machine guns. They included the wife and children of Aharon Harkavy, who had known Serafinowicz before the war. He told the Australian police that: 'the Head of the Byelorussian police, Serafimovich was present and helped the Germans to select which Jews would be killed and which would be sent to work at the camp at Nowy Swierzen [Harkavy escaped from the camp on 29 January 1943 shortly before it was liquidated].'[10]

In July 1993, the Russian-speaking historian Alasdair Macleod, who worked in tandem with Martin Dean, examined the trial records of a *Schutzmänner* called Konstantin Nos, who had been arrested by the NKVD in December 1944. He told them that he had joined the Mir auxiliary police under the command of Serafinowicz. The trial heard from witnesses—some of whom had known Serafinowicz before the war—that: 'Serafinowicz was in charge of everything – training, expeditions and battles, arrests and shootings, looting. All [i.e. the police] wore black uniforms, received free rations and took the oath.'[11]

After finding Serafinowicz's name amongst the files of the Polish Resettlement Corps at Hayes in West London, the police felt they had

[9] Police Exhibit No. HC/171.
[10] Statement of Aharon Harkarvi, Yad Vashem no. 2104/96 SIU 5612 or PU443.
[11] Hartley Library Special Collections, Archive file MS 408_A1057 2/17, p. 901.

enough information by June 1993 to warrant questioning him though not nearly enough direct evidence of killing to arrest him for murder. He was first seen at his home in Banstead in Surrey by Detective Inspector Howard Chapman and Detective Constable David Lloyd of the War Crimes Unit. Chapman said Serafinowicz 'appeared to be expecting police and there was no secret concerning the allegation of war crimes...Serafinowicz, apart from being a little hard of hearing, seemed to be in possession of his faculties.'[12]

Following a search of the house, Serafinowicz was asked to present himself at Epsom police station in Surrey on 22 July, accompanied by his legal team of Nicholas Bowers and Edward Dancey. The interview session, and two subsequent ones in November 1993 which we shall discuss, were recorded on both video and audio cassette. Serafinowicz was then 82 but showed notable stamina for a man of his age, refusing all offers of a drink or break. He spoke in broken, heavily accented English interspersed with clarifications in Russian offered through an interpreter (Fig. 5.1).

Serafinowicz Speaks

It is a truism that the scale of the Holocaust cannot be 'understood' through numbers alone. Eleven million dead, six million Jews—these are awe-inspiring statistics but they are also an aggregation of personal experiences of victims, survivors, bystanders, and, yes, perpetrators. The latter have been chiefly represented through documented trials, whether the defendant was the vainglorious Hermann Goering in the Nuremberg courtroom or the seemingly colourless bureaucrat, Adolf Eichmann, behind his glass cage in Jerusalem.

The value of observing Serafinowicz, not yet arrested, let alone charged, in a police interview room is the opportunity to put generalization to one side and inhabit the psychopathy of one individual, faced with allegations that he killed. As the Dutch scholar of genocide and mass violence Uğur Ümit Üngör, has written: 'The study of low-level

---

[12] Prosecution unused material Hartley Library Special Collections, Archive file MS 408_A1057.

Fig. 5.1 Szymon Serafinowicz pictured at the time of his first police interview, 1993. Jon Silverman.

perpetrators has moved way beyond differing cliches of faceless, banal or sadistic killers, undifferentiated and unexplained, who murder people for no apparent reason or out of pure hatred and malignance.'[13]

Serafinowicz was interviewed under caution, meaning that he was told he was not obliged to say anything if he so wished. At various times, his solicitor, Nicholas Bowers, intervened to try to prevent him incriminating himself but, over the course of twenty-one hours of interviews, Serafinowicz spoke freely: 'I am very pleased to sit here and talk to you and tell you the truth.' Crucially, he admitted being in the *Schutzmannschaften* in both Turets and Mir during the period of the *Aktionen* against the Jews, thus the issue of identification was dealt with satisfactorily. But he claimed that all the killings were carried out by the Germans. 'I stayed in

---

[13] Üngör, 2019 'Perpetration as a Process: A Historical-Sociological Model', in *Perpetrators of International Crimes*, ed. Smeulers et al., p. 128.

Turets until the Germans came and shot all the Jews.' His interviewer, Detective Inspector Howard Chapman, asked:

How were you regarded in Turets?

A. Very well, including by some Jews.

Q. When you left Turets, there weren't any Jews left because they had all been executed. You shot a person called Chaimovitch [the director of a mill].

A. It's not true. It's lies.

Serafinowicz explained his decision-making when the Germans invaded Turets in June 1941 as follows:

Bandits [i.e. pro-Soviet partisans] killed my best friend. This was the start. I went to the Germans six days after the invasion to ask for protection and that was when I armed myself. Local people, including Jews, knew that I had been in the (Polish) army and I was asked to organize a volunteer defence force. It was made up of people whose relatives had been deported by the Bolsheviks.[14]

The interviews make clear that Serafinowicz's course of action was set by his hatred of the Russians, who occupied western Belorussia under the terms of the Nazi–Soviet pact:

The village Soviet could arbitrarily decide who should be jailed. One day in the winter of 1939–40, the police came to the flour mill [at Obrina where he was the manager] and accused the mill owner of contaminating the flour. I was arrested and ordered to be deported to Wolodna in central Russia with all of my wife's family, her parents, two sisters and two brothers. As the train was about to depart, I was freed because my wife, Jadwiga, was ill. The rest of her family was deported. Her parents did not survive.[15]

---

[14] Serafinowicz WCU interview tape 4, 11 November 1993.   [15] Ibid.

Serafinowicz claimed that the group of *Schutzmänner* had come together spontaneously as a response to the threat from Russian partisans. One admission he was not prepared to make—on the advice of his lawyers— was that he had been in a position of command, despite conceding that he was referred to as 'commandant'. When DI Chapman asked: 'Were you in command?' he said, 'I don't want to answer.' In a later statement which his lawyers drew up ahead of the trial, he elaborated:

> It is not true to say that I formed a group of people of which I was in charge. I simply visited the local villages and asked for people to volunteer to help me protect everybody....I state that no local Police force made up of Belarussians was established by the Germans....After Turets, I moved to Mir. I did not go there as a Policeman. I went there as a private citizen to try to talk to people and stop them fighting against themselves....I would point out that at this time there was total anarchy in the area.[16]

Serafinowicz was adamant that:

> At no time did I wear a uniform whilst I was in Mir. I did not want to wear a uniform since I felt it was inappropriate. In addition, these uniforms [which he agreed some of the *Schutzmänner* wore] were often the wrong size. I wore civilian clothes at all times.[17]

This assertion was easily disproved by photographs showing him wearing the *Schutzmann*'s distinctive black uniform with grey or beige collar and cuffs (Fig. 5.2). A witness added that: 'He wore military style knee-length boots and carried a pistol.'[18] Serafinowicz also told his police interviewers that he wasn't paid for his service. But a document written by the head of the Mir gendarmerie, Reinhold Hein, in July 1942, shows this to be untrue. Discussing the amount of death benefit to be paid to the father of a *Schutzmann* killed by partisans, it states that *Schutzmänner*

---

[16] Serafinowicz statement for committal hearing, January 1996.   [17] Ibid.
[18] Hartley Library Special Collections, Archive file MS 408_A1057 2/38 NS/136.

Fig. 5.2 Serafinowicz in his *Schutzmann*'s uniform, with young son, also Szymon. Mir/Turets *c*.1942. The shoulder flashes indicate his status as a 'commander'. Source unknown.

were paid 1RM (one reichsmark) per day at that point, though the rate was revised later that year.[19]

What Drove Serafinowicz?

It is difficult to be certain about Serafinowicz's motivation. Unlike his compatriot, Andrzej Sawoniuk (see Chapter 6), he did not appear to be anti-Semitic per se. His barrister, William Clegg QC, believes that had his case come to a full trial, credible evidence could have been adduced

[19] Hein report to the Gendarmerie Regional Commander, Baranovichi, 6 July 1942, Hartley Library Special Collections, Archive file MS 408_A1057 2/9, p. 63.

that he saved some Jews from the Nazis. In his police interview of November 1993, Serafinowicz was shown a copy of a German document translated into English, which listed the names of *Schutzmänner* put forward for bravery awards in July 1943. Asked by DI Chapman what it was for, he replied: 'I got this award for saving 100 lives in a village four kilometres from Obrina called Sinyavskaya Sloboda. I prevented the Germans from shooting the villagers.'[20]

This claim may be somewhat counterintuitive—why should the Germans confer an award for saving villagers from the Germans? But its veracity appears to be borne out in notes of a visit by the defence team to Belarus in November 1996, which recorded a witness saying: 'Everybody in the village of Sinyavskaya Sloboda believes that Serafinowicz saved us from execution in the summer of 1942.'[21]

The truth about the saving of some lives was not contested by the prosecution. Indeed, it was used to bolster the case against the defendant. At one of the pre-trial hearings, the Solicitor-General, Sir Derek Spencer QC, told the court: 'We have served three statements on the defence to the effect that on occasions, Serafinowicz saved lives. We say he had the power of life and death. Indeed, people were petrified of looking him in the eye in case he made up his mind about their fate.'[22]

Nechama Tec, in her biography of Serafinowicz's German-speaking interpreter, Oswald Rufeisen, who became a key witness against him, argued that the crimes he committed were transactional in nature:

> Serafinowicz was convinced that by excelling on the job and specifically by following German orders, he would be able to fulfil his ambitions. When they wanted him to kill Jews, he did it almost indifferently. When they wanted him to find Communists and murder them, he did it gladly.[23]

[20] Serafinowicz WCU interview tape, 11 November 1993.
[21] Note NS/136 19 November 1996 in Hartley Library Special Collections, Archive file MS 408_A1057 4/2.
[22] Abuse of process hearing, Sheffield Crown Court, 17–19 December 1996.
[23] Tec, 1990 *In the Lion's Den*, p. 80. Tec told Jon Silverman in June 1995 that Serafinowicz had said that 'all his troubles were because of that Tec woman'.

In this, Serafinowicz's behaviour could be compared to that of the collaborationist Polish Blue Police in the Subcarpathian region, described by Tomasz Frydel as men of 'two faces' whose behaviour was 'more situational than it was ideological'.[24] Nevertheless, Serafinowicz was not a mere cipher. Underlying this willingness to comply was a commitment to Belorussian nationalism and he remained wedded to the cause of a Belorussia, whose identity was distinctive from both Russia and Poland, not only during the war but long after he arrived in the UK. We discuss his post-war involvement with Belorussian nationalist organizations later in this chapter but in a pre-trial deposition he set out his belief:

> I have always considered myself to be a native of Belarus which is, in my view, a separate country in its own right. It is true that over the years my country has been occupied by various other countries but I feel I was always a Belarussian with my own language and nationality.[25]

During his first interview with the police in 1993, Serafinowicz revealed that he had had contact with the Belorussian nationalist politician Radoslaw Ostrowski as early as 1943. After the battle of Stalingrad, Ostrowski set up the Belorussian Central Council, which was tolerated by the Germans as an anti-Soviet puppet. He held a 'Belorussian Congress' in Minsk with 1,150 hand-picked delegates shortly before fleeing westwards as the Germans retreated in July 1944.[26] Serafinowicz told his interviewers:

> In September 1943, I was summoned by Ostrowski to go to Baranovichi to help organize and train volunteers. There were 22–24 men in the *Jagdzug* [a hunting group formed to root out escaped Jews and partisans]. I went there with my wife and son, Simon. While I was there, 'bandits' killed a woman and I took her two children with me

---

[24] Frydel, 2019 'Ordinary Men? The Polish Police and the Holocaust in the Subcarpathian Region', in *Collaboration in the Holocaust and World War II in Eastern Europe*, ed. Black et al., p. 73.

[25] Serafinowicz statement for committal hearing, January 1996.

[26] Dallin, 1981 *German Rule in Russia, 1941–45*, p. 222.

when I went to the West. I said to them 'one day we will return to Belarus and it will be free'.[27]

The importance of the *Jagdzug* (or *Jagdkommando*) in hunting down Jews who had managed to escape the various *Aktionen* should not be underestimated. Though these hunting parties were often led by the German gendarmerie, only the members of the *Jagdzug* had the necessary local knowledge to lead them to likely places of concealment and identify potential victims. As a statement of their contempt for, and perhaps fear of, the partisans, the Mir *Schutzmannschaft* posted up a letter (undated), in response to threats made against them, headed:

> Bandits!
>
> We are sending you this letter in reply to your awful letters and would advise you not to write any more of your stupid bandit orders.... This will help you as it helped the Jewish vermin who are only capable of speaking and writing but when it comes to fighting, your Jews just run away, you are all pigs and on top of everything else you are now robbing the people and mobilise bandits in your ranks.
>
> We are still in our right minds but will behave like beasts of the forest unless everyone agrees.
>
> The Police (*Schutzmannschaft*) from the village of Mir.[28]

The deputy head of the Mir gendarmerie, Sergeant Willi Schulz, led a number of *Jagdzug* operations, for example one at Stolpce in September 1942, an account of which he wrote up for the 'Main Commissar' in Baranovichi, Captain Max Eibner:

> approximately 750 Jews of both sexes, though more female ones, were shot. On the whole, these were Jews who were no longer fully fit for work [a further 850 Jews in the ghetto hid in underground hiding places and elsewhere]. In a search operation and seizure of Jewish mobile

assets...the following numbers were rounded up. 24 September – 131; 25 September – 103; 26 September – 71; 27 September – 32; 28 September – 36; 29 September – 38; 30 September – 64; and 1 October – 13. These Jews, mostly women and children, were taken to the execution site by bus in the evening and shot under my supervision.[29]

The Evidence

Oswald Rufeisen was a Jew who survived by concealing his true identity and posing as a Catholic. He worked for Serafinowicz and lodged with him and his family for several months in their home on Wilenska Street. By the summer of 1942, those Jews who had not been killed in the previous November's *Aktion*, some 700–800, had been forced into the grounds of a castle on the outskirts of Mir, which was the family seat of Count Mirski. By chance, Rufeisen overheard a telephone conversation between the head of the Mir gendarmerie, Reinhold Hein, and his regional superior, Max Eibner, setting the date for the next liquidation as 13 August. Two days before it was carried out, Rufeisen got a message to the Jews and supplied them with some captured Russian firearms, enabling a significant number of people to escape to the forest. Rufeisen went into hiding but was apprehended.

In the Brest State Regional Archive, investigators found a report which Hein, known to his subordinates as *Meister* Hein, wrote in order to absolve himself of responsibility for what had transpired. It was written a week later on 20 August:

On 11 August, a Jew from the local ghetto reported to me that Rufeisen had betrayed the *Aktion* planned for 13 August. I questioned Rufeisen and he admitted he had done so because he was a Jew. On hearing this, I immediately took away his weapons and myself took him into detention. [Hein recorded that he placed Rufeisen in the custody of a

[29] Report by Sgt. Willi Schulz, 18 October 1942, E1195 State Archives, Brest Oblast 995 (Hartley Library Special Collections, Archive file MS 408_A1057 2/6).

corporal called Marten and said]...I am now going into the forest where the grave is being dug.[30]

Hein wrote that on his return from the forest, he was told that Rufeisen had escaped. As a postscript, and to assure his superiors that the work of making the region *judenrein* (Jew-free), had merely suffered a hiccup, he added '560 Jews shot in *Aktion*, 65 Jews captured later.'

It is possible that Serafinowicz had suspected that Rufeisen was Jewish but hid it from the Germans because he was useful as an interpreter and Serafinowicz seemed to have some genuine affection for him. Nechama Tec's book was published in 1990 but at the time of the two police interviews with Serafinowicz in 1993, the WCU was unaware of Oswald Rufeisen and how the prosecution case would be immeasurably strengthened by his inside knowledge, as a credible cohort witness, of the crimes committed. In the event, Rufeisen's testimony of what happened in a village called Dolmatowszczyzna on 2 February 1942 was considered to be compelling by prosecutors.

Two groups, one of German gendarmes (led by Hein, according to a report he wrote of the *Aktion*) and the other of *Schutzmänner* commanded by Serafinowicz, set out on sleds from Mir and collected forty-one Jews from a number of villages along the route. Rufeisen, who was present, said that once they had reached their destination, the Jews were ordered to lie in the snow face down in lines. The shooting lasted for about thirty minutes. Some of the victims needed to be dispatched with a second bullet. The killers departed and the dead were left lying in the snow for burial by the villagers (Fig. 5.3).

Serafinowicz's defence team went to the village in November 1996 to try to find surviving witnesses to test the evidence. A note in the file says: 'Day 6 (of the visit), November 23. Arrive Dolmatowszczyzna. We talk to a group of three elderly male villagers. They are all extremely drunk and cannot assist or remember Serafinowicz.'[31]

[30] Copy (*Abschrift*) of Hein report to the Baranovichi Gendarmerie Regional Leader SIU 5770, pp. 183–4.
[31] Hartley Library Special Collections, Archive file MS 408_A1057 4/2 NS/136.

Fig. 5.3 Members of the Voronovitch family murdered in the village of Krynichno (Kriniczne) 16/17 January 1942 by the Mir schutzmannschaft commanded by Serafinowicz. Source unknown.

Rufeisen recounted that a fortnight before the massacre at Dolmatowszczyzna, on 17 January, the Mir police headquarters had received an order to liquidate those Jews remaining in outlying villages and hamlets. He said Serafinowicz was 'in charge of the policemen, who were all armed with pistols or automatic rifles'. The execution site was the village of Kryniczne on the River Niemen, not far from Mir. According to a prosecution accompanying note, four families were lined up in the snow outside a barn with the:

policemen positioned behind them. Serafinowich [note the alternative spelling of his surname] was the last policeman in the line.... The Jews were then shot; and afterwards each policeman verified that the Jews at whom he fired were dead. The method of checking was for each policeman to lift a leg of the bodies for whom he was responsible. If the leg fell like a piece of wood there would be no need for a second bullet. If there was any resistance when the leg was raised, the policeman would fire a second bullet at the dying Jew. Rufeisen testifies that Serafinowich played his part in this process.[32]

A number of surviving witnesses provided evidence implicating Serafinowicz in the massacre in Mir on 9 November 1941 in which up to 1,800 Jews were murdered in a nearby sand pit. Serafinowicz admitted that he was in Mir that day and heard the shooting but claimed that he had tried to save lives. He told his police interviewers: 'I try my everything to save that people [sic]...I didn't shoot anybody. I didn't give any orders to shoot.'[33]

Rufeisen was not a direct witness to the 9 November killings but four others were, including a woman called Regina Bedynska, whose allegations against Serafinowicz were the subject of a post-war investigation in the UK, discussed later. In 1941, she was the 16-year-old daughter of a schoolmaster and close neighbour of Serafinowicz. She testified that she was on her way to draw water from a communal well when she noticed four adult Jews and a child of about seven, identifiable by the yellow Star of David pinned to their clothing. They had also been spotted by Serafinowicz, who was standing with some other *Schutzmänner*. Mrs Bedynska drew a map for the investigators showing where she was standing in relation to the defendant.[34] She said she saw Serafinowicz raise his rifle and fire at the Jews, hitting a woman who fell to the ground covering the child with her body:

> The child then crawled out from under the body of the woman crying 'get up mother, get up'. Regina Bedynska could bear to look no longer, collected her bucket and returned home. Serafimovich was within a distance of about twenty metres from Regina Bedynska....Regina Bedynska knew Serafimovich well....She identifies correctly the house in which Serafimovich lived and knew Rufeisen to be his lodger.

---

[32] 'The Crown Against Semyon Serafinowich' drawn up by John Nutting QC for the committal hearing, 4 January 1996.

[33] From the prosecution draft opening for the committal hearing CPS Copy, John Nutting QC/John Kelsey-Fry, 22 December 1995.

[34] Exhibit Identity No. RFB/2 no. 8326 in Bundle 16 March 1995.

She has no doubt that the policeman she saw shooting this Jewish woman was Serafimovich.[35]

Why Didn't Serafinowicz Stand Trial?

By the spring of 1995, all of the substantive evidence against Serafinowicz had been gathered and the CPS was satisfied on balance that it had a solid case to submit to the Attorney-General, Sir Nicholas Lyell, who alone could authorize a charge. But according to the then CPS head of War Crimes Casework, Paul Harrison, no decision was made for several months:

> The AG sat on it for some time, perhaps because he couldn't make up his mind [Lyell was thought to have been sceptical from the beginning about the wisdom of war crimes prosecutions]. The particular reason for the delay though was that he wanted a number of extra checks made. But I stress that no more information was added to the file whatsoever after I submitted it.[36]

Thus more time was lost as officers from the WCU were sent back to Belarus to re-interview several of the witnesses in order to 'consolidate' statements to the satisfaction of Treasury Counsel. Even then, according to Robert Bland, of the CPS Casework team, more persuasion was needed: 'John Nutting originally said "no way" to prosecution but I said to him "look, if the case wasn't fifty years old, on the strength of the evidence, would you prosecute?" That persuaded him.'[37]

Finally, on 12 July 1995, with the fiat (i.e. legal assent) of the AG, Serafinowicz was arrested and charged with four counts of murder under the War Crimes Act 1991. At this point, he was 84 and deemed to be sufficiently healthy, both physically and mentally, to stand trial.

---

[35] From the Draft Opening for the committal (note: there were variable spellings of the defendant's name throughout the pre-trial period).

[36] Paul Harrison interview with author, 27 June 1996.

[37] Robert Bland conversation with author, 3 September 1998.

His counsel, William Clegg QC, has given an excellent description of him at that time: 'When I first met Szymon Serafinowicz, he was a bright sparkling old man with penetrating blue eyes. He had a strong personality and even at 83 or 84, he dominated his sons. He was no-one's fool'.[38]

On 13 July, Martin Dean informed the expert historian engaged to provide context for the trial, Christopher Browning, that Serafinowicz had been charged, adding in his letter: 'John Nutting is keen to have a preliminary draft from you by about mid-August if possible, *as events may move rather quickly here...* [authors' emphasis]'.[39]

Dean's prognosis seems to have been built more on hope than expectation. It is necessarily a moot point but had the trial taken place later in 1995 or in the first part of 1996, it is possible that a historic conviction could have been obtained. However, the normative legal process put an 'obstacle' in the way of that happening. It was called the committal.

The committal is an occasion for the strength of the prosecution case to be tested before a magistrate, sitting without a jury, who decides if there is sufficient evidence on which a reasonable jury, properly directed, can convict on any or all of the charges. It is self-evident that holding what is, in effect, a 'mini-trial' (though technically it is an 'inquiry' not a trial) before the substantive event causes delay and an extra logistical hurdle to be overcome. The Hetherington-Chalmers Inquiry, when it reported in 1989, recognized that:

> The difficulty of securing the attendance of witnesses from abroad in relation to these [i.e. war crimes] cases would be magnified if it was necessary for them to attend twice, that is for the committal proceedings and then for the trial. This would be particularly burdensome for frail elderly witnesses from abroad, who would in any event be unfamiliar with the procedures of the courts.[40]

---

[38] William Clegg speech at the British Academy of Forensic Sciences Friends' Dinner, Law Society, 26 February 1998 reported in *Journal of Medicine, Science and the Law* 38(3).

[39] Dean letter to Browning, 13 July 1995, Hartley Library Special Collections, Archive file MS 408_A1057 2/43, p. 505.

[40] *War Crimes: Report of the War Crimes Inquiry* 1989 Cm 744 para 3.33, para 9.43.

Accordingly, it recommended that, in the event of a War Crimes Act being brought into law:

> Certain procedural changes will also be desirable.... In England and Wales, we recommend that the procedure of transfer to the Crown Court *without any committal proceedings* [authors' emphasis], which was introduced for serious fraud cases by sections 4–6 of the Criminal Justice Act 1987, also be applicable to war crimes trials.[41]

But this did not happen. There were press suggestions that this was because of a bureaucratic slip-up by the Home Office, which was said to have omitted to bring forward a piece of enabling legislation to allow the committal stage to be bypassed.[42] Others hinted at darker motives: that the 'establishment' hoped that further delay and possible attrition of witnesses, would render a case unviable. The truth is rather different. The law, even as it stood in the mid-1990s, would have permitted the Serafinowicz case to proceed swiftly to a full trial, with the evidence examined in a 'paper' committal, in other words, the pre-trial examination conducted by written testimony alone. However, the prosecution wanted a full 'old-style' committal, with the witnesses present, as Treasury Counsel, Sir John Nutting, explains:

> We said that there had never been an English criminal prosecution like this one before and we would allow the defence every latitude in testing our evidence *at the earliest opportunity* [authors' emphasis]. I regarded that as only fair. We believed that having an old-style committal, giving us two goes at it, would also be of enormous benefit to us in ensuring that we had a cogent and credible case to put forward, and one which had been examined by a senior legal mind, i.e. a magistrate. The full committal also offered the defence the earliest chance to get their client acquitted.[43]

[41] Ibid., para 10.4.
[42] Stephen Ward, 'War crimes case is thrown into chaos', *The Independent*, 27 September 1995.
[43] Nutting interview with author, 28 May 2021.

This decision had consequences. The committal, at Dorking magistrates court in Surrey, formally opened in January 1996 and did not end until 15 April when Serafinowicz was committed for trial at the Old Bailey on three charges of murder, the fourth having been dropped because the evidence did not meet the criminal standard of proof. There was a further delay when the defence attempted to have the case dismissed in an 'abuse of process' hearing at the end of 1996. By this point, Serafinowicz, now 86, was suffering from Alzheimer's and the prosecution was formally halted in January 1997, eighteen months after he had been charged. Nutting added (Fig. 5.4):

> We didn't anticipate that Serafinowicz would put forward a defence that he was unfit to stand trial but if the charge is that we bent over backwards to favour the defendant I can live with that. And if people say 'he got away with it', one could reply that it also deprived us of a possible conviction.[44]

It is fruitless to speculate on whether Serafinowicz would have been found guilty if he had been fit to stand trial. His barrister, William Clegg QC, remains of the opinion that there were weaknesses in the prosecution case which he could have exploited. But it is germane to the thesis advanced in this book to wonder why the considered judgements of two distinguished prosecutors, Sir Thomas Hetherington and William Chalmers, were sidelined by those responsible for prosecuting suspects under the War Crimes Act. This applies not only to the question of the committal but also to whether other procedural modifications should have been adopted, or at least considered in light of the uniqueness of the cases.

One such was the question of admissibility of witness evidence captured on video or audio tape or taken down in some other form in a foreign jurisdiction for a trial in the UK. The Inquiry accepted that some potential witnesses in say, Eastern Europe, would be unable through ill health, or unwilling, to travel to the UK for a trial. It pointed to existing

[44] Ibid.

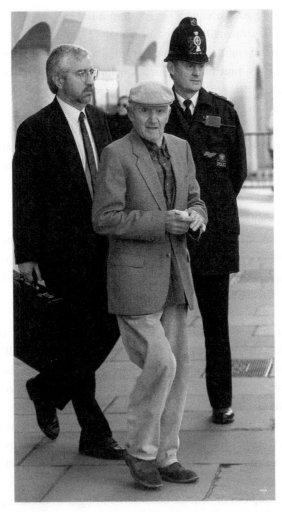

Fig. 5.4 Szymon Serafinowicz outside court in London 1996. PA Images/
Alamy Stock Photo.

provisions in the 1988 Criminal Justice Act for such evidence to be
made available in other forms with the leave of the trial court. For
instance, the Act allowed for Letters of Request to be sent, with the
authority of a judge or magistrate, asking for testimony to be taken in a
foreign jurisdiction:

This method of taking and receiving evidence is clearly a possibility in the context of any war crimes trials in this country. It thus seems desirable that arrangements should be made with the authorities in the countries in question, and in particular the Soviet Union, where potential witnesses are available so that evidence could be taken in pursuance of a letter of request.[45]

It is true that the use of video evidence had not gone smoothly in the Australian prosecutions and Sir Thomas Hetherington later qualified this recommendation by saying that 'I don't think a video link could be used for crucial evidence.'[46] And, although it would not have required the enactment of fresh legislation, neither did it appeal to the Crown Prosecution Service. Thus, when the acting Director of Public Prosecutions, Michael Bibby, wrote to his counterpart in Latvia in 1991 requesting assistance, he implicitly ruled out the giving of evidence in this manner:

> I think it only right to point out that, in my view, the more important the evidence that the witness can give, the less likelihood there is that a judge will allow it to be given in any way other than orally by the witness who is physically in the presence of the jury. Someone, for instance, who was an eye witness to an atrocity would be expected to give evidence in this way.[47]

It is impossible to miss the inconsistency here. Bibby also told his interlocutor that under the 1988 Act, it was permitted—with the approval of the trial judge—for a witness to give evidence in a homicide case via video link. Yet even though the CPS insisted that war crimes cases should follow the normative procedures of a murder prosecution, with no concessions to the extraordinary context in which the alleged crimes were committed, this was, apparently, the exception that proved the necessity of the rule!

---

[45] *War Crimes: Report of the War Crimes Inquiry* 1989 Cm 744 para 3.33, para 9.35.
[46] Hetherington interview with author, 5 July 1995.
[47] Bibby letter to the General Procurator of Latvia, 6 November 1991, Doct DPP 2/13571 UKNA.

The Retreat from Mir

By the end of June 1944, the Nazi occupation of western Belorussia was threatened by the Red Army advance, and the German gendarmes and locally recruited *Schutzmannschaften* began an evacuation westwards. Serafinowicz told his police interviewers that: 'My wife, Jadwiga and son, Szymon, left with me on a horse-drawn cart as we crossed the border with Poland. The Germans gave us uniforms, I had the uniform of an infantryman.'[48]

In East Prussia, the Mir cohort, along with many other *Schutzmänner*, were absorbed into the 30 Waffen SS Grenadier Division which had been formed by merging volunteer units of Ukrainians, Russians, and Belarussians from the *Siegling* punitive brigade. The makeshift force was then transported by train to France: 'Meister Hein and Schulz came to France with us.'[49]

In his interviews, Serafinowicz omitted all mention of the Waffen SS and, probably aware that appearing to have been anything but a foot solider would increase his chances of being prosecuted, he said nothing about his promotion in the autumn of 1944 to *Zugführer*, platoon leader. He said that he and his unit were taken from eastern France to Dachau, near Munich, and, at some unspecified time afterwards, they surrendered to French forces. But this version left out, for self-serving reasons, an episode in which he went missing from the division during an engagement with French forces in the Vosges. The division, which had numbered some 15,000 men at its peak, was now severely depleted through casualties and desertion in the face of a better motivated enemy. A German army Loss Report, dated 28 November 1944 was filed on Serafinowicz, whose police rank is described as 'Sgt/SS Rank Untersturmführer. Last Address—Field Post no.31251B'. It records that:

> The above was with 1st Squad of Reconnaissance Detachment 1 defending the village of Balschweiler...the enemy with a large tank force and superiority in infantry numbers managed to strike Balschweiler on two sides and in the second attack to get into the village...According

---

[48] Serafinowicz WCU interview, 22 July 1993.   [49] Ibid.

to some men who were able to get out of Balschweiler during the night, the missing person was taken prisoner.[50]

Serafinowicz was shown a copy of this document by DI Chapman and became rather agitated. 'Everything a liar' was his response. 'Are you saying you were never there?' 'We were never involved in fighting. We surrendered to the French after Dachau.' 'Were you given uniforms/firearms?' 'No comment.'

In fact, a police search of Serafinowicz's house had turned up contemporaneous notes, in his handwriting, of this episode. It is not clear why he kept the notes, nor why, when confronted with them, he denied they were his. As Martin Dean has written: 'The history of the 30 Waffen SS Division as a fighting unit is less than glorious. Soon after their arrival in France (in late August 1944), there was a mutiny in which some of the Belorussians killed their officers and fled to join the French partisans.'[51]

This chequered history was of great assistance to the war crimes investigators because an examination of the Loss Report section (*Verlustmeldungen*) of the Division 'showed a large number of traces for suspects allegedly living in Britain and also for possible members of the *Schutzmannschaft* in the Baranowichi/Slonim areas.'[52]

Like many of his police compatriots, Serafinowicz was absorbed into the Free Polish forces (the so-called Anders Army) fighting alongside the British and he spent time in Egypt and Italy before arriving in the UK through Glasgow at the end of June 1946. Research conducted for the War Crimes Unit shows that 104 members of the Mir/Turets *Schutzmannschaft* post escaped to the West, at least forty-six of them coming to the UK, in the last few months of the war. Eleven were NCOs, including Serafinowicz.[53] He was recruited into the Polish Resettlement Corps (PRC), in his case, serving in the Wielkopolska Armoured Brigade, based at Barkford Camp in Sussex. Having calculated that it was better to be taken for a Pole than a Belorussian. Serafinowicz's recruitment

---

[50]   Report by SS Haupsturmführer, Capt. and squadron commander, Hartley Library Special Collections, Archive file MS 408_A1057 2/10, p. 550.

[51]   Dean, 2000 *Collaboration in the Holocaust*, p. 152.

[52]   Dean report 27 November 1992 on WAST (Berlin) Germany Army personnel and POW records.

[53]   Source: WCU 93/1 Appendix II/1–11.

form shows that he concealed the truth about his origins: 'Army Form B271 (Polish) Army No: 30008035. Enlisted – 19.9.1946. Parents – Polish. Born in Bozek, near Stolpce [he was actually born in Skomorski which in 1910 was part of Russia]. Character – very good. Served in Egypt – eight months. Italy – eight months.'[54]

Serafinowicz Under Investigation

Amongst the troops in the Polish Resettlement Corps (PRC) there were many who had sanitized their wartime activities in the hope that they were unlikely to come under close scrutiny once in the UK. Naturally, Serafinowicz disclosed nothing about his service as a Belorussian *Schutzmänner*, but the files show that his past caught up with him when three fellow PRC soldiers accused him of war crimes. The allegations were grave enough to be passed on by the Polish General Staff to Whitehall where they landed at the door of the Security Service, MI5 and the Home Office. The files make sobering reading in light of the subsequent failure to secure any form of redress for the crimes committed under Serafinowicz's command in Mir and surrounding villages.

The complainants were a Corporal Kucharczyk, Sergeant Leon Sawicki, and Private Tomasz Acecki, the latter two serving at Cark Camp near Barrow in Lancashire. Sawicki made a statement on 17 December 1946, alleging that 'during the German occupation, Serafinowicz collaborated closely with the Gestapo in the localities of Turka [i.e. Turets], Mir and Baranowichi.' Sawicki said he had been arrested on the orders of Serafinowicz and taken to a concentration camp.

In his statement, Acecki said he had met Serafinowicz at the beginning of 1942: 'Serafinowicz was initiator of all reprisals, chicanery and pacification of whole villages in the Mir district…He showed also a great zeal in the extermination of Poles and of the intelligentsia in particular.'[55]

[54] Hartley Library Special Collections, Archive file MS 408_A1057 2/30, p. 7124.
[55] Files of Polish Resettlement Corps, Hayes. Hartley Library Special Collections, Archive file MS 408_A1057 2/44, pp. 43–4.

The commanding officer at the PRC camp (no name attached) sent a summary of the allegations to the War Office in February 1947:

Serafinowicz is said to have taken part in arrests, executions and burning of villages and to be guilty of the death of numerous persons. He is also said to be holder of German decorations.

As Serafinowicz should be *treated as a war criminal* [authors' emphasis] I should appreciate to have your decision as what steps should be taken in this matter. I should like to add that SERAFINOWICZ has not been interrogated yet.[56]

It may be significant that at this point, MI5 became involved, as illustrated by a letter from J. L. Irvine of the Security Service to an official in the Home Office (Aliens Department), S. H. E. Burley:

CONFIDENTIAL

> Box No. 500
> Parliament Street B.O.
> London SW1
> 18th February, 1947.

Dear Burley,

L/Sgt. Szymon SERAFINOWICZ

Reference our telephone conversation of 14th February and yours with my secretary last night. I enclose a copy of the information [this is the summary above] which I have received from my Polish source alleging that Serafinowicz is a war criminal.

I have written to my contact recommending that the Poles should prepare the case against him and submit it to the British Advisory Staff for forwarding to the appropriate quarter.[57]

On the same day as that letter was sent, Irvine wrote to Lt. Col. W. Zarembski, Security Section of the Polish General Staff:

---

[56] File Gen./B.2.a./JLL no. 4198/4199, Hartley Library Special Collections, Archive file MS 408_A1057 2/44.
[57] WO Gen./B.2.a./JLI Hartley Library Special Collections, Archive file MS 408_A1057 2/44.

Headed L/Sgt. Szymon Serafinowicz

I have discussed this case with the Government department concerned [presumably the Foreign Office] and they advised me that it would be a matter to be submitted to the International War Crimes Commission for consideration. As I explained in my letter (Gen.1508), dated 4.2.47 about the case of Dr. Dering, we are not normally concerned with war criminal cases in this office, unless there is a counter-espionage interest.[58]

MI5's view was that, as the alleged crimes related to Polish territory, they were 'of no concern to the British'. But for whatever reason, the case was not submitted to the UN War Crimes Commission. Had they been, Serafinowicz might have been traced and prosecuted in the 1990s rather earlier.

One of the recipients of Irvine's letters, Burley (of the Home Office) appears to have sent a copy of the denunciations to the War Office on 26 February 1947 and the response, though it came within twelve days, reflects the mixture of scepticism and buck-passing characteristic of the approach to war crimes issues in 1940s Whitehall: 'A good deal of the information in the statements appears to be based on hearsay, and some of the first-hand statements are in rather general terms but we shall have to try to sift them, or have them sifted.'[59]

The fact that MI5 was involved in the chain of correspondence about Serafinowicz is a strong indication that Whitehall suspected there might be some truth in the accusations and officials were concerned at possible repercussions, not least at Westminster. The archive files contain a letter sent to Major A. R. J. Hewitt, of the British Advisory Staff—the sender's identity is not clear but his/her government department appears to be the Foreign Office. The letter betrays a sense of unease: 'This is the sort of case that is always likely to be raised in a Parliamentary question and we are anxious to dispose of it without delay.'[60]

---

[58] WO Ref: Gen.1520, 18 February 1947, Hartley Library Special Collections, Archive file MS 408_A1057 2/44, p. 155.

[59] WO/CDCR response, 10 March 1947, Hartley Library Special Collections, Archive file MS 408_A1057 2/44, p. 3.

[60] FO s66787, 20 May 1947, Hartley Library Special Collections, Archive file MS 408_A1057 2/44.

The 'solution' was to put the investigation into the hands of Lieutenant Colonel Alexander Paterson Scotland, the officer commanding the London Cage, which, during the war, had mainly focused on gathering intelligence on German strategic intentions. Between 1945 and 1948, the role of its premises at Kensington Palace Gardens had changed to become the home of the War Crimes Investigation Unit, which the historian Helen Fry has called 'the most important centre outside Germany to deal with high profile Nazi war criminals'.[61] These included the commandants of concentration camps, SS generals, and a Field Marshal, Albert Kesselring. Serafinowicz arrived in this 'distinguished' company in April 1947, and, as another sign that, on paper at least, the allegations against him were being taken seriously, he was interrogated by Scotland himself, who, according to Fry, was a formidable and committed inquisitor:

> Pitted now against the Nazi war criminals, Scotland was determined to bring them to justice for their crimes, if it was the last thing he did. It became a very personal mission. He vowed to track down every name on the London Cage's list of wanted war criminals.[62]

Scotland does not mention the Serafinowicz case in his memoirs but it is reasonable to infer from the three-page report he sent to Major F. W. G. Thompson of the Judge Advocate General's office that the feared interrogator did not regard the denunciation of a low-level auxiliary policeman, who wasn't even German and not on any recognized war crimes list, as worth anything more than superficial consideration:

> Serafinowicz was brought to the London Cage on 30 April. Serafinowicz makes a good impression, he is a pleasant and easygoing type, has a somewhat sly character, possessing a slightly shifty eye, but could not be described as anything approaching a brutal type. Obviously, because of his strong physical development and his ability to adopt an authoritative manner, he made a considerable impression on the German occupying forces in Poland...The force [i.e. the

[61] Fry, 2017 *The London Cage*, p. 123.   [62] Ibid., p. 126.

Schutzmannschaft] did not wear uniforms [untrue] but were issued
with red and white armbands...[63]

Amongst the allegations made against Serafinowicz was the claim that
he had been responsible for the arrest of the Communist president of an
agricultural association in the district of Mir, and of the former school
principal, a man called Balicki. Balicki's daughter was Regina Bedynska,
whose eyewitness testimony that she saw Serafinowicz shoot a Jewish
mother became one of the principal charges against him in the 1990s.
Both of the arrested men were sent to a concentration/labour camp at
Koldichevo, where Balicki was amongst a number of people gassed in
specially adapted trucks. The Communist prisoner was apparently shot.
Scotland reported that:

> Serafinowicz denied all knowledge of the shooting of a Russian subject
> as described. Claimed that two men [i.e. Sgt. Sawicki and Pte. Acecki]
> were drunkards who had taken a deep personal dislike to Serafinowicz
> and had spread reports calculated to damage his character. [Serafinowicz]
> knows nothing about the murder of a Polish family by Pankiewicz [his
> deputy in the Mir cohort, who also came to the UK after the war]. The
> Jews killed in the district of Mir were killed by German soldiers.[64]

Without any independent digging into the allegations, Scotland declared
that Serafinowicz was not responsible for Balicki's arrest. And without
any real insights into the nature of the German occupation of Belorussia,
he described the *Schutzmannschaft* as 'a protective police force' (i.e.
offering protection against partisans), concluding that:

> I do not believe that Serafinowicz was a member of the Gestapo...It
> cannot be a criminal offence to have served in the *Schutzmannschaft*,
> otherwise the Polish Government would by now have tried all its
> members. Serafinowicz obviously assisted the power [i.e. Nazi Germany],

---

[63]   Ref: MD/JAG/FS/0173/500 April 1947 Hartley Library Special Collections, Archive file
MS 408_A1057 2/44, p. 27.
[64]   Ref: MD/JAG/FS/0173/500 April 1947.

which, for its own purposes, was eager to maintain an *orderly state of life in Poland* [authors' emphasis] and unless there is much more conclusive evidence forthcoming…no blame can be laid at this man's door more than at others who did no more than he did.[65]

On the basis of Scotland's assessment, the Judge Advocate General's Office declined to pursue the matter further, though a note in the files dated 13 May 1947 suggests more than a lingering suspicion that Serafinowicz had not been exonerated, merely that the evidence was not robust enough, and that his permanent presence in the country could prove an embarrassment:

> In light of this report, it is difficult to see what further steps could be taken against Serafinowicz as an alleged war criminal…The man is not on the UN War Crimes Commission lists. We might find out in the usual way what plans Serafinowicz has made for his future, e.g. emigration or enlistment in the corps [the Polish Resettlement Corps]. The former course would be the most satisfactory one, no doubt, from our point of view. In addition, it would be helpful if BAS [British Advisory Staff] obtained particulars of the man's military record and character. On the facts available at present, we do not feel there is any further actions we can take in this case…[66]

The hope that Serafinowicz would spare the authorities any potential embarrassment by emigrating might have been encouraged by the fact that he had written on a pre-demobilization questionnaire in September 1946 that he would like to settle permanently in Canada, with the UK as his second choice. His change of mind can probably be explained by the presence in the UK of other members of the Mir cohort and a burgeoning number of Belorussian social/political organizations.

The war crimes allegations had originally been channelled to Whitehall through the British Advisory Staff (BAS) attached to the Polish Resettlement Corps and on 20 May 1947, Major Hewitt of the BAS

---

[65] Ibid.
[66] Unidentified official, Hartley Library Special Collections, Archive file MS 408_A1057.

received a letter either from the Foreign Office or the Judge Advocate General's Office (the sender is not noted):

Dear Hewitt, since February last, a certain amount of time has been spent in investigating accusations made against Staff Sgt. Szymon Serafinowicz and we have now received a copy of the report made by Colonel Scotland on his interrogation of Serafinowicz on April 30. The report seems to us to reveal nothing very damning in Serafinowicz's record and Colonel Scotland seemed disposed to take a lenient enough view of it...[67]

Finally, at the end of May 1947, the letter chain about the war crimes allegations looped back to S. H. E. Burley of the Home Office Aliens Department. He received this from P. F. Hancock of the Foreign Office: 'Colonel Scotland is a most able and experienced interrogator and in view of his report, I am sure that no British Military Court would look at this case. It seems to me that the only thing to do is to drop it.'[68]

Even if the British authorities no longer had an interest in pursuing Serafinowicz for war crimes, the Polish army was not prepared to let the matter drop. In the files of the Polish Resettlement Corps is a report on 'initial proceedings towards a court martial under Art. 100 para 1 of the Polish Criminal Code', concerning Serafinowicz's collaboration with the Germans between 1941 and 1943. It is written by the Legal Adviser to the Inspector-General of the PRC:

12th Field Court Martial of PRC, Delamere Park Camp.

Proceedings instituted against junior Sgt Serafinowicz of the 14th Gt. Poland Armoured Brigade.

...namely during the war in Nowogrudok province in Poland [sic], he acted to the advantage of the enemy in that being appointed police

---

[67] File ref: s66787 Hartley Library Special Collections, Archive file MS 408_A1057 2/44, p. 14.
[68] FO/Ref: N5467/2815/55, 29 May 1947, Hartley Library Special Collections, Archive file MS 408_A1057 2/44, p. 23.

commander by the German occupation authorities for the purpose of their arrest or deportation for forced labour, and ordered the pacification and burning of villages.[69]

The rest of the documentation relating to the court martial has since disappeared and it is not possible to determine whether any evidence, either for or against the accused, was heard. All that seems to have survived is a note from the Acting Head of the Court, Adam Szediwy, written on 22 April 1948, which declares: 'By the same instructions... the bringing of the charges against junior Sgt. Serafinowicz is postponed until his demobilization, in view of his joining the PRC.'[70]

Serafinowicz was discharged from the PRC on 12 April, ten days before this note was written. And there the investigation into his wartime activities in Belarus seems to have come to a halt.

Belorussian Emigres and Nationalism

In November 1947, having apparently shrugged off the taint of war crimes accusations, Serafinowicz decided to rectify a deliberate falsehood on his recruitment form to the PRC. He completed an application to change his nationality: 'I testify that in my record sheet... I am entered as a Pole which is not in accordance with the truth. I respectfully request that an amendment be made in the above space [to change] from Polish nationality to White Russian.'[71]

It is impossible to be certain about why he did this but the Poles had already noted Serafinowicz's active involvement with the Belorussian émigré nationalist movement based in London. In July 1947, the security officer for 34 Brigade Group, Captain Radziukinas wrote to PRC headquarters that:

---

[69] PRC file Index no. KW:100/47 Hartley Library Special Collections, Archive file MS 408_ A1057 2/44, p. 96.
[70] Ibid.
[71] PRC File, 29 November 1947, Hartley Library Special Collections, Archive file MS 408_ A1057 2/30, p. 7219.

According to the information that has been gathered, a group of Belorussians live there [a hostel at 50 Onslow Square, South Kensington SW7], who are also nationally active with respect to plans for the future. They are said to be receiving assistance from Belorussian organisations. While in the Brigade, L/Sgt. Serafinowicz maintained correspondence with displaced persons in Germany, and in the regiment, the Belorussians gathered around him but without showing any indication of subversive activity.[72]

This information must have been passed on to the Home Office because there is a handwritten note on Serafinowicz's file from December 1947 which reads: 'This alien is associated with the Byelorussian Liberation Movement.'[73]

Serafinowicz's relationship as an acolyte of the head of the Belorussian nationalist movement, Radoslaw Ostrowski, began during the period of the German occupation, as stated earlier, and continued once Serafinowicz had come to London. A highly partisan pro-Communist publication from 1982 declared that:

Towards the end of the Occupation, he was Ostrowski's right-hand man. Serafinowicz rarely went to Minsk. For that reason, Ostrowski often used to send his people to see him in Mir and ask his 'expert' opinion about many questions of a kind relating to the forcible Germanisation of Byelorussia. Serafinowicz was also his adviser on military matters.[74]

Given its provenance and aims, which were to skewer 'the detestable activities of the Byelorussian bourgeois-nationalists who, during the Great Patriotic War, cooperated with the Nazis', this propaganda work can hardly be relied upon for historical accuracy. But its picture of Serafinowicz's political activities and connections in London seems to

[72] PRC Historical Records Ref: 933/96 Radziukinas letter, 7 July 1947, Hartley Library Special Collections, Archive file MS 408_A1057 2/44, p. 197.
[73] HO Minute sheet/Ref:S.66484, 17 December 1947, Hartley Library Special Collections, Archive file MS 408_A1057 2/44, p. 3.
[74] Extract from Bazhko Ales, 1982 Total Bankruptcy, 2nd edn., Minsk BBK 66.5/WCU Ref:288.

accord with some of the observations of the Polish security officer cited above. The author claimed that Serafinowicz:

> was quietly running the KhABR [the Belorussian Central Council] in London and assiduously 'selling himself short' to his fellow country-men, insisting that he was 'only small fry'. It was only after Ostrowski moved to London from West Germany that Serafinowicz went a bit quieter.... The KhABR was a focal point of interest to the British and American intelligence services.... Serafinowicz was, so to speak, an adviser to the British and Americans with the KhABR.[75]

These somewhat florid assertions reflect the Soviet view that the West provided a refuge for war criminals because they were passing on useful anti-Communist intelligence. Records of MGB (forerunner of the KGB) interviews with citizens of Soviet republics who had been in the UK and imprisoned on their return, show a continuing interest in the émigré nationalist organizations. One such was the interrogation of a Belorussian, Ivan Grigoryevich Lyakhov, who was questioned repeatedly between April and July 1951. At his first interview, which took place in Riga in Latvia, he was asked to supply the names of Soviet 'displaced persons' living in England. Serafinowicz was number six on the list of seven which he disclosed.

In July 1951, he was questioned again, in more detail, in Baranovichi in Belorussia. He admitted that during his stay in England, he had been a member of 'the anti-Soviet nationalist organization, the CBU, the Christian Byelorussian Union of Workers of Great Britain'. He named Boris Suravy, a close confidant of Ostrowski, as the president of the London committee of the CBU, whose deputy was 'Sarafinovich [sic] Semyon, aged about 40, a native of Nesvizh district, Baranovichi province... during the German occupation of the BSSR he served in the German police in Nesvizh district, he served in Anders' army. At present, he lives in London, he works as a labourer building houses.'[76]

[75] Ibid.
[76] Lyakhov interrogation by Head of Section 3 of the Investigation Dept. of the MGB Directorate for Baranovichi province, 16 July 1951, pp. 1155–69, Minsk KGB Archive.

Asked what the aims of the CBU were, Lyakhov replied: 'the main aim of the organization is the struggle against the Soviet authorities in Byelorussia in order to tear the Byelorussian SSR away from the Soviet Union and form an independent, separate Byelorussian bourgeois state with the help of American and British forces'.[77]

Why and how Lyakhov returned to the Soviet Union after his post-war stay in London is not clear. Ostrowski was also in the UK for several months, seeking to galvanize the Belorussian liberation movement and help organize a convention of the supranational body, the Anti-Bolshevik Bloc of Nations, which took place in Edinburgh in June 1950.[78] The Security Service, MI5, and MI6 kept a close eye on such gatherings and it is known that Ostrowski strove to establish a liaison with UK (and US) intelligence. The police investigating Serafinowicz in the 1990s were denied access to MI6 files but Professor Anthony Glees, an adviser on intelligence and security to the Hetherington-Chalmers Inquiry, believed it was more than likely that some of the émigré nationalists were per-suaded or induced to provide intelligence for the British.[79] If so, it is not inconceivable that Lyakhov had agreed to become an agent for MI6, as his interrogator accused him of being: 'It is clear to the investigation that you came to the USSR with the task from British intelligence and the CBU of carrying out anti-Soviet activities in the BSSR [i.e. Belorussia]. Is that not so?'

Lyakhov's denial would not have helped him and the file does not spell out his punishment. If he was lucky, it would have been a term in the gulag, possibly commuted after Stalin's' death. Ostrowski moved to London permanently in 1954 after a two-year interlude in Juan Perón's Argentina and he played host to a conglomeration of nationalist groups, according to one Belorussian activist: 'Serafinowicz and I were on the committee of the White Ruthenian Workers Association in the 1950s. It used to meet at no 57 Cathnor Rd, Shepherd's Bush, which was Ostrowski's home. It was also the headquarters of the Belorussian Liberation Movement.'[80]

---

[77] Ibid.   [78] Alexander, 2015 *Nazi Collaborators*, pp. 86–7.
[79] Glees interview with author, 18 June 1996.
[80] Nicholas Sienko interview with author, 17 October 1996.

This skein of connections between the émigré nationalists, many of whom had been ardent collaborators of the Nazis, has prompted speculation that some arrived in the UK as part of organized networks rather than 'atomized' individuals and that this was missed by the security agencies.[81] The first evidence of an assessment by the British Security Service can be found in the records of the major screening exercise on some 213,000 foreigners who had been admitted to the UK after the war under the European Voluntary Workers scheme. It was called Operation Post Report.

Operation Post Report

Such was the acute labour shortage after the war that the Labour government knowingly admitted hundreds of thousands of foreign workers about whom minimal background information was available. But even where their provenance was quite clear, for example, in the case of an entire Ukrainian Waffen SS division, some 8,000 men, shipped to the UK from a DP camp at Rimini in Italy in May 1947, there was astonishing complacency in Whitehall. Eventually though, at the insistence of the Deputy Director-General of MI5, Guy Liddell, the Home Office initiated a screening programme which took place between 1950 and 1952 (with a later resumption following the Hungarian uprising of 1956).

By the time Operation Post Report (OPR) was underway, the UK's interest in holding war crimes trials had ceased and, in the view of Professor Glees, the objective of OPR was not to root out Nazis and collaborators: 'It must…be said that OPR's prime purpose was not to spot war criminals but to identify possible Soviet sympathizers, seen as a potential security threat and to gain for the Security and Intelligence Services agents with a knowledge of Soviet affairs and the Russian language.'[82]

But even had there been a serious intention to identify Nazi collaborators, the woeful lack of resources and half-hearted direction offered by

[81] Glees interview with author, 18 June 1996.
[82] Glees, 1992 'War Crimes: The Security and Intelligence Dimension', p. 260.

MI5 to the cadre of immigration officers tasked with carrying out the screening would have ensured failure. Little has been written about the way OPR was actually implemented, the unremitting and unrewarding drudgery of it for those who conducted the interviews. Peter Tomkins was one of the 300 or so immigration officers deployed over two winters in 1951 and 1952:

> The Security Service gave us this job without telling us what it was about. At the time of OPR, both MI5 and MI6 would have treated us immigration officers as clods and very naïve so they didn't share anything with us. I remember we used to joke about catching Martin Bormann but, although we were briefed about the Waffen SS, we knew nothing about what had happened in Eastern Europe and the massacres of Jews. When I joined the Immigration Service in 1951, I was 20 and we carried out the interviews in some of the worst conditions I have ever worked in. We were doing about thirty interviews a day, twelve-hour days, in mill towns in the north of England – Burnley, Blackburn, Huddersfield and Bradford – in freezing village halls and unheated rooms in police stations, with only thirty minutes allotted for each interview. Our supervisor would be walking up and down, saying 'you've got to hurry up' so that we could reach the next appointment. The job was regarded as a chore. We saw no value in it.[83]

The interviewees were contacted via the Aliens Registration Scheme and asked a set of very basic questions about their family tree and what their fathers and brothers had done during the war. At the conclusion of the session, they were supposed to be placed in one of two categories: 'No security interest' or ' Specially Submitted'. If a subject was in the former category, as the overwhelming majority were, the form would go directly to the Home Office. If the latter category, the case would be passed over to MI5 who would submit it for further consideration to the Metropolitan Police Special Branch. That, at least, was the theory:

---

[83]   Peter Tomkins interview with author, 2 January 1997.

I must have done about 2,000 interviews and never had a single question or follow-up query from any of them. Frankly, to interrogate a trained ex-Nazi you would have needed a week's debriefing. We had no more than half an hour to prepare for an interview. You would ask 'were you a member of the Waffen SS or any Nazi organization?' Of course, they would say 'no' and that would have been the end of it.[84]

Serafinowicz's Operation Post interview took place at Lion House in London on 2 June 1951. Because of previous MI5 involvement in his case, the file shows that a copy of the form went to the Security Service as well as the Home Office. Otherwise, the interviewer seems to have taken Serafinowicz's answers to questions about his wartime service completely at face value:

Home Office doct. 24.8.51   Port and date of arrival—Glasgow 28.6.46
HMCI(2)

Police,

Box 500

When the Germans occupied the town (Mir), he joined the White Russian Police and later the Byelorussian army, when he fought the Russians…Alien is now employed as a labourer…He belongs to the United Christian Byelorussian Workers Association [founded by Radoslaw Ostrowski] and does not correspond with anyone in Europe [this contradicts the assessment made by Capt. Radziukinas of the PRC, as stated above]. He has no desire to return to home country while it is occupied by Russians or Poles: is in the usual position of Byelorussians—against everybody!

No security interest.[85]

Serafinowicz's wife, Jadwiga, was interviewed on the same day as her husband by HM Immigration Officer Austin Holton, who later provided information to Professor Glees for the Hetherington-Chalmers Inquiry.

[84] Ibid.
[85] HO doct.Bulk Entry Report, 24 August 1951, Hartley Library Special Collections, Archive file MS 408_A1057 2/44, p. 16.

Holton's terse assessment of Jadwiga illustrates how the priorities of the Cold War shaped the focus of Operation Post Report: 'She has never heard of any Communist propaganda, has no desire to return to Poland under present conditions. Her husband's home is in Byelorussia so is always occupied by somebody.'[86]

Conclusion

The Operation Post Report files (or, more correctly, card indexes) 'which might have provided essential evidence for tracking down war criminals in Britain' remained secreted in a Home Office archive, to which only MI5 had access, for forty years.[87] Had it not been for the Hetherington-Chalmers Inquiry, which made use of them in an unpublished annexe to its influential report, they would almost certainly still be hidden away in keeping with the secrecy still shrouding this part of the UK's post-war history.

Thus Serafinowicz came to the attention of the British police only in the 1990s, principally through the diligent research of the historians who discovered that more than forty *Schutzmänner* from the Mir district had immigrated to Britain after the war and that at least half of those were still alive. Once it had been established that Serafinowicz was amongst them and living in London, 'the focus of the investigation shifted rapidly from pursuing several of his subordinates, who were less prominent, to putting a case together against the man who was in charge.'[88]

After a period of hesitation, the Attorney-General finally authorized charges against Serafinowicz in July 1995 and he was arrested only hours after a report into his alleged crimes on BBC Television News by one of the authors of this book. For forty years, the prevailing 'official' narrative that the war crimes issue had been settled remained intact. This comforting illusion had now been overturned.

---

[86] HO doct.Bulk Entry Report form no. 3195, 11 July 1951, Hartley Library Special Collections, Archive file MS 408_A1057 2/3, p. 63.

[87] Cesarani, 1992 *Justice Delayed*, p. 132.

[88] Dean, 2005 'Soviet War Crimes Lists and Their Role in the Investigation of Nazi War Criminals in the West, 1987–2000', in *NS-Gewaltherrschaft: Beiträge zur historischen Forschung und juristischen Aufarbeitung*, ed. Gottwaldt et al., p. 465.

6

Sawoniuk, the Unexpected Conviction

Introduction

The trial of Anthony (Andrzej) Sawoniuk in 1999 was unique in English legal history and has attracted a modicum of scholarly curiosity from researchers such as Bloxham, Fraser, and Laputska. David Hirsh, a sociologist, has observed how the memories of survivor witnesses were required to fit a normative juridical process, leaving some feeling short-changed. Anderson and Hanson's *The Ticket Collector from Belarus* (2022) offers a breezy blow-by-blow account of the proceedings, based on the court transcript. But perhaps because the case was the only Commonwealth war crimes prosecution to result in a conviction, it has been treated as something of a legal outlier, notable mainly for the rarity of an accused speaking in his own defence. For Marouf A. Hasian Jr this ill-judged decision was an attempt—in the event, a failed one—to portray Sawoniuk 'in a particular historical narrative of "resistance", which constructed both Nazis and Soviets as oppressors'.[1]

However, the significance of the case can be measured by much more than courtroom strategy and prosecutorial success. As one of the thousands of low-level *Schutzmannschaft* whose local knowledge was essential to eradicating Jewish life in Belorussia, Sawoniuk's contribution to the Holocaust was far from negligible. Thus, there is much value to be gained by asking how and where the evidence against him was obtained. This process of inquiry situates the case within the investigatory landscape of war crimes, stretching geographically from the Soviet Union to the

---

[1] Hasian, 2006 *Rhetorical Vectors of Memory*, cited by Fraser, 2010 *Daviborshch's Cart*, p. 105.

Safe Haven: The United Kingdom's Investigations into Nazi Collaborators and the Failure of Justice.
Jon Silverman and Robert Sherwood, Oxford University Press. © Jon Silverman and Robert Sherwood 2023.
DOI: 10.1093/oso/9780192855176.003.0007

UK and temporally from 1943 to 1993. The finality of the prosecution—it was the last in any Commonwealth jurisdiction—led the War Crimes Unit historian, Martin Dean, to throw down a challenge: 'It is now left for historians to ... see what light they can shed on both the implementation of the Holocaust and also on Soviet investigations of these crimes.'[2]

We have already given a sense of the sheer ambition of the project undertaken by the Soviet Extraordinary State Commission to make an inventory of the crimes committed by the invading Nazis and those who assisted them. Through an examination of some of the documents previously held in closed archives, this chapter relates that relentless tracking of suspects to the trajectory of a single individual, providing insights into how that information was harnessed and exploited by Western investigators. As Martin Dean discovered, some of the documents known as Search Files contained over 100 pages of interviews and interrogations.[3] Sawoniuk's file was double that size.[4] Through the serendipity of timing, the outcome of his investigation confounded predictions, based on the experiences of other Commonwealth countries, particularly Australia, that there would be no 'successful' inquiries in the 1990s. But there is reason to believe that in the UK there could have been more.

The historian Christopher Browning, author of the celebrated work, *Ordinary Men* (1992), was an expert witness for the prosecution, which might have contributed, albeit unwittingly, to a somewhat reductive view about Sawoniuk and his place in the typology of perpetrators. David Hirsh, who sat through the trial, observed: 'Sawoniuk himself was in many ways unremarkable yet he became, for a few years only, a sadistic mass killer before reverting to an invisible life as a railway worker' (Fig. 6.1).[5]

[2] Dean, 2005 'Soviet War Crimes Lists and Their Role in the Investigation of Nazi War Criminals in the West, 1987–2000', in *NS-Gewaltherrschaft: Beiträge zur historischen Forschung und juristischen Aufarbeitung*, ed. Gottwaldt et al., p. 470.

[3] Dean, 2010 'Crime and Comprehension, Punishment and Legal Attitudes: German and Local Perpetrators of the Holocaust in Domachevo, Belarus, in the Records of Soviet, Polish, German, and British War Crimes Investigations', in *Holocaust and Justice*, ed. Bankier and Michman, p. 266.

[4] The Search File was a dossier on a suspect, updated as more information was gathered and only closed when it was known definitively that the suspect was outside the jurisdiction of the USSR.

[5] Hirsh, 2001 'The Trial of Andrei Sawoniuk: Holocaust Testimony Under Cross-Examination', p. 529.

Fig. 6.1 Convicted war criminal Andrzej Sawoniuk entering the Old Bailey during his trial in March 1999. PA Images/Alamy Stock Photo.

Analysing Sawoniuk

David Hirsh's observation seemingly cast Sawoniuk in a preordained 'mould' as an ordinary man like the disparate group of middle-aged Germans plucked from mundane civilian lives to become the killers of Reserve Police Battalion 101 in Poland before returning to obscurity. Browning ascribed the behaviour of the Order Police to the situation in which they found themselves rather than any innate 'dispositional' factors. He derived his 'social psychology' model from a painstaking study of the whole careers of his subjects. By contrast, Sawoniuk's designation is based only on what was learned of him through his eight-week trial. It is an approach with serious limitations, as Bouwknegt and Nistor point out: 'what can we actually *know* [authors' emphasis] about the ordinariness or extraordinariness of these perpetrators...when our knowledge is informed by snippets of their lives, presented via anecdotal evidence and through the hermetically sealed black and white of the judicial arena?'[6]

This chapter goes beyond the trial to argue that, although the German invasion of Belorussia in 1941 presented Sawoniuk with the opportunity to kill, his own personality and background predisposed much of his behaviour. This is a long way short of endorsing Goldhagen's 'eliminationist' thesis (1996) but it reinforces the 'nuanced and complex picture of dispositional and situational factors' behind 'low-level killing' identified by Jensen and Szejnmann in their work on 'perpetrators'.[7]

The earliest personality profile available of Sawoniuk was an assessment made by the commander of his squadron in the Polish 10th Hussar Regiment, after he had deserted from the German forces in late 1944. It reads: 'requires supervision in his work, no initiative, reckless, superficial, unreliable, likes to drink, constantly dissatisfied and insubordinate'.[8] In 1998, Robert Bland, a CPS casework officer, remarked that of all the suspects he had investigated, Sawoniuk was the only one about whom nobody had a good word to say. His own lawyer, Martin Lee, described him as a 'horrible man'.[9] William Clegg QC, his barrister, commented that the prosecution was lucky to have found 'such a completely obnoxious defendant as Sawoniuk'.[10] His rancid truculence was demonstrated during the trial itself when, according to prosecuting counsel, Sir John Nutting, outside the courtroom, he 'came up to a witness with his fists raised and threatened to punch the "Jew boy's" lights out'.[11] The woman

[6] Bouwknegt and Nistor, 2019 'Studying "Perpetrators" through the Lens of the Criminal Trial', in *Perpetrators of International Crimes*, ed. Smeulers et al., pp. 91–2.

[7] Jensen and Szejnmann (eds.), 2008 *Ordinary People as Mass Murderers*.

[8] Cited in Anderson and Hanson, 2022 *The Ticket Collector from Belarus*, p. 92.

[9] Interview with author, 17 May 2021.

[10] Clegg interview with author, 28 April 2021.

[11] Nutting interview with author, 28 May 2021.

he married when he arrived in the UK, Christina Maria van Gent, told the police that Sawoniuk was a 'nasty, violent individual', hinting strongly that he beat her.

The role which ideology plays in mass killing has provided fertile ground for analysis by authors such as Bartov, Mann, Smeulers, and others. And Jonathan Leader-Maynard has produced a compelling comparative theory relating the ideology of mass violence to security politics.[12] But specialists in perpetrator studies searching for an ideological root cause of Sawoniuk's behaviour will find little ammunition in either his police interrogations or our interviews with his lawyers. They depict a man of little native intelligence, a volcanic temperament but, unlike his compatriot Szymon Serafinowicz (see Chapter 5), no discernible trace of ambition beyond surviving and profiting from the opportunities afforded by the Nazi occupation.

The Soviet Union's 'Most Wanted'

If Sawoniuk's personality is important to understand, even more so is the assiduity with which he was tracked, over more than four decades, by the security agencies of the Soviet Union. Indeed, Sawoniuk's London lawyer, Martin Lee, was shown about twenty KGB files on a pre-trial research trip to Belarus (they were stored in the KGB offices in Brest), which indicated that Sawoniuk headed the list of the Soviet's 'most wanted' suspects in the UK for part of the 1950s.[13] In this chapter, we provide detail of the witness interrogations, painstakingly conducted, initially by the Extraordinary State Commission and then taken over by state security organs, which lasted from 1944 until the early 1980s. It is a record of unflagging dedication to pursuing a perceived enemy of the motherland.[14]

---

[12] Leader-Maynard, 2022 *Ideology and Mass Killing*.
[13] Lee interviews with author, 3 September 1998/17 May 2021.
[14] The formal, overly prolix title was 'The Extraordinary State Commission for Ascertaining and Investigating Crimes Perpetrated by German-Fascist Invaders and Their Accomplices', often referred to by its Soviet shortened name, ChGK.

But first it is necessary to explain how the eyewitness evidence gathered against Sawoniuk and the context within which the crimes were committed, distinguished this inquiry from many others and enabled the prosecution to meet the normative juridical expectations of a UK murder trial. At the time the War Crimes Act passed into law in 1991, this outcome was so much against the odds that a gambler would not have risked much on this 'ordinary man' being traced, let alone brought to court.

A Border Town Under Occupation

At one level, Sawoniuk's background is the biography of a single individual but it is also illustrative of that broader canvas which weaves together the iniquities committed in a pre-war backwater, characterized by Alexander Dallin as 'the least-known country of Europe', with a judgement delivered in the world's most famous court in the closing year of the twentieth century.[15] Andrzej Sawoniuk was born in March 1921 in the small town of Domachevo, which was then in Poland but now, as a result of the reconfiguration of borders during and after the Second World War, to be found in the south-western corner of Belarus, close to the River Bug. Poland is about ten miles to the west and Ukraine is to the south. Anne Applebaum described Domachevo memorably as 'a border town in a borderland, an odd bit of Europe where it was once possible to find, in one village, Poles, Russians, Germans, Belarussians and Jews.'[16] When one of the authors visited in early 1997, the town, surrounded by pine forests and sandhills, could hardly have changed in profile since Sawoniuk's birth—wooden houses, water drawn from the well, and farming carried out largely by scythe and plough. Heavy rain would turn the many unpaved roads into quagmires. Sawoniuk's house, number 6 Sverdlov Street, behind its picket fence, was still there.

Sawoniuk was the illegitimate son of a schoolmaster, thought to have been called Yakub, who disappeared from the scene before his son's

---

[15] Dallin, 1981 *German Rule in Russia, 1941–45*, p. 224.
[16] *Sunday Telegraph*, 14 February 1999, p. 35.

birth. His mother died when he was young and he and his half-brother, Nikolai, were brought up in a two-room wooden shack by their grandmother. The family was poor and Sawoniuk's schooling was rudimentary. One witness described him and his brother as 'street children', largely illiterate. From an early age, Sawoniuk was known locally as Andrusha. This was to become significant during the evidence-gathering phase for his trial at the Old Bailey because a number of elderly witnesses told the police that the diminutive was so fixed in their minds that, though they could not recall either his first name or surname, they remembered him vividly as the only person called Andrusha.[17]

Domachevo's population in the 1920s was around 5,000, approximately 3,000 of them Jews. Belorussia was part of what had been promulgated in Tsarist times as 'the Pale of Settlement', that portion of the Russian Empire where Jews were concentrated (perhaps corralled is more accurate). Thus the town in which Sawoniuk grew up had a long-standing Jewish presence.

In common with many other parts of pre-war Eastern Europe, most of the adult Jews were merchants or tradespeople but, because of its proximity to the River Bug and its warm summers, Domachevo was known as a spa town and a proportion of working Jews ran boarding houses catering for the tourist trade. They lived around the town centre, kept the Sabbath and worshipped at one of two synagogues, one near the main square, the other near the bakery to the east of town. Many of the poorer and younger gentiles, the youth, Andrusha among them, earned a pittance as 'shabbas goys', performing those tasks forbidden to Orthodox Jews on the sabbath, such as lighting fires, chopping wood, and drawing water from the well. Sawoniuk confirmed these facts in interviews with the Metropolitan Police in April 1996 and that during his youth he spoke some Yiddish. This was the confined small-town world in which he came to adulthood.

That world was dramatically upended in June 1941 when Nazi Germany launched its surprise attack on the Soviet Union, Operation Barbarossa. Shortly after 3 a.m. on the 22nd, a Wehrmacht artillery barrage destroyed about half of the houses in Domachevo and set other

---

[17] From the Opening Note for the Jury at Sawoniuk's Old Bailey trial in 1999.

dwellings alight. The ground invasion began at 4 a.m. and, given its proximity to the border and the fact that the military post on the bridge over the River Bug was only lightly guarded by about forty Soviet soldiers, the town was overrun within minutes. The invading force, led by the 487th Infantry Regiment and the 22nd Cavalry Regiment, encountered no enemy fire once they had crossed the river.

Sawoniuk had spent his first twenty years living on the margins, looked down on and because his parents had never married, routinely described as 'the bastard'. The dramatic upheaval of June 1941 presented an unexpected opportunity for self-advancement. Martin Dean has written that: 'Due to the shortage of German personnel, the Nazi police structure in the east relied heavily on local manpower to carry out its various tasks.'[18] During 1942, some 55,000 Belorussians joined, or were conscripted, into police and self-defence militias.[19] The locally recruited units were called *Schutzmannschaften* (often abbreviated to *Schuma*) and were integral to the Nazi's master plan to make Eastern Europe *judenrein* (free of Jews). The local population often referred to them as 'crows' because of their black uniforms.[20]

Sawoniuk volunteered within days of the invasion, amongst other 'early' recruits to the occupiers. Seven of the Domachevo police arrested and put on trial by the NKVD at the war's end had thrown in their lot with the Nazis in 1941.[21] Volunteers had many incentives to join. They were paid daily and given free food, and from 1942, they and their families were exempted from forced labour. They were armed with rifles, Russian-made, and each given a bicycle. A Jewish survivor told the WCU detectives, 'the volunteers were, in my opinion, bandits and murderers'.[22] The precise number of locally recruited police in Domachevo is undocumented but witnesses whose evidence led to Sawoniuk's UK

---

[18] Dean, 2000 *Collaboration in the Holocaust*, p. 60.

[19] Cesarani, 1992 *Justice Delayed*, p. 27.

[20] Gilbert, 1986 in his magisterial work *The Holocaust: The Jewish Tragedy*, p. 298 refers to them as 'ravens'.

[21] Dean, 2010 'Crime and Comprehension, Punishment and Legal Attitudes: German and Local Perpetrators of the Holocaust in Domachevo, Belarus, in the Records of Soviet, Polish, German, and British War Crimes Investigations', in *Holocaust and Justice*, ed. Bankier and Michman, p. 266.

[22] Ibid., p. 271.

prosecution spoke of between ten and fifteen in the early phase of the occupation. One witness, perhaps the only Jew to have survived in Domachevo until it was liberated, Ben Zion Blustein, provided the WCU with the names of eight of the police. It was Blustein, familiar with Andrusha since schooldays, who gave the trial its most memorable quote when he said that, to the Jews, Sawoniuk 'was a man of power, a master, a lord'. This line was picked up pointedly by the trial judge, Mr Justice Potts, in his sentencing remarks.

Anti-Semitism

The influence of anti-Semitism in pre-war Europe has its own place in the historiography of the Holocaust and construction of post-war Jewish identity. A shibboleth for many Jewish communities in the West and implicit in the Israeli and Zionist 'framing' of the Holocaust is 'the assumption that it was the culmination of antisemitism. Antisemitism is itself viewed as an essential part of the human nature of all Gentiles.'[23]

Applied to those independent states carved out of the Austro-Hungarian and Tsarist empires—Poland, Hungary, Ukraine, the Baltic States, and Romania—this judgement holds that the Final Solution may have been conceived by Germany but it was aided by a pre-war hatred of the Jews, which was endemic in those lands. In the case of Latvia, which is extensively discussed in the context of the Arãjs Kommando in Chapter 4, this belief coloured the attitude of prosecutors who ascribed the primary motivation of the killing squads to anti-Semitism. Whereas, for the Soviet Union, seeking ideological advantage wherever it could find it, the murderers were said to be driven by a Fascist-inspired resistance to Communism. Putting crude reductionism aside, recent scholarship has advanced some interpretations based on differences of geography and demographics rather than imprecise generalizations.

Yehuda Bauer has suggested, albeit tentatively, that Jews in those regions of Ukraine which had previously belonged to Poland were at far greater risk from Nazi collaborators than those in the eastern half of the

---

[23] Silverman and Yuval-Davis, 2002 'Memorializing the Holocaust in Britain', p. 109.

country which had been 'Sovietized'.[24] Diana Dumitru's examination of the Holocaust in Romania has found that violent anti-Semitism was more prevalent in Bessarabia (roughly corresponding to present-day Moldova) than in Transnistria, which had a predominantly Ukrainian population before the war and was more heavily conditioned by Soviet ideology.[25] In Latvia, during much of the period of the First Republic, 1918–40, the Jewish community flourished and anti-Semitism was far less virulent than it was in neighbouring Lithuania or Poland.[26]

In Belorussia, as suggested in the Introduction, the picture was mixed but it was certainly not immune to the virus of anti-Semitism. Memoirs by survivors speak of the growing influence of Nazi thinking amongst portions of the Polish-speaking population in the years before the war. Indeed, a National Socialist Party (PBNS) was set up in 1933 under Fabiian Akynchits, described by Dallin as 'a pathological fanatic, ex-Bolshevik turned fascist'.[27] Its direct influence is hard to gauge but seemingly it 'was so insignificant that not even the Germans put any faith in it'.[28] The Free Poles Party, known as the 'Endeks', advocated a boycott of Jewish trade, banning Jews from public office, and limiting Jewish admission to universities. Berl (Jack) Kagan, who grew up in Novogrodek and assisted the WCU investigators with historical background, has written:

> Physical injury, beatings and even pogroms became more common towards the end of 1938. I remember the rumour that spread through Novogrodek just before Passover of 1939 that the Poles were planning a pogrom for the night of the seder.... Peasants from surrounding villages flocked to the town in their carts or on foot, carrying large sacks for the expected plunder.[29]

Given the wisdom of hindsight, it might appear that, as the 1930s progressed, Jewish existence seemed increasingly precarious in the shadow

---

[24] Bauer, 2010 *The Death of the Shtetl.*
[25] Dumitru, 2016 *The State, Antisemitism, and Collaboration in the Holocaust.*
[26] Plavnieks, 2013 'Nazi Collaborators on Trial during the Cold War: The Cases Against Viktors Arājs and the Latvian Auxiliary Security Police', PhD dissertation submitted to the University of North Carolina at Chapel Hill.
[27] Dallin, 1981 *German Rule in Russia, 1941–45*, p. 213.   [28] Ibid., p. 213.
[29] Kagan and Cohen, 1998 *Surviving the Holocaust with the Russian Jewish Partisans*, p. 33.

of 'a ubiquitous violence-inducing ideology'.[30] Nevertheless, historians such as Dean, Browning, and others are wary about ascribing inherent anti-Semitism as a prevailing motive for the involvement of locally recruited police and the (German) Order Police in massacres. As Dean puts it: 'It remains doubtful…that those who participated in Nazi atrocities acted *purely* [our emphasis] from motives of racial hatred. A similar bloodthirstiness and indifference to human life was applied by the local police towards many victims who were not Jews.'[31]

This is probably an accurate characterization of someone like Szymon Serafinowicz but Sawoniuk's own admissions leave little doubt that his anti-Semitism, perhaps born out of resentment and hatred of Jewish neighbours, was deeply rooted and long lasting. His lawyer, William Clegg QC, said: 'In private meetings I had with him, Sawoniuk frequently referred to prosecution witnesses as "Jew boys" and I had to warn him that if he said that in the witness box his case was doomed from the outset. He also denied the Holocaust. According to him, no Jews were killed in Domachevo.'[32]

During his police interviews in 1996 Sawoniuk blamed the Jews who had employed his mother to do chores, saying that her early death was due to overwork. Some of the evidence suggests that he felt he was owed a 'payback' for his wretched start in life. A witness said he overheard Sawoniuk dismiss concerns about what might happen to him if the Germans were defeated: 'In the meantime, I'll try to do what I want – to have a good life, to kill, to drink, and to take what I can.'[33]

There is a wealth of evidence that Sawoniuk derived satisfaction from inflicting indignity and cruelty on his Jewish fellow-townsfolk. One witness told Soviet investigators that Sawoniuk was known as 'a most bloodthirsty person and that many people died at his hands'.[34] According to a member of his own police cohort whose comments were recorded

[30] King, 2012 'Can There Be a Political Science of the Holocaust?', p. 324.

[31] Dean, 2000 *Collaboration in the Holocaust*, p. 163.

[32] Clegg interview with authors, 28 April 2021.

[33] Testimony given by Ben Zion Blustein at the committal hearing held in London, 28 May 1998.

[34] Dean, 2005 'Soviet War Crimes Lists and Their Role in the Investigation of Nazi War Criminals in the West, 1987–2000', in *NS-Gewaltherrschaft: Beiträge zur historischen Forschung und juristischen Aufarbeitung*, ed. Gottwaldt et al., p. 469.

in Sawoniuk's Search File, he 'was the most active policeman in all the repressive measures... who went to the executions of his own accord'.[35]

Whether this innate propensity for violence was why he was held in high regard by the Germans must be a matter for speculation but according to a German-speaking clerk at the police station, Ludwig Trybuchowicz, the German gendarmerie frequently asked Sawoniuk to accompany them on operations and *Aktionen*. And unlike some of the other *Schutzmänner*, Sawoniuk was allowed to carry a firearm at all times. In February 1943, when the German army was defeated at Stalingrad, it is estimated that some 12,000 Belorussian police seized the opportunity to defect to the partisans.[36] It is likely that some of the lower-level *Schutzmänner* had maintained contacts with the partisans even before then as an insurance against a German withdrawal. Not so Sawoniuk who remained at his post at the gendarmerie.

The Circumstantial Evidence

The Domachevo *Schutzmänner* were stationed in a building (still there in 1997) which before the war had been a shop belonging to a Jew called Hershel Eisenberg. The Jewish ghetto was established in 1942 and the police station stood close to its eastern side. The ghetto, bounded by barbed wire, with access restricted to two gates, was roughly square in shape and its contours could still be discerned when one of the authors was speaking to witnesses in 1997. Perhaps fittingly, it had become the municipal graveyard after the war.

A survivor called Miriam Soroka, born in Domachevo in 1909, spoke of the precarious nature of existence for Jews after the invasion. She said that anyone who refused to wear the designated white armband would be summarily killed. She and her children survived the first round-up of Jews by hiding first in a hayloft and later in a hole in a basement dug below a stable. She would venture out only at night to beg for food in

---

[35] From a Search File held in the KGB Brest *oblast*, cited by Dean, ibid.
[36] Snyder, 2010 *Bloodlands*, p. 243.

nearby villages.[37] Ben Zion Blustein told the WCU investigators that there was very little food in the ghetto and many starved. He said that anyone who approached the barbed wire to throw over food would be beaten back by the police if they were spotted. The only time that the Jews were allowed to leave their confinement was for forced labour assignments, such as cutting wood in the forest. A strictly enforced curfew began every night at 7 p.m.

Frequently, both German gendarmes and local policemen, including Sawoniuk, conducted raids on Jewish homes with the object of confiscating valuables. Sometimes this was done by deception. On one occasion, the Jews were told to assemble with all their possessions because they were being transported to the administrative capital, Brest-Litovsk. The assembly place was an empty plot of land where sports competitions had once been held. Blustein and his family joined many other Jews and were made to throw anything of worth into a large sack being held by two armed policemen. The Jews were then kept for hours in heavy rain on the pretext that vehicles were being sent to collect them. None arrived and eventually the captives were released and told to return home. When they did, they found their houses had been systematically looted in their absence.

Blustein's characterization of the policeman, Sawoniuk, as 'a man of power, a master' was corroborated by a witness at the Old Bailey trial, Ivan Yacovlevich Bagley, whom the BBC interviewed in Domachevo in 1997. Bagley (sometimes spelled Baglai) went to the same village school as Sawoniuk so there was no issue over identification. He said he saw Sawoniuk shoot a mother and her daughter, aged about seven, with a machine gun after breaking the woman's arm with a heavy stick. 'Everybody spoke of him as the most cruel killer of them all.'[38]

Bagley's father, Jakov, had built a house which Sawoniuk ordered to be dismantled, removed from the ghetto and erected elsewhere in the town for him to occupy. (When the trial jury made its historic visit to Domachevo in February 1999, they were shown the wooden house with its picket fence.) When Jakov asked for payment, Sawoniuk is said to

---

[37] Soroka interview in Jerusalem, 18 February 1990.
[38] Bagley interview in Domachevo, 28 July 1997.

have pulled out a pistol and warned: 'If you come here again, the first bullet will be yours.' As Martin Dean has written: 'A definition of terror is when most crimes are committed by the police.'[39]

Several witnesses testified that Sawoniuk carried out his police duties conscientiously. Blustein, on his journeys in and out of the ghetto, was frequently searched by him. In his evidence, he said that if Sawoniuk found any forbidden item—which covered an infinite range of possibilities—he would invariably resort to violence. A Jewish girl returning from work on a farm tried to smuggle some potatoes into the ghetto. Sawoniuk beat her savagely and placed her in detention in the police cells. The *Judenrat* (the local Jewish-run administration) had to pay a fine to secure her release.

The *Aktion*

It is estimated that between 1941 and 1943, about two million Jews were killed within the borders of the Soviet Union, as they were constituted in May 1941.[40] Indeed, in the earliest phase of the Nazi invasion, from June to December 1941, more Jewish civilians were killed than Soviet soldiers.[41] Probably the majority were dispatched by the mobile killing units, the *Einsatzgruppen*, the oft-remarked 'Holocaust by bullets'. But in the summer and autumn of 1942, what Dean calls a 'Second Wave' of killings took place in western Belorussia and Ukraine in the areas under German civil administration.[42] In Domachevo, the cataclysm arrived on Yom Kippur (19–20 September), 1942. The official report, recounted in the Opening Note for the trial of Sawoniuk, read: 'On 19 and 20 September 1942, a Jewish *Aktion* was carried out in Domachevo and Tomaschevska by SD *Sonderkommando* in conjunction with the mounted squadron of gendarmerie stationed in Domachevo and the *Schutzmannschaft* [sic]. A total of 2900 Jews were shot.'

[39] Dean, 2000 *Collaboration in the Holocaust*, p. xiii.
[40] Hilberg, 1961 *The Destruction of the European Jews*.
[41] Fritzsche, 2008 'The Holocaust and the Knowledge of Murder', p. 600.
[42] Dean, 2000 *Collaboration in the Holocaust*, p. 161.

As a prelude to the *Aktion*, the ghetto was surrounded by troops, supported by a mounted squadron, and police, under the overall command of a Gestapo officer. The police clerk, Trybuchowicz, saw the Domachevo police leaving the station to participate, Sawoniuk among them. The Jews were ordered onto the streets and told to assemble in the sandhills for a roll call. Those who didn't and tried to hide in their homes were later rooted out and shot.

The Jews, escorted by police carrying sub-machine guns, were marched to the killing ground in batches and shot. The massacre lasted from early morning until about five in the afternoon. Ivan Bagley heard the firing as he was walking from Domachevo to Borisey to buy bread but others were made to witness the event. Galina Puchkina told the UK investigators that she and her sister were ordered to stand next to the Catholic church on Lenin Street, at the edge of a hill, where they could see the victims below, in groups of between fifty and seventy, men, women, and children. Despite a gap of half a century, she said she remembered the cries and screams as the Jews were ordered to undress and throw their clothes on to a pile. The police and Germans used rifle butts to push them towards the pits which had been ready dug (by the victims themselves). A set of concrete kerbstones placed in a circle now stands as a memorial to the massacre.

Ben Zion Blustein described how he survived the *Aktion* by hiding under floorboards for eight days. During his concealment, he heard Sawoniuk, whose voice he recognized, searching his home. On the eighth day, he crept out and found a new hiding place in the attic of an empty house close to the eastern gate of the ghetto, opposite the police station. From this vantage point he saw police searching for Jews and witnessed several being discovered and shot on the spot. He also recalled a specific incident in which he saw Sawoniuk among a group of police taking an 80-year-old Jew called Shaya Idel into the street, setting fire to his beard and stabbing him with bayonets.

The clerk, Trybuchowicz, placed Sawoniuk at the scene on the day of the *Aktion*, and in view of what is known about his enthusiastic complicity in other killings, it is more than probable that he took part in the massacre. But in the absence of eyewitness corroboration, this was not one of the charges he was required to answer at the Old Bailey. Neither was an allegation made by an elderly couple, when interviewed by lawyers on a pre-trial visit to Domachevo, that Sawoniuk had killed two Jews and buried them close to the town bakery.[43] This goes to the important point about the strict interpretation of the rules of evidence, which excluded anything that could not be corroborated by live witness testimony.

It is worth reflecting that had Sawoniuk been tried in Germany, post-2011, these close circumstantial associations with Holocaust murders would, on their own, have been sufficient for prosecutors. This significant development arose from the Demjanjuk case, which, as Mary Fulbrook makes clear, meant that:

> No longer were eyewitnesses deemed necessary to secure a conviction. Documentary evidence of a particular role and presence in a place of mass murder would suffice. Rather than treating mass murder as an individual crime, for which subjective state of mind was crucial to proof of culpability, the court had finally decided that simple function within a wider machinery of mass murder was sufficient for conviction.[44]

Identification and Eyewitnesses

When the War Crimes Bill was being debated in the UK Parliament, opponents of the legislation deployed a number of arguments: that a definitive line had been drawn after the war against further prosecutions; that the proceedings would be stacked unfairly against the defendant and become an 'un-English' show trial; that the legislation would be retrospective and thus offend against common law precedent; and that the lapse of time, of at least half a century, would produce unreliable evidence. Uppermost in the minds of many sceptics was the recent trial of John Demjanjuk, which, when it opened in Jerusalem in 1987,

---

[43] They even offered to point out the exact spot where the killings had happened (Martin Lee interview).

[44] Fulbrook, 2018 *Reckonings*, p. 349.

was 'seen as a tool of collective memory'.[45] After he was arrested in the United States in 1980, investigators had been confident that they had found the notorious Ukrainian operator of the gas chamber at Treblinka, 'Ivan the Terrible' (Ivan Marchenko). Yet the identification, by more than one witness survivor, was flawed and, although he was later convicted of being a guard at another camp, the original premise was disproved amid considerable embarrassment and soul-searching.

Demjanjuk's original conviction was overturned in 1993, at a time when British lawyers believed that there was at least a fighting chance of mounting a war crimes prosecution and the Demjanjuk case served as a powerful warning to senior Treasury Counsel, Sir John Nutting and his team of what could go wrong:

> We were very much influenced by those awful scenes in the Israeli trial where a succession of elderly witnesses were convinced that the man standing in the dock was 'Ivan the Terrible'. That weighed heavily on my mind and one thing which was absolutely clear to us right from the start was that we would not proceed with a case which depended on identification.[46]

There was a sound legal reason for this caution. In 1977, the Court of Appeal had ruled that where the defence challenged a case on the grounds that it depended wholly or substantially on identification of the accused, the jury would be given a warning, known as a *Turnbull* direction.[47] In the minds of Nutting and his team, this might have tipped what was seen as a fine balance against them.

The trials of John Demjanjuk also illustrate the perception, fostered by the reification of survivor experiences over several decades, that the dominant motif of the Holocaust is the concentration and death camp. Increasingly, cultural representation has designated Auschwitz, 'the site of all evil' (Raul Hilberg) a metonym for the Holocaust itself, pushing to the margins the role played by the other Polish sites dedicated in

---

[45]   Douglas, 2001 *The Memory of Judgment*, p. 186.
[46]   Sir John Nutting interview with author, 28 May 2021.
[47]   *R v. Turnbull* [1977] QB224.

Operation Reinhard exclusively to killing—Belzec, Sobibor, and Treblinka. Within this framing, the risk of misidentification of a perpetrator in the maelstrom of a camp, with its constantly shifting population, clearly concerned UK parliamentarians as they argued over such a consequential law change. However, as Charles King points out, millions died, not in camps but 'through mass executions, typically shootings over ravines, tank traps and pits'.[48] It seemed inconceivable that a member of an *Einsatzgruppen* squad could be identified to the criminal standard of proof by a witness who may have glimpsed the unknown shooter momentarily from a (safe) distance. In fact, as we reveal in Chapter 2, one case involving a Georgian member of a Caucasian killing unit which committed atrocities in Ukraine, came close to a prosecution but it was the only one to have progressed to a late stage. As Detective Chief Inspector Dermot McDermott, who led the WCU after 1994, put it: 'Many of the allegation[s] related to mass murders carried out by mobile killing units. Clear and uncontroversial identification was always an issue.'[49]

By contrast, the idea that, in the event of a trial, a witness could be found who had known the suspect well years before the war, indeed might have grown up alongside him in the same town or village, is largely absent from the Hansard record of proceedings or in the opinion columns of newspapers.[50] For the war crimes investigators, there were two ways to ensure reliable identification. One was to persuade a surviving member of Sawoniuk's Domachevo police cohort to give evidence. At the time that Sawoniuk was traced in 1993, a small handful were still living in Canada and the United States. But, according to Robert Bland, the Crown Prosecutor who worked most closely with the police team, none was prepared to be interviewed, let alone testify: 'The other way to achieve our purpose was to find witnesses who had known him intimately, some since schooldays, so that a jury could be confident the identification was solidly based. It helped enormously that he was the only person in Domachevo known as Andrusha.'[51]

---

[48] King, 2012 'Can There Be a Political Science of the Holocaust?', p. 326.
[49] McDermott email, 5 March 2018.
[50] Hansard is the daily official record of proceedings in both Houses of the UK Parliament.
[51] Bland conversation with author, 3 September 1998.

Ben Zion Blustein had played in the same streets as Sawoniuk as a youngster and though his evidence was regarded as circumstantial, it supported the prosecution case that the right person was in the dock. Ivan Stepaniuk, a bakery worker, recounted seeing Sawoniuk on many occasions escorting victims to an execution site in the sandhills beyond the town. But as we have shown, identification of the suspect had to be accompanied by credible live eyewitness testimony to reach the evidential threshold. This meant that three of the five murder charges which Sawoniuk originally faced—all dependent on one eyewitness—were ruled out, one at the committal stage and two more during the Old Bailey trial.[52] Thus the success or failure of the prosecution rested on the credibility of two key witnesses, Fedor Zan and Alexander Bagley.

Bagley testified that, at a distance of no more than three or four metres, he had seen the defendant shoot two Jewish men and a girl of about 20 and push their bodies into a pre-dug grave. Both he and his brother, Ivan, knew Sawoniuk well. Zan (Fig. 6.2) was a year younger than Sawoniuk and had been at school with him. In 1997, before the trial, the BBC interviewed Fedor Zan in a pine forest at the spot where he said he had seen Sawoniuk murder fifteen Jewish women by machine gun. In the televised report, he re-enacted the scene, even down to mimicking the staccato rat-a-tat of the weapon. Zan described Sawoniuk as 'always in the forefront of police activities'.

Zan's evidence on Count Three of the indictment occupies a small but memorable place in British legal history because, at the request of the defence, the judge agreed that the court should visit the scene of the alleged crime, the first and only occasion on which part of a criminal trial has been heard abroad. Zan's evidence was that one day in September 1942 he was returning from visiting his sister when he took a shortcut from the railway station through the pine forest. He heard the sounds of female crying and, concealed by bushes, saw the women of various ages, all with yellow stars pinned to their clothes, huddled in front of an open grave and Sawoniuk standing behind them with a

---

[52] The committal hearing is held before a magistrate to determine whether there is a *prima facie* case to go to full trial. There is a fuller discussion of the important role played by the committal hearing in the Serafinowicz case in Chapter 6.

Fig. 6.2 Fedor Zan, a key witness against Andrzej Sawoniuk, outside his home in Domachevo, 1997. Jon Silverman.

sub-machine gun. Zan said Sawoniuk ordered them to remove their clothing and then shot them. As they died, they collapsed into the grave.

Sawoniuk was allegedly alone when this took place, with no Germans or other policemen present. This potentially damning testimony presented the defence with a challenge to which they responded by arguing that Zan would have been the length of a football field, about 75 yards, from the defendant when the shootings took place, too far to be certain it was Sawoniuk. On a freezing February day in 1999, judge, jury, and press corps, including one of the authors, stood above-ankle deep in snow drifts while Zan described what he had seen and where he had been hiding, saying that: 'I recognized him by his size, his face. He was famous.' The jury believed him and Sawoniuk was convicted on this count and one other.

As the testimony showed, Sawoniuk was alone at the time he committed this crime so the disputed fourth criterion for prosecution, 'proof that the defendant was in a position of command', had little or no relevance. Indeed, the former head of casework at the CPS, Rajka Vlahovic, has confirmed that the issue of command responsibility played no part in the evidence put forward during the trial.[53] So it is even more puzzling that the members of the Metropolitan Police WCU set such store by it and is yet another question which could have been settled definitively had a final report been published.

The Killers Retreat

When the British police began interviewing Sawoniuk under caution on 1 April 1996, they had already spent nearly two years amassing a wealth of incriminating information about him through 431 interviews and 120 statements. Eventually, a staggering 90,000 pages of evidence was submitted to the Crown Prosecution Service. Thus his version of what he did in Domachevo—or rather did not do—and afterwards could not withstand any sustained scrutiny. Sawoniuk claimed that he had no knowledge of any massacre of Jews and, moreover, that life for the Jews did not change under the occupation. There was no ghetto and neither Jews nor any other townsfolk were subject to a curfew.

He claimed that between the time of the Nazi invasion in June 1941 and spring 1942 he had no job and lived a hand-to-mouth existence, subsisting on an apple here or a tomato there provided by a well-meaning neighbour. He said there were no locally recruited police, merely certain civilians who acted as lookouts to warn of the proximity of Russian soldiers or partisans lurking in the forest. In reality, at the time of the Yom Kippur massacre and the hunting down and shooting of Jews who had escaped, he was probably deputy to the police commander, Tribunko, and after Tribunko's death in a partisan attack on the police station in November 1943, he was placed in charge.

Sawoniuk seemed naively unaware that his lies could easily be undermined by the townspeople whom the police had tracked down and interviewed. His brother Nikolai, still living near Domachevo in 1994, demolished the story that he had never been in the police. And Sawoniuk's claim that he had not been married in Domachevo was

---

[53] Vlahovic conversation with author, 25 February 2020.

easily disproved because it was common knowledge locally that, in late 1941 or early 1942, he had wed a Russian midwife called Anna Maslova who was later killed in a partisan attack. This was a pointless lie since the police were able to show him a number of legal documents dating from 1946 and 1947, describing him as a widower. These forms were signed by him prior to his (second) marriage on 30 January 1947 in West Sussex to a Dutch woman, Christina van Gent. (After the trial, she told reporters that Sawoniuk was 'a horrible man – vile and violent… he used to attack me'.)[54]

Sawoniuk knew that he had to establish an 'alibi' for the period during which the worst atrocities were carried out, above all the Yom Kippur massacre. Accordingly, he claimed that he was not present in Domachevo from the spring or early summer of 1942, having been deported to Germany to work as a forced labourer on a farm. He was unable to tell the police the location of the farm or name others from Domachevo who were supposedly deported with him. His story was that he had escaped from the farm, made his way to the border with France and crossed over. He then offered his services to the Polish Army in exile—having insisted that he had always been Polish not Belorussian. Thereafter, he said he was recruited in Italy and sent for training in Egypt, returned to Italy and fought for the Free Poles until the war's end.

The truth is that Sawoniuk was the police commandant in Domachevo until the advance of the Red Army in July 1944 forced the Germans to retreat across the River Bug. Sawoniuk accompanied them and in August, he joined the 30 Waffen Grenadier Division of the SS in East Prussia and served until November 1944 when he deserted in south-east France. He was not alone among the *Schutzmänner* in joining the Waffen SS but he could have taken the alternative option offered by the retreating Germans of remaining in East Prussia to work on defence construction or local farms.[55] His desertion eventually provoked a Missing Person's Report, dated March 1945, which the prosecution sought to admit in evidence at the trial to support the case that he had remained loyal to the Nazis until he found it expedient to abandon the cause. The judge,

[54] Anderson and Hanson, 2022 *The Ticket Collector from Belarus*, p. 341.
[55] Dean, 2000 *Collaboration in the Holocaust*, p. 151.

Mr Justice Potts, described this document, stamped with the eagle and swastika emblem of the Third Reich, as 'potentially explosive'. Nevertheless, he ruled it inadmissible on the grounds that there was no one left alive to authenticate it. This, despite an archivist at Berlin's Deutsche Dienststelle archive confirming that it was genuine.[56]

The only part of Sawoniuk's story which contained any truth was that in the latter six months of the war, from December 1944, he did join the Free Poles, attached to the British army as the 10th Hussar Regiment. Like many collaborators from Eastern Europe, he entered the UK ostensibly as a Pole with few if any questions asked about his past, other than a cursory screening carried out by immigration officers in 1950 under the MI5-led Operation Post Report. This murky period of Britain's immediate post-war history has been admirably researched by the late David Cesarani in his ground-breaking work, *Justice Delayed* (1992).

Sawoniuk and the Extraordinary State Commission

Sawoniuk's trial was conducted under the normative rules of a murder prosecution. In other words, he was charged with murder contrary to common law. The only difference from the many murder trials held at the Old Bailey was that his crime constituted 'a violation of the laws and customs of war' (in the wording of the 1991 War Crimes Act). Thus, apart from being told the historical context of the case and reminded of the criteria laid down by the War Crimes Act, the jury did not need to weigh up more than the witness evidence and the defendant's rebuttal to reach a verdict.

But for historians and anyone interested in a broader paradigm of 'justice' and the tracking down of perpetrators, there is more to be said about this case and the war crimes process in the UK. Although Sawoniuk was not positively identified by the WCU until 1993, his status as a suspect was known to the Soviet security organs even before the end of the war. In late 1944, after the Germans had been forced out of Domachevo, a unit of the Extraordinary State Commission arrived in

---

[56] Sawoniuk's lawyer, Martin Lee, has no doubt that it was genuine.

the town to seek intelligence on who had collaborated with the Nazis. With the Soviet Union still at war in 1944, the Sawoniuk inquiry was stalled but in March 1947, at the height of Stalinist reprisals against anyone suspected of collaborating, witnesses in Domachevo were questioned again. This evidence is contained in a thirteen-page dossier found in the archive of Group 10 of the First Directorate of the KGB in Brest.

Dated 11 March 1983, the dossier is headed 'Record of Examination of archive investigation case no: 2259 regarding Savanyuk Andrei Andreyevich'. As will become clear, the Russian/Ukrainian spelling of the surname was later to take on a heavy significance for the UK war crimes team in the 1990s. The examination was headed by 'the senior investigator of *particularly serious cases* [our emphasis], Colonel Osintsev, on the instructions of the deputy head of the department, Lieutenant Colonel Manyakov'. The allegations were that 'while serving in the German police, Savanyuk A.A. took part in arrests, beatings and executions of Soviet people, and also in operations against partisans'.

The dossier reveals that, over a period of years, starting in March 1947 and ending in December 1960, witnesses living in and near Domachevo were questioned periodically about Savanyuk/Sawoniuk. Indeed, he was the first named individual to be investigated in connection with the killings in Domachevo (files on other suspects were not opened until 1951). The first recorded witness was Vera Tribunko, widow of the police commander whose position Sawoniuk had taken over in 1943. She stated that in 1942 she had seen Sawoniuk beating up a Jew because that person had strayed outside the ghetto. But she made no further allegations against him (at least none that were recorded in the file). However, when next interrogated, in July 1955, she revealed that Sawoniuk had admitted killing two *Schutzmänner* who had defected to the partisans in 1944 and that she had seen the corpse of one of them lying on a wagon near the gendarmerie (police) building.

The dossier says that this incident had also been attested to by a former *Schuma*, Mikhail Kozlovskiy, who made a deposition in October 1948. It seems odd that, in the immediate aftermath of the war, the widow Tribunko would have recalled a comparatively minor incident rather than this far more damning evidence of murder, unless the interrogators had shown her Kozlovskiy's statement and asked her to 'refresh her memory'. This apparent discrepancy draws attention to the difficulty faced by the WCU team and defence lawyers of 'isolating a witness's own memory from collective memory, e.g. village history' (Robert Bland). As William Clegg put it: 'By the 1990s, these accounts had been handed down orally hundreds, perhaps thousands of times. So were the witnesses remembering what they had actually seen or what they had been told?'[57]

It is also true of course, that age itself can make memory fallible. As the British novelist, Julian Barnes, put it: 'You [also] mistrust memory more than when you were younger: you realise that it resembles an act of the imagination rather than a matter of simple mental recuperation.'[58]

In the 1955 file, Tribunko goes on to accuse Sawoniuk of involvement in the killing of two other policemen because they 'did not want to flee with the retreating Nazi troops [in the summer of 1944] and intended going over to the partisans'. She also took the opportunity of this interview to amend her 1947 evidence regarding the beating of a Jew outside the ghetto to say that the attack had been committed not by Sawoniuk but by another policeman, Mikhail Kotelnyuk.

The dossier contains a number of other witness statements which show, if the evidence presented is to be believed, that Sawoniuk was guilty of murdering at least a dozen civilians (in addition to those crimes for which he stood trial in the UK) as well as ten or more Soviet prisoners of war (Fig. 6.3). Hence the designation of the case as 'particularly serious'. The Domachevo investigation was finally discontinued on 3 December 1960 when it was 'ascertained that he was living in England'. The file was placed in the Brest archives of the KGB in March 1961.

Of course, we don't know what pressure may have been put on the witnesses to tell the investigators what they wanted to hear and do their 'duty' as Soviet citizens who lived through the Great Patriotic War. As Martin Dean has pointed out: 'Such immediate postwar Soviet interrogations are not the most reliable source material, containing some inaccuracies.'[59] Sawoniuk himself, during his trial, alleged that his

---

[57] Interview with author, 28 April 2021.
[58] Barnes, *The Guardian*, 12 June 2021, p. 26.
[59] Dean, 2005 'Soviet War Crimes Lists and Their Role in the Investigation of Nazi War Criminals in the West, 1987–2000', in *NS-Gewaltherrschaft: Beiträge zur historischen Forschung und juristischen Aufarbeitung*, ed. Gottwaldt et al., p. 469.

Fig. 6.3 Andrzej Sawoniuk pictured in London, 1948. PA Images/Alamy Stock Photo.

accusers were in the pay of the KGB and argued that no credence should be given to their stories. But from what is known of the verified wartime history of the occupation in Domachevo, there is every reason to believe the evidence compiled by the Soviet post-war inquiry.

The members of the All-Party Parliamentary War Crimes Group offered further support for this view, concluding that:

> In the overwhelming majority of cases where the OSI [the US Office for Special Investigation] has tendered Soviet depositions, the court has credited the depositions, either placing reliance on them as principal inculpatory evidence or as corroborative of other inculpatory evidence. No United States judge has ever found that a witness made available by the Soviet Union has lied in connection with his or her testimony.[60]

---

[60] 'Nazi War Criminals in the United Kingdom: The Law', para 5.14 (p. 35), February 1989.

Historical research has perhaps under-appreciated the meticulousness with which the Soviet authorities tracked collaborators who had fled with the Nazis. In thousands of handwritten pages stitched into leather-bound files and held in archives in cities such as Brest and Minsk, lies evidence of a monumental enterprise. Sawoniuk's lawyer, Martin Lee, believes he was probably the first Western defence lawyer to gain access to this material:

> I was astonished at the level of detail contained in some of these files. I recall one was an instruction to an agent to locate the collaborator's sister, who worked in a hairdressing salon, to find out as much information on the suspect as he could and return at such and such a date, at a precise time, to deliver his report to a KGB official.[61]

The continuing Soviet interest in Sawoniuk bears out Lee's assertion that for some years after the war, certainly from the time that the authorities could be sure he was still alive, he was regarded as a high-profile suspect. The fact that Sawoniuk had survived the war was confirmed in 1951, when the KGB intercepted a letter from him in the UK to his brother, Nikolai—who had served in the *Schutzmannschaften* with him—revealing that he was living with his then wife, Christina van Gent, on the south coast of England.

There is every reason to suppose that during the Cold War, the KGB's extensive network of agents in the West were feeding back real-time intelligence on 'persons of interest', including wanted war criminals, which would explain why in 1983, almost forty years after the war, the Soviet authorities were still taking a close interest in Sawoniuk. And we know for certain that in 1986 there was further confirmation that he was still alive in the UK when another letter was intercepted. This was written from London by Stefan Androshuk, who, according to a document in the Yad Vashem archive in Jerusalem, was listed at number four on the police roster for Domachevo. It is believed that Androshuk made his way to the UK with Sawoniuk as a member of the Polish Corps.

---

[61] Martin Lee interview, 17 May 2021.

In January 1986, Androshuk wrote to his sister, then still living in or near Domachevo, and mentioned that Sawoniuk was alive and in the UK. By coincidence, the UK's interest in Nazi war criminals—long dormant since the start of the Cold War—was reawakened in 1986 by a list of possible suspects presented by the Simon Wiesenthal Center to the government of Margaret Thatcher.[62] It was this list and a subsequent inquiry by the Parliamentary All-Party War Crimes Group which can be said to have set in motion the process which led, via the Hetherington-Chalmers report, to the passage of the War Crimes Act in 1991.

In 1988, the Soviet embassy in London, taking advantage of this renewed interest and of *glasnost*, the thawing of East–West relations under the presidency of Gorbachev, presented its own list in the form of a diplomatic note to the Foreign Office. The list, which had originated in the Moscow Procurator's office, contained the names of ninety-six suspected war criminals, who were thought at some stage to have been in the UK. Prominent amongst them was one, Andrzej Andreyevich Savanyuk.

Enter (Belatedly) the Historians

Despite the close attention of the Soviet authorities, Britain was a safe haven for Sawoniuk for more than forty years. But since he was on the 1988 Soviet list and amongst seventy-five cases picked up from the Hetherington-Chalmers Inquiry which the WCU was 'duty-bound' to pursue, it is legitimate to ask why he almost slipped through the net after the detectives began work in earnest. Indeed, in April 1992, frustrated at the lack of progress in tracing him, the police informed the CPS and Home Office that he was almost certainly no longer in the UK, possibly no longer alive. The CPS agreed to close the case.

Scotland Yard's lack of success in tracing Sawoniuk at this point had echoes of the difficulties encountered by an equally celebrated police force, the Royal Canadian Mounted Police, in the case of a German

---

[62] Cesarani, 1992 *Justice Delayed.*

war crimes suspect named Helmut Rauca. Rauca, a *Hauptscharführer* (Master Sergeant) who committed war crimes in Kaunas, Lithuania, was the subject of an extradition request to Canada by the West German authorities in 1962 but, according to the writer, Sol Littman:

> although Rauca was living openly under his own name, drove a car, possessed an Ontario driver's licence, received an old age pension, paid his taxes, had several bank accounts, owned a cottage and travelled regularly on a Canadian passport, it took Canada's legendary police force another ten years to find him.[63]

Like the Mounties, Scotland Yard's difficulties in tracing Sawoniuk arose from their reliance on the kind of standard techniques familiar from most routine criminal inquiries. Taking the name Savanyuk from the Soviet list, they entered the first three letters, SAV, and a date and place of birth into the computerized files of more than fifteen government agencies, including the Immigration and Naturalization Service (INS), Inland Revenue (now Her Majesty's Revenue and Customs), and Department of Social Security (DSS). The latter was usually reliably swift in providing a match, if one existed, according to Detective Inspector Dave Drinkald: 'To the best of my recollection, the DSS was fairly instant. I think we had a named contact there who we dealt with.'[64] However, no match came up.

'Routine' murder cases usually start with a body and detectives then work 'forward' to identify the name of the perpetrator/s. The WCU was being asked to work 'backwards' from a name and link that person to a crime—moreover a crime committed in another era and a completely alien historical context. This required a different skillset and the application of knowledge which most police officers understandably do not possess. In short, it needed the expertise of a historian.

As we have demonstrated, no member of the WCU appears to have read the Hetherington-Chalmers Inquiry report, so it was unfortunate,

---

[63] Littman, 2015 *War Criminal on Trial*, p. 137.
[64] Former Detective Inspector David Drinkald of the WCU. Email to authors, 12 October 2018.

to say the least, that, for the first eighteen months of its existence, the unit was without the dedicated input of someone used to working in the archives. This was because the Belorussia specialist, Martin Dean, was still contracted to the Australian Special Investigation Unit, although the crossover between the two national inquiries did lead to an exchange of information, where relevant. It was only when Dean and Alisdair Macleod, who between them knew German, Yiddish. and Russian, were seconded to the WCU in 1992 that the databases began to yield important clues. The first breakthrough came when Macleod, whose Russian was so good that archive staff in Eastern Europe thought he was a Russian native, spotted that the INS had been supplied with the transliteration of the name from Russian rather than the Polish spelling and realized that the misleading 'v' should be read as 'w'.

In the spring of 1993, there was an even more significant development when Dean was able to check the priority WCU cases against files held in the main index catalogue of the former Stasi archives in the Dahlwitz-Hoppegarten complex to the east of Berlin:

> In particular, I found a number of positive traces for those WCU cases linked to Belarus. The index cards included the rough dates of service in the local police for these men and usually a Germanized (or Polish) spelling of the name.... Among the names included... was an allegation for Andrzej Sawoniuk, clearly identical with the person on the 1988 Soviet list.[65]

Another piece of the puzzle fitted into place when Sawoniuk's name was found in the archive of the Polish Resettlement Corps in London and in an immigration file at the INS. Thereafter, it didn't take a great deal of detective work to locate his address in the London borough of Southwark where he had lived since 1975. The hunt for the suspect was over but the search for inculpatory evidence went on.

---

[65] Dean, 2005 'Soviet War Crimes Lists and Their Role in the Investigation of Nazi War Criminals in the West, 1987–2000', in *NS-Gewaltherrschaft: Beiträge zur historischen Forschung und juristischen Aufarbeitung*, ed. Gottwaldt et al., p. 468.

Conclusion

The problem with Soviet 'cooperation' on war crimes is that it only ever went so far. The most useful evidence against suspects who had fled to the West after the war was the Search File compiled by the KGB. But for reasons which are not entirely clear, the Soviet authorities were initially reluctant to allow access to these files or even to admit that they existed, as Martin Lee discovered:

> When we first went to Belarus, the KGB lied to us. First they said the files on Sawoniuk did not exist. Then they conceded that they did exist and were all stored either at their headquarters in Minsk or even in Moscow. But I did some research which showed that there were 20 files in a safe in their archive in Brest.[66]

Treasury Counsel in London still required more evidence in order to strengthen the case for prosecution, so the influence of this obfuscation can hardly be overestimated. It was not until April 1997 that Martin Dean was granted access to the Central Card Index of the Belarusian KGB in Minsk where he found the index card for Sawoniuk's file and later the original Search File. As he explained, it contained 200 pages of potentially damning testimony gathered over decades:

> The significance of obtaining the summary of the KGB Search File at a key juncture in this case, just at a time [1997] that the Metropolitan Police War Crimes Unit was also beginning to wind down its remaining investigations, begs the question whether more war criminals would have been prosecuted in the West if greater access had been granted...before it was too late.[67]

It is certainly true that the inquiries conducted in the 1980s and early 1990s by countries such as Australia and New Zealand might have

---

[66]   Lee interview, 3 September 1998.
[67]   Dean, 2005 'Soviet War Crimes Lists and Their Role in the Investigation of Nazi War Criminals in the West, 1987–2000', in *NS-Gewaltherrschaft: Beiträge zur historischen Forschung und juristischen Aufarbeitung*, ed. Gottwaldt et al., p. 470.

progressed more swiftly if earlier access had been granted to files held in Soviet archives and those of post-Soviet republics such as Belarus and Ukraine. By an accident of timing, some of those bureaucratic obstacles had been lowered by the mid-1990s after the collapse of the Soviet Union, granting the UK investigators a level of cooperation denied their Commonwealth colleagues. However, this 'window of opportunity' was tantalizingly brief, as states such as Belarus became increasingly nationalist and inward looking. Thus, for the reasons presented in this chapter, Sawoniuk's conviction, achieved against expectations, will always stand alone as tribute to a historic juridical endeavour.

7

Slonim, Secrets and Spies

Introduction

Over the years since the War Crimes Act was passed, it has been alleged periodically that the failure to prosecute more suspects was because it would have caused embarrassment to the security and intelligence agencies, MI5 and MI6, which had sought to recruit collaborators with certain skills and an abiding hatred of Communism. The fact that Scotland Yard's War Crimes Unit was denied access to confidential case files held by those agencies has further fuelled these suspicions. Without documentary proof of any kind, such claims remain unsubstantiated and there is no definitive basis for saying that x or y was not prosecuted because of previous involvement with the 'spooks'.

However, here and there, the emergence of intriguing fragments—like shards of pottery found at an archaeological dig—has added to what we know and what we might plausibly surmise about the relationship between some of the collaborators and the so-called 'deep state'. This chapter traces the outline of a connection between the world of intelligence and a suspect whose case was unique.

Slonim

Of all the Nazi collaborators who found a home in the UK after the war, only one was being pursued by Germany's investigative agency at Ludwigsburg, which goes by the cumbersome title of Central Office of the State Justice Administration for the Investigation of National Socialist Crimes (aka *Zentrale Stelle*). The man was a Belorussian called Stanislaw Chrzanowski (Fig. 7.1) and his alleged crimes did not involve

Safe Haven: The United Kingdom's Investigations into Nazi Collaborators and the Failure of Justice.
Jon Silverman and Robert Sherwood, Oxford University Press. © Jon Silverman and Robert Sherwood 2023.
DOI: 10.1093/oso/9780192855176.003.0008

Fig. 7.1 Stanislaw Chrzanowski pictured in his seventies. John Kingston.

German victims, which makes it all the more surprising that in June 2017, on application from the Attorney-General for Baden-Württemberg, the 2nd Criminal Senate of the Federal Court of Justice gave its approval to a full investigation. The reasons stated in the court's published decision were that:

> He is suspected of having shot civilian D. and other civilians in a mass shooting on 28 October 1942 on a hill (Berg P.) near what is now the Belarusian city of S., and on at least two other days before or after taking part in mass shootings and having shot at least thirty people personally. As an auxiliary policeman, the person concerned belonged to a protection team formed by the Germans from locals. These protection teams were in the German police structure and were also used for mass killings.[1]

---

[1] Federal Court of Justice Decision 2 Ars 252/17 2AR 142/17.

Unpicking the linguistic circumspection of German criminal inquiries, the initial D refers to a woodsman, Jan Daletsky; the hill P to a notorious killing ground called Petralevichi (there are various spellings of this site); and the city S to Slonim, which came under the command of district commander (*Gebietskommissar*) Gerhard Erren, from August 1941. By the time he moved on almost three years later, Erren expressed pride in having overseen one of the most thoroughly systematic killing operations carried out by the Germans and their local accomplices anywhere in Eastern Europe:

> Upon my arrival, there were about 25,000 Jews in the Slonim area, 16,000 in the actual town itself, making up two thirds of the total population of the town. It was not possible to set up a ghetto as neither barbed wire nor guard manpower was available. I thus immediately began preparations for a large-scale action.[2]

Erren's efficiency in reducing the Jewish population of Slonim to a few dozen by the war's end led to his arrest in the British zone of post-war Germany but, unaccountably, he was allowed to go free (after becoming a teacher, he eventually stood trial in Hamburg in 1974 for war crimes and was sentenced to life imprisonment).

A *Volksdeutsche* living in the city, Alfred Metzner, provided an almost unbearably graphic account of the slaughter of Slonim's Jews in a detailed statement to prosecutors when arrested in 1947. Metzner, who was executed in Poland for war crimes in 1950, worked as a driver and interpreter for Erren. Metzner reported that the first *Aktion* took place in the summer of 1942, although there is undisputed evidence—substantiated by Erren himself—that several thousand were killed the previous November:

> The men, mothers and children were pushed into the trench. At first the children were beaten and then kicked into the trench. As the next lorries [carrying the victims] came up, the Jews could see the bloody

[2] From Gerhard Erren's situation report, 25 January 1942 in *The Good Old Days* (1988), ed. Klee et al., p. 178.

bodies in the grave and recoiled from it. The Operation Kommissar shot these recoiling Jews and the rest were beaten to go into the trench... There were very many mean sadists involved in the extermination Kommando. So, for example, pregnant women were shot in the stomach for fun and thrown into the graves.[3]

Perhaps under pressure from his interrogators, Metzner does not hesitate to implicate himself in the massacres. At a suburb of Slonim called Schirowits, some 1,400 Jews were executed:

I was also present at these executions and I also shot people.... It was astounding how the Jews went into the trenches with just some mutual words of comfort in order to encourage themselves and to make the work of the Execution Kommando easier. The executions themselves lasted for three to four hours. I was involved in the executions for this whole period. The only pause I had was when my rifle ran out of bullets and I had to load it again. It's therefore not possible for me to say how many Jews I personally killed during this three to four hours... During this time we had drunk rather a lot of schnaps in order to keep our appetite for the work... Because schnaps was continually distributed, our fighting spirit was increased.[4]

The practice of plying the killers with alcohol and tobacco both to anaesthetize them against the work and to reward them for doing it is a common feature of accounts of the 'Holocaust by bullets' in Eastern Europe. While the available transcript of his affidavit is over-full of physical detail, Metzner offers no insights into his state of mind while participating in the slaughter. We do not know, for example, whether his behaviour was, as Mary Fulbrook (2018) suggests, like that of many killers in:

detaching the self that acted in a particular situation from the 'authentic' self and suggesting that the person who acted or behaved in certain

---

[3] Wiener Library Doct. Series, Metzner Affidavit, October 15 1947 NO5530 1655/2713 Statement no. 5558.
[4] Ibid.

ways was not the 'real me'. The 'real' self is the moral inner self; the outwardly visible self that acted was prompted by external considerations over which it had little or no control.[5]

That outwardly visible self was fortified not just by alcohol but, no doubt, by Himmler's directive, sent to commanders throughout the occupied territories in 1942, that it was 'their solemn duty to see to it personally that none of our men who have to fulfil this *hard duty* [authors' emphasis] ever becomes brutalized or suffers damage to his mind and personality'.[6]

This touching concern for the welfare of the German killers did not apply to locally recruited collaborators, such as Stanislaw Chrzanowski, alleged to have murdered between thirty and fifty people in Slonim, both Jews and non-Jews. The fact that he became of interest to German war crimes investigators speaks to the widened scope of inquiries as a result of the judgement in the trial of John Demjanjuk in Munich in 2011. Demjanjuk, originally accused, wrongly, of being the infamous operator of the gas chamber at Treblinka, 'Ivan the Terrible', was convicted in a later trial of being a guard at the death camp, Sobibor, although as Fulbrook has pointed out:

> Demjanjuk was eventually found guilty despite the lack of irrefutable witness testimony directly linking his actions or state of mind with any particular killings...From now on it was possible to try someone merely for having worked at a site where atrocities had occurred. This dramatically altered the scope of those who could be brought to court.[7]

The Chief Investigator of the *Zentrale Stelle*, Thomas Will, said that following the judgement, his unit re-examined the files in the central registry relating to a thousand cases which had not been prosecuted for lack of direct evidence of killing. In 2013 alone, they handed over thirty cases to the Public Prosecutor's Office, including that of the Auschwitz

---

[5] Fulbrook, 2018 *Reckonings*, p. 417.
[6] Directive signed H. Himmler, Reichsführer SS, received by the Police Garrison Commander, Libau (Liepāja) Latvia, 23 January 1942.
[7] Fulbrook, 2018 *Reckonings*, pp. 348–9.

'book-keeper' Oskar Gröning, who was later convicted as an accessory to murder. Will has also revealed that investigators made several visits to Britain's National Archives in West London seeking information on perpetrators from a number of countries still thought to be living. They were looking mainly for suspects who had worked at a concentration or death camp where the intended outcome was that no one should be left alive:

> It has been wrongly suggested that we are prosecuting anyone who worked at a camp but that isn't so. We are pursuing only those people who worked at facilities where death was almost certain and which we therefore regard as part of the Nazi crime complex. Because Chrzanowski was a functionary for a German unit, whose purpose was to kill, it could be seen as a German crime and within our remit to investigate.[8]

A Stepson's Suspicions

The uniqueness of the Chrzanowski case lies not only in German intervention in a UK inquiry but also in the fact that the initial suspicions about his wartime activities came from within his own family. The psycho-dynamics of familial relationships is a comparatively recent field of interest for those researching the legacy of Nazism. In the 1980s, the Israeli psychologist Dan Bar-On began his study of the children of Nazi criminals.[9] More recently, Niklas Frank has written about the tortured legacy of his father, Hans, the governor-general of Poland who was executed after the war for presiding over mass murder.[10] As a counterpoint, Tania Crasnianski writes that the offspring of Himmler, Goering, and Hess refused to acknowledge that their notorious parent had been complicit in the iniquity of genocide and poses the question: 'Must anyone feel responsible or even guilty, for the crimes of his parents? Family life leaves an indelible mark on every child. An inheritance as sinister as

---

[8] Will interview with authors. 30 March 2022.   [9] Bar-On, 1989 *Legacy of Silence.*
[10] Frank, 2021 *The Father: A Revenge.*

theirs cannot come without consequences...How did they live with such macabre facts?'[11]

Gitta Sereny, in her ground-breaking book, *Into That Darkness*—a study of the sometime commandant of Treblinka, Franz Stangl—interviewed the wife and son of Gustav Münzberger, a non-commissioned SS officer, whose job was to drive Jews into the gas chambers at the extermination camp. The son, Horst, expressed his conflicted feelings when his father was arrested in the 1960s:

> Oh, I had an idea that everything hadn't been as it should have been...But I didn't know anything. I wish he had prepared me, talked to me, told me the truth...Yes, I know now what he was accused of and sentenced for...But I don't know it from *him* [original emphasis]. Now I just wish, for his sake, that he would ease his mind by talking about it.[12]

This sense of half-knowing and the unsated need to know much more was present in John Kingston, Chrzanowski's stepson, for much of his adolescent and adult life. Crasnianski could almost have been referring to him when she described the second generation of perpetrators carrying 'the past from day to day like a ball and chain; it is impossible to ignore'.[13] It was this unresolved anguish which eventually drove him to contact Scotland Yard. Kingston and his stepfather came into contact for the first time in 1954 when Kingston was aged nine. His mother Barbara, divorced from John's birth father, met Chrzanowski at a dance in Birmingham where there was a Polish expatriate community. Of his background in Slonim, he said he had worked at a sawmill until 1943 when the Germans made him a civilian guard. He claimed to have escaped the city in 1944 and, after a brief period as a prisoner of war, joined the Polish military. The boy and his new 'father' immediately bonded: 'I was looking for a father figure and he was looking for a kind of ready-made family. I found him fascinating. He told me stories about

---

[11] Crasnianski, 2016 *Children of Nazis*, p. xii.
[12] Sereny, 1995 *Into That Darkness*, pp. 222–3.
[13] Crasnianski, 2016 *Children of Nazis*, p. xii.

where he had grown up in Poland and recounted some of the things he had done during the war—like making petrol bombs to throw at Russian tanks when he said he was a commando. I was spellbound.'[14]

But Kingston's adult recollections suggest a Hitchcockian unfolding of clues which gradually, over time, began to tarnish the heroic image he had developed of his stepfather, creating a more sinister picture:

> We used to have chicken for Sunday lunch and if you pulled the leg off to eat, it would spark him off to talk about the war and bodies being burned, with the tendons distorted into grotesque shapes. He would talk about having to climb over piles of bodies lying by barbed wire and so on. Later he would discuss how to kill people. He said to kill a small child you would grab it by the ankles and smash it against a wall. He would actually mime doing it![15]

Stan (or Stasik as he was sometimes called) Chrzanowski was, by all accounts, a troubled and sometimes violent figure within the family. There were allegations of brutality inflicted on both Kingston and his sister, Barbara, a factor which shouldn't be ignored when considering the stepson's relentless campaign to expose Chrzanowski's wartime activities. As Crasnianski has written of her own research: 'Love that is stretched thin is more porous to judgment. This may be one reason why the least-loved children in this study, the ones who received little affection from their fathers... judge their fathers the most severely.'[16]

Kingston's growing private suspicions about Stasik found an outlet in the very public focus on war crimes in the 1980s when it became known that the UK government had set up an inquiry into allegations made by the Simon Wiesenthal Center. This was a period when a number of separate internationally publicized issues had awakened apparently dormant concerns about the legacy of the Nazi era and its implications for modernity.

---

[14] This and subsequent Kingston quotes come from conversations with Jon Silverman in February and March 1996, including a journey to Slonim together.
[15] Kingston-Silverman conversations.   [16] Crasnianski, 2016 *Children of Nazis*, p. 196.

They included a visit made by President Ronald Reagan to a military cemetery outside Bitburg in West Germany, where, it was revealed, a number of Waffen SS soldiers were buried; the controversy over the wartime past of the Austrian president (and former United Nations Secretary-General) Kurt Waldheim; and the trial of the Ukrainian John Demjanjuk. For John Kingston, many of the inchoate anxieties which had troubled him since childhood crystallized when he saw images of Demjanjuk on the television news and remarked on the physical similarity he bore to Chrzanowski:

> During our conversations over the years, Stan had hinted that he was harbouring a secret, and I was always convinced that he had done something much worse than he had done in Slonim. The Belarusian consul drew to my attention the likeness between Stan and Demjanjuk and I mentioned that perhaps he had been at Treblinka or that he had helped put down the Warsaw uprising. I pressed him about these suspicions and he told me to keep very quiet.[17]

It was at that point, in April 1988, that he wrote to the secretariat at the Hetherington-Chalmers Inquiry which had placed advertisements in national and regional newspapers seeking information and names of possible suspects:

> I believe I may have some evidence on a possible perpetrator of war crimes who has been living in Britain since 1946/7. This evidence is mainly circumstantial, his profile matching that of some war criminals I have learned of lately through the media. In addition, since the war he has acted like a man frightened of being caught by certain European authorities, has exhibited great brutality and cruelty at times ... Because he is 'family' and because I may be wrong in my suspicions, I require to know what sort of person you are looking for and what magnitude of crime concerns you. Does the suspect need to be German?[18]

---

[17] Ibid.   [18] Kingston letter to the Secretary, War Crimes Inquiry, 11 April 1988.

Within a fortnight, he received a reply from the Secretary of the Inquiry, David Ackland, enclosing the terms of reference:

> Thank you for your letter of 11 April. It is not necessary that the perpetrator be German: he should, however, now be of British citizenship or resident in this country. If you believe that the person of whom you wrote has committed war crimes that fall within the Inquiry's purview, I should be grateful for details so that investigations may be pursued.[19]

Kingston responded with a lengthy and detailed statement 'giving circumstantial evidence regarding possible war crimes of "S"' and an assessment of his character:

> Stan is anti-Jewish in general disposition (like many Poles?) but did not refer to them with any great animosity. He seemed rather reticent and subdued on the rare occasions when they were mentioned.[20] ... He spoke of playing cat-and-mouse with interrogators. He had been trained to resist interrogation and talked of giving a false name. ... He has spoken of not fearing British authorities but only Polish/Russian ones. ... he hinted at his cleverness and guile in persuading the British to believe him.[21]

The Inquiry passed Chrzanowski's name, along with 370 others, to the War Crimes Unit at Scotland Yard when it started work in 1991. Kingston had also supplied a photograph which he discovered by accident when sifting through a linen box hidden under a bed in his mother's house. Taken in March 1942, it showed a youthful Stan wearing the black uniform of a *Schutzmänner* (Fig. 7.2). At this early stage in the war crimes inquiry, the police knew next to nothing about the Holocaust in Slonim and Kingston's suspicions were quickly dismissed in a letter he received from the WCU head, Detective Chief Superintendent Eddie

---

[19] Ackland letter to Kingston, 22 April 1988, released under FOI request.

[20] Though Kingston told one of the authors that 'Stan spoke about Jews always moaning about the War and about how many of them had died'. Kingston interview, 29 November 1995.

[21] Letter to the War Crimes Inquiry, 15 May 1988 released by the Home Office under Freedom of Information Request.

Fig. 7.2 Stanislaw Chrzanowski in the uniform of a *Schutzmänner*, Slonim 1942. John Kingston collection.

Bathgate: 'No further action will be taken in this matter owing to the fact that no direct allegation of murder or manslaughter was made and there was no supporting evidence.'[22]

The 'Evidence'

As stated earlier, the initial D. in the German legal authorization to investigate Chrzanowski was a reference to Jan Daletsky, a woodsman or

---

[22] Bathgate letter, 21 October 1991, Ref: 25/WCU/91/79.

forestry official, who was arrested in June 1942 in a large-scale round-up
of Slonim citizens perceived by the Germans to be a 'threat' to the occupiers if not overtly sympathetic to the partisans. He was not Jewish. On a
visit to Slonim in March 1996, one of the authors, Jon Silverman, interviewed his widow, Alexandra, in her modest wooden home. This and
other first-person recollections from witnesses in this section were
recorded on that visit:

> On 23 June, a group of ten people wearing civilian clothes—they were
> not German—arrived at the house at night and said 'give us your
> weapons'. My husband had a hunting rifle for his job. They took him
> away and I ran outside to protest. There were many other women cry-
> ing and shouting as their men were taken prisoner. About 120 were
> arrested. They were the elite, doctors, lawyers and so on, import-
> ant people.
>
> Q. Did you know Chrzanowski?
>
> I knew him. He lived on Sovietskaya Street with his sister, aunt and
> grandmother. His father often visited us after his wife died. Stasik was
> not important to us, he was just a young guy, about seventeen. Nobody
> would think he would accept such a dirty rotten job when he joined
> the *Schutzmanshaft*. Later, I saw him in his uniform.

Olga Danielyuk lived next door to the Chrzanowski family. She said her
brother was arrested for possessing lists of Communists and taken to the
prison, where he was tortured in a crude version of 'waterboarding', having cold water forced down his throat. Stasik was a guard. Shown John
Kingston's photograph of him, found in the linen box, she exclaimed:

> Yes, that's Stasik. When I went to the prison to take my brother some
> food and a parcel of clothes, Stasik didn't treat me well, even though
> I was a neighbour and friend of his sister Vera. I said 'Stasik could you
> give my brother a message?' He refused. He said 'I'm not here for that'.
> That was his arrogance and bad temper.

The prisoners were held under severe conditions, regularly beaten, for
nearly four months before a decision was taken to execute them at a

nearby hamlet overlooked by a hill called Petralevichi which had become one of Slonim's two principal killing sites. Alexandra Daletsky was outside the prison with other wives that day:

> Chrzanowski and the other guards would beat us away with their whips if you got too close to the walls. On that day, 28 October, we saw the gates open at about 7.30 a.m. and a number of camouflaged trucks, with canvas covers, came out. They headed for Petralevichi and later we heard machine gun fire. There were two guards with that consignment of condemned men, Chrzanowski and a man called Kolbasinksi.

Alexandra's version of what happened next was necessarily treated as hearsay because she was not an eyewitness and, for that reason, was discounted by the CPS when assessing the strength of the evidence against Chrzanowski. Moreover, even had she witnessed Jan's death with her own eyes, it would not have passed the arbitrary threshold for prosecution set by Treasury Counsel, i.e. that the case would not be considered strong enough if the victims had not been Jewish civilians. Once again, historical 'truth' and the requirements of law had to part company:

> When they came to Petralevichi hill, there were maybe five Germans standing and watching, smoking cigarettes. Chrzanowski and Kolbasinksi told the prisoners to lie down in a trench in order to kill them with machine guns. It was 'our' men doing the shooting. The Germans didn't want to cover their hands in blood. Jan managed to run away towards the village and came to Makar's house when Chrzanowski shot and wounded him in the yard. Makar told me later that Jan had said 'tell my wife they are killing me'. Jan was dragged to the trench and thrown in with the others. I went there later and tried to dig him out with my hands. I managed to get half of his body out of the earth. I had to make sure it was him.

There was at least one credible eyewitness to the behaviour of Chrzanowski the killer. Kazimir Adamovitch (Fig. 7.3), who became a Catholic deacon at Slonim's St Andrew's Cathedral, knew Stasik well because, as a boy, he often saw him visiting his aunt:

Fig. 7.3 Father Kazimir Adamovitch, eyewitness as a boy to a massacre in Slonim. Pictured at St Andrew's Cathedral, Slonim 1996. Jon Silverman.

We were with the cows in the fields close by Petralevichi and saw how he was killing people, at least thirty over the course of three days. Most of his victims had been in the prison and were connected to the partisans. The trenches were already dug and I saw him using his automatic on three occasions, maybe more.

Q. You actually saw Chrzanowski killing?

Yes, that's true. I saw it with my own eyes. I was only about thirty metres away. It was very easy to recognize Stasik. He was tall and tough and serious. He loved to kill people. For him to kill was the same as spitting. He was swaggering around like a hero and was in a very good mood.

At another killing site, Chepilova, Jews were murdered systematically in police-led *Aktionen* in the early stages of the Nazi occupation. In a single day in 1941, 10,000 died. But by 1942, increasingly frequent partisan incursions from the surrounding forests made it too risky for the *Schutzmannschaft* and thereafter the bulk of the massacres were carried out at Petralevichi. Some 22,000 non-Jewish Belorussians were also killed, among them, Kazimir Adamovitch's grandmother.

The KGB archives in Minsk is a repository of information about wartime collaboration with the Nazis and one list, headed Slonim *Schutzmannschaft* contains 116 names. Chrzanowski's is number 21 on the roster.

Chrzanowski Post-War, the Missing Years

When the Germans were forced to retreat from Belorussia in the face of the advancing Red Army, Stasik's 'after-life' bore many similarities to those of his sixty or so *Schutzmänner* compatriots from Slonim who fled westwards in 1944. Like many of them, he was conscripted into the 4th regiment of the 30th Waffen SS Grenadier Division, known as the Waffen Stürmbrigade Belarus. The Loss Report Section (*Verlustmeldungen*) of German army personnel and POW records held in Berlin in the early 1990s showed that a substantial number of those who subsequently emigrated to Britain had been in the Slonim *Schutzmannschaft*.[23] Chrzanowski deserted from the German forces after defeat by a Free French armoured division in the Belfort Gap in Eastern France. The Slonim men surrendered to the Americans in September 1944 and later joined the Second Polish Corps, attached to a Signals Company, which fought alongside Allied troops in the Italian campaign. Chrzanowski's serial number was 141921/111. He arrived in the UK at Liverpool in September 1946 and within two months had been transferred to the Polish Resettlement Corps (no. 30051647). He was finally demobilized in July 1947.[24]

In common with the thousands of East Europeans who had arrived in the UK as part of the European Voluntary Workers scheme, Chrzanowski was interviewed under the belated scrutiny programme, Operation Post Report. He was called to Oldham borough police station in January

---

[23] Martin Dean report, 23–27 November 1992, Hartley Library Special Collections, Archive file MS 408_A1057 2/35, p. 935.

[24] Information from Chrzanowski's application for naturalization, 12 June 1961. Chief Constable of Birmingham's office ref: CID no. 61/12813. Copy supplied by Dr Stephen Ankier.

1951 where he was questioned by an immigration officer. Chrzanowski gave an artfully 'redacted' version of his biography, which was written up in the card index as:

> alien was living in Slonim until the beginning of the war when he left school to join the army. He was taken prisoner by the Russians but escaped home after two months and remained at home *working in a factory* [authors' emphasis] during the German occupation…He appears to be of average intelligence, reliable and no security interest. He speaks Polish, Russian and some Italian, German and English.[25]

As we have discussed earlier, Operation Post Report was little more than a fig leaf to cover the fault lines in the open-door immigration policy which had encouraged into the UK thousands of East Europeans with wartime affiliations to the Nazis. The interviews were cursory and superficial and it was easy to fool the 'interrogators' whether they were immigration officers or police.

Moreover, a clean bill of health from Post Report also acted as an insurance against later accusations of bad faith or worse, a kind of bureaucratic exoneration which in post-war Germany was known as *Persilscheine*.[26] The fact that Chrzanowski told the same story in 1951 and in 1961, when he made his application for naturalization, clearly carried weight with the Hetherington-Chalmers Inquiry when John Kingston wrote with his suspicions. This led to a seriously flawed evaluation of Kingston's allegations: 'There are no inconsistencies between his [Chrzanowski's] stories in 1951 (79C) and in 1961 (79D). When in the German forces, he appears to have served on the Western front, which is not where most war crimes were committed.'[27]

Not only did the Inquiry team seem to 'validate' Chrzanowski's sanitized version of his past, it is clear from the correspondence that it also found fault with Kingston as a credible 'accuser'. He had written of his stepfather: 'he often expressed a fear of authorities in Poland and

---

[25] Bulk Entry Report 40498, 20 June 1951, Home Office file no. C39016/3.
[26] This was the popular German term for letters defending the character and integrity of Nazi functionaries called before denazification panels.
[27] War Crimes Inquiry Case number 79. Copy supplied by Dr Stephen Ankier.

[possibly] Russia, forcing him to return to Poland. In 1964, he returned to Poland, near the Russian border. Although he took——[name redacted] with him, he expressed rather fatalistically that he might not return [i.e. to the UK].'[28]

The secretariat's assessment was dismissive:

> There are inconsistencies in John Kingston's allegations. His major reason for believing Chrzanowski to be a war criminal is Chrzanowski's fear of return to Poland but, by his own admission, Chrzanowski returned to his home town in 1964 (79B, page 1) and made subsequent visits to Poland (79A, Annex, page 2)…. There is no direct allegation or evidence of war crimes. The circumstantial evidence given is disproved by the person making the allegation.[29]

Almost five years after the Hetherington-Chalmers Inquiry reported, the case against Chrzanowski still appeared to lack substance. In May 1994, the WCU asked the office of the Procurator in Warsaw to check for information but no trace was found.[30] Whereas some of the other Belorussian cases, from Mir, Turets, and Baranovichi, with their much smaller populations, had yielded promising leads to suspects, the size of wartime Slonim appeared to militate against reliable witnesses, who had known the suspect, being located. Chrzanowski had also made the investigators' task harder by falsely claiming to have joined the *Schutzmannschaft* in 1943, after the main massacres had taken place. However, by the summer of 1994, evidence was beginning to emerge, from 'traces' in both German and Byelorussian archives in Minsk as well as some UK press reporting, that Chrzanowski had been a Slonim *Schutzmänner* during the period of anti-Jewish *Aktionen* and had participated. In October 1995, Martin Dean found three oral testimonies from a Slonim family called Derman in the archive at the United States Holocaust Memorial Museum. Without implicating Chrzanowski

---

[28] Kingston letter to War Crimes Inquiry, 15 May 1988.

[29] War Crimes Inquiry internal assessment Case number (Stanislaw Chrzanowski): 79, 26 May 1988.

[30] Dean report, 7 May 1994, Ref: 5423 Hartley Library Special Collections, Archive file MS 408_A1057 2/35, p. 1011.

by name, they provided further contextual proof of the Jewish Holocaust in the city.

It was learned that after the war, Stasik's sister Vera, who worked at the textile factory, was interrogated by a team from the Extraordinary State Commission on suspicion of collaborating with the Nazis and, it is believed, sentenced to exile deep into Russia. The archives in Brest, Moscow, and elsewhere continued to yield information about the crimes committed in Slonim so that, even at a relatively late stage of the WCU investigations, Chrzanowski remained amongst the ten to twelve names still being considered for prosecution if the witnesses could be found.

John Kingston, meanwhile, refused to let go of the belief that his step-father was concealing incriminating information about his past. Remarkably, for many years he had been routinely recording their tele-phone conversations, hoping that Stan might let slip a crucial clue. On a number of occasions, Stan had discussed 'secrets' which he wouldn't divulge but in one call, in 1994, he had referred repeatedly to an 'English secret' and claimed to have been a double agent, working for the British. Despite being something of a polyglot, his spoken English was fractured: 'They, no... want this publicity. They waiting if we all dead, it is true... You take it, the secret, keep it with you all time... maybe even to the dead.'[31]

Kingston put this together with the numerous occasions during his younger years when Stan had talked of carrying out espionage on behalf of the Germans and wondered whether, with Stan's good grasp of three European languages, German, Polish, and Russian, he might have been considered useful by British intelligence after the war.

The speculation began to take on more substance with a chance dis-covery by a BBC reporter, Nick Southall, of some archive film footage shot at Marienfelde refugee camp in Berlin in late 1953.[32] The footage was filmed by the US army as part of a newsreel titled 'This is Berlin' depicting the work taking place in West Berlin at the height of the Cold

---

[31] A portion of the recording was played on *The Nazi Next Door* presented by Nick Southall and first broadcast on BBC Radio 4, 23 March 2021.

[32] Southall came across the footage by accident as he was searching for the identities of POWs at the Regensburg camp. Email to author 12 December 2018.

War. It was shown on American television in March 1954.[33] Southall, whose news patch covered Telford in Shropshire, where Chrzanowski was then living, thought he recognized a much younger Stan in the nine seconds of footage which opens the documentary. His suspicions were confirmed by a forensic team, expert in facial recognition comparative mapping. They concluded that there was a 99.9 per cent match. Further examination of a longer unedited sequence of the film revealed the presence at Marienfelde of four other men whose photographs were discovered in Chrzanowski's collection, two of whom had served with him in the *Schutzmannschaft* in Slonim.

So, what significance should be attached to the discovery that Stanislaw Chrzanowski was in Berlin in 1953? First, this conflicts with the report drawn up by Birmingham police in 1961 when he applied for naturalization: 'Since his arrival in the United Kingdom in 1946, the applicant asserts he has not made any visits abroad. He agrees, however, that about 1950, he applied for a Home Office Travel Document with a view to emigrating to the United States of America. The application was later cancelled.'[34]

The Berlin newsreel footage showed this statement to be untrue. The second salient point is that although there is documented information about where Stan lived and worked between his arrival in Liverpool in 1946 and December 1951, when he attended a friend's wedding in Oldham, thereafter there is an informational void until Chrzanowski met John Kingston's mother, Barbara, in Birmingham in early 1954 and settled down with her. Of course, without further evidence, this gap in his timeline and appearance at Marienfelde is not conclusive of involvement with the foreign intelligence service, SIS, but it raises some interesting questions.

Professor Anthony Glees, who acted as an expert adviser to the Hetherington-Chalmers Inquiry on security and intelligence, has little doubt that someone with the background of Chrzanowski would have been courted by SIS:

---

[33] https://www.criticalpast.com/video/65675045315_passengers_children_play_people_eat_food_people_with_belongings.
[34] From Chrzanowski's application for naturalization, 12 June 1961. Chief Constable of Birmingham's office ref: CID no 61/12813.

the presence of such refugees from central and Eastern Europe – that is to say, from areas of Europe which had, after 1945, become satellites of the Soviet Union – might well be supposed to have excited the interest of the secret intelligence service, both because of the specialized knowledge such people might possess and because they might be useful to the intelligence service in other ways.[35]

And one of those ways would have been to act as a 'spotter', helping to screen the new arrivals for those sympathetic to and prepared to actively help the anti-Communist cause. It is well documented that Marienfelde attracted interest from the Western intelligence agencies as well as the Stasi and that SIS had its largest European station, Yorkshire House, near the Olympic Stadium in West Berlin.[36] The camp opened in 1953 as an emergency reception centre for the incessant flow of refugees from the German Democratic Republic who, from the late 1940s until the building of the Berlin Wall in 1961, sought a new life in the so-called Golden West. The historian Eric Limbach has written that in 1953 alone, 330,000 arrivals from the East passed through the camp:

To receive their residence and work permits...they endured a health examination, inspections and a gauntlet of interviewers, with representatives of the Federal Republic and the potential destination *Länder*, as well as with the *intelligence services* [authors' emphasis] of all three Western Allies, a process faced by every individual who had crossed the Iron Curtain.[37]

What Role Did MI6 Play?

The historian Martin Dean has confirmed that the war crimes investigators were denied access to files held by either MI5 or MI6. Neither was

[35] Glees, 1992 'War Crimes: The Security and Intelligence Dimension', p. 243.
[36] Aldrich (ed.), 1988 *Espionage, Security and Intelligence in Britain 1945–1970*.
[37] Limbach, 2011 'Unsettled Germans: The Reception and Resettlement of East German Refugees in West Germany, 1949–1961', dissertation submitted to Michigan State University, pp. 4–5.

he granted security clearance to see relevant records held by the Foreign Office. According to Anthony Glees, more than 100,000 files on those who had immigrated to the UK after the war were destroyed in the late 1980s and early 1990s. This may have been routine 'housekeeping' but in the absence of verified information from the security and intelligence agencies, suspicions that there were ulterior motives will linger. As David Cesarani has written: 'In the world of secrets where such covert activities take place, anything is possible and suspicion is fuelled by the bizarre restrictions on access to British material pertaining to "national security".'[38]

Stephen Dorrill, who has studied the history of MI6, has no doubts that the intelligence agencies played a significant role in thwarting extradition requests for certain people:

> Some of the collaborators and war criminals were highly prized by MI6 and were protected and given a form of immunity from extradition. They were allowed safe haven, provided with funds and new passports. If the Soviets asked for certain people, their existence in the UK was denied. And if specific evidence was produced, it was dismissed as propaganda.[39]

During the debates on the War Crimes Bill in 1990, the Conservative MP—and writer on espionage matters—Rupert Allason said that he had personal knowledge that some of the émigrés with dubious pasts, principally Ukrainians, had been sent to the Joint Services School for Linguists, RAF Crail in Scotland, for purposes likely to have been of benefit to the intelligence services:

> I have obtained evidence from people who served there and were taught Russian by people who openly boasted about atrocities that they had committed against Jews in the Baltic countries during the war. Those boasts were known to British national servicemen going

---

[38] Cesarani, 1992 *Justice Delayed*, p. 160.
[39] Stephen Dorrill interviewed in *Forgotten Nazi*, a documentary broadcast by BBC Frontline Scotland in 2001.

into the Intelligence Corps and they must have been known to the British government in subsequent years.[40]

One document which is clearly authentic and throws a shaft of light on these matters is a Home Office letter from January 1970 concerning the case of a Georgian called Yuri Epifanovich Chapodze, who the Soviet Union sought to extradite from the UK for war crimes. We dealt with the specific allegations against Chapodze and his role in the notorious Caucasian Company which murdered thousands, especially in Ukraine, in Chapter 2. We also discussed in detail the Soviet extradition requests. Chapodze, who owned a guesthouse in the seaside resort Bournemouth, became a British citizen in 1956. Kay Coates, of the Home Office, sent a note to an official in the Eastern European and Soviet Department of the Foreign Office, to bolster the government's justification for refusing the Soviet request (there was, in any case, no extradition treaty between the two countries). MI6 involvement in such cases was the secret that 'dare not speak its name' in written form and the coy euphemism, 'our friends', was employed instead:

> Mr Chapodze, who has been known since 1956 as George Chapell, was granted naturalization on 16 March 1956 and became a citizen of the United Kingdom & Colonies on taking the oath of allegiance on 10 April 1956. I should mention that he was at one time an interest of *our friends*.... The information before us contains nothing to show that Mr Chapodze was implicated in war crimes. His application was supported by *our friends* and it was decided to grant his naturalization. We have no information beyond that given by Mr Chapodze at the time of his interview by an officer of Special Branch, Metropolitan Police, in connection with his application for naturalization.[41]

The letter also contains the line: 'The circumstances [i.e. of Chapodze's case] are indeed very similar to those of Mr Pardzhadnadze.'[42] Avtandil

---

[40] HC Deb, 19 March 1990, vol. 169, cols. 950–1.
[41] Letter written by Kay Coates, Home Office ref: C.45064/4, on 30 January 1970 to Mr. P Shaw, FCO ref: 28/1156.
[42] Ibid.

Pardzhadnadze—whose case we examined in Chapter 2—was another member of the Caucasian Company (*Kaukasier Kompanie*), formed from Red Army soldiers taken prisoner by the Nazis and later attached to *Einsatzgruppe D*. It is obvious that MI6's support for Chapodze's application was a 'reward' for past services, or perhaps for ongoing collusion. The historian Stephen Tyas who has specialized in researching the war in the Caucasus, claims that both me: 'were brought to Britain by the British secret service, MI6, for training as possible agents to be parachuted into their homelands'.[43]

The reason that MI6 showed such interest in the two Caucasians can be traced back to what happened after they were captured by the Germans and before they were assigned to the extermination campaign against the Jews of southern Ukraine. Martin Dean made a short oblique reference to this under-researched episode when he was drafting a review of cases in 1994. Benefiting from intelligence gained from German sources, he wrote that Pardzhadnadze, 'was taken and trained in Auschwitz and Eupatoriya espionage schools' in the summer of 1942.[44] These were specialist camps or 'reconnaissance schools'—known in German as *Schleusungslagern*—set up as part of Operation Zeppelin (sometimes known as Zeppelin Command), with the aim of training suitable civilians and selected POWs in sabotage and subversion to act as a 'fifth column' behind Russian lines. There was a particular focus on those of non-Russian heritage, with no historic loyalties to the Communist regime, such as the Caucasians. According to the historian Andrej Angrick, the first camp was established near Auschwitz, with others set up:

> along the entire eastern front, in the south, including in Yevpatoria [in western Crimea]. (Probably) all of the contemporary material has been preserved and is located in Moscow; copies have been handed over to the State Security (Stasi) in Berlin, which itself carried out investigations. Since sick spies were murdered in Auschwitz, the

---

[43] Tyas, 2020 'The Kaukasier Kompanie ("Caucasian Company"): Soviet Ethnic Minorities, Collaborators, and Mass Killers', in *Beyond the Pale*, ed. Brooks and Feferman, p. 112.

[44] Martin Dean case review notes, 14 July 1994, Hartley Library Special Collections, Archive file MS 408_A1057 2/35, p. 1017.

Hamburg public prosecutor carried out an investigation in the post-war period, which included further material.[45]

Material found in the Russian and Stasi archives supplemented information provided by the head of the Auschwitz reconnaissance school, Guido Huhn, which had emerged from a trial in Dusseldorf in 1966. Huhn, a member of *Einsatzkommando 5*, who committed multiple murders in occupied Ukraine, claimed to have received and trained groups of up to fifty Caucasian POWs during the summer of 1942.[46]

Although the clandestine skills learned by Pardzhadnadze and Chapodze made them privileged assets, there is no documentary evidence to suggest that they did return to their homeland after arriving in the UK. However, Britain's SIS continued to make the recruitment of émigrés integral to its plans to undermine the Soviet state. Two secret operations, known as Climber 1 and Climber 11, were launched against the Soviet southern flank in the late 1940s. Both involved the infiltration of Georgians into Soviet Georgia with the aim of making contact with anti-Russian resistance groups and reporting back to SIS on military and naval installations in the Black Sea region. The official historian of SIS, Keith Jeffery, wrote that in the second of the operations, in the spring of 1949:

> two émigrés, one apparently in his late forties, the other in his early thirties, were recruited in France and brought to England for training. They were given a special tradecraft course, with a particular emphasis on secret writing and two weeks' physical 'hardening up', walking on Dartmoor.... While the actual intelligence product was relatively modest, Climber 11 was adjudged to have been a success, and a useful basis for further such ventures to penetrate the Soviet Union.[47]

Any audit of the value of such missions would have to conclude that, in the context of the Cold War, they achieved little. Likewise, German

[45] Angrick email to author, 16 February 2022.
[46] Martin Dean email, 14 February 2022.
[47] Jeffery, 2010 *MI6: The History of the Secret Intelligence Service 1909–1949*, pp. 709–11.

espionage plans involving the Caucasians had a nugatory impact. According to Stephen Tyas, a number of Georgians were dropped by parachute into Georgia and Azerbaijan during the war but much of the military information they sent back by radio was intercepted by the UK Signals Service at Bletchley Park, passed on to the Soviets and most of the would-be agents and fifth columnists were killed.[48]

Frustratingly, the secrecy surrounding the MI6 files makes it impossible to be certain to what use Pardzhadnadze and Chapodze might have been put. And whether this had any bearing on their status as war crimes suspects.

The Belarus Secrets

In February 1947, an official of the Security Service, MI5, wrote:

> As I explained in my letter (Gen.1508) dated 4.2.47 about the case of Dr. Dering [the Polish doctor who had been accused of carrying out medical experiments at Auschwitz], we are not normally concerned with war criminal cases in this office, unless there is a *counter-espionage interest* [authors' emphasis].[49]

As explained in Chapter 5 on Serafinowicz, there was undoubtedly a British interest in the Belorussian émigré community which coalesced around the wartime puppet leader Radislaw Ostrowski. It is difficult to ascertain what intelligence benefits accrued although the former OSI investigator John Loftus wrote confidently—and controversially—that he had uncovered a conspiracy to bring ex-Nazi collaborators to the US and UK:

> *Knowledgeable sources* [authors' emphasis] confirmed that leading Byelorussian Nazis were transported to London in 1945, given a

---

[48] Tyas, 2020 'The Kaukasier Kompanie ("Caucasian Company"): Soviet Ethnic Minorities, Collaborators, and Mass Killers', in *Beyond the Pale*, ed. Brooks and Feferman, p. 97.

[49] Letter from J. L. Irvine dated 18 February 1947 to unknown recipient, Hartley Library Special Collections, Archive file MS 408_A1057 2/44.

stipend of five hundred pounds, provided with police transportation and employed as government translators as cover for their covert operations.[50]

In the summer of 1950, Ostrowski visited the UK ostensibly to organize a conference of the newly formed Anti-Bolshevik Bloc of Nations. The historian Mark Alexander has made a study of US intelligence efforts during the Cold War to undermine the Soviet Union through the use of Belorussian Nazi collaborators. He argues that files held by the CIA suggest that Ostrowski also harboured the hope that the political struggle would be matched by a military, or para-military one, to be spearheaded by the Byelorussian Liberation Movement (BLM): 'an underground guerrilla army sponsored by British intelligence designed to be subordinate to Ostrowski and the Byelorussian Central Council....They [the Belorussian activists] remained active in postwar Europe's Displaced Persons camps, published propaganda, and whitewashed their Nazi pasts.'[51]

So how might Stanislaw Chrzanowski, with his knowledge of German and Russian and his apparent obsession with military hardware and killing, have fitted in to the anti-Soviet machinations of the foreign intelligence service, SIS?

A possible clue lies in John Kingston's account of how, from the time they met in 1954, he was exposed to his stepfather's 'wartime experiences'. He found it bizarre that someone living in peacetime Birmingham continued to behave as though he was a commando caught in the midst of an ongoing conflict:

Stan used to pace up and down on a plastic mat with spikes poking through so that his feet were hardened. He was constantly on the alert and on buses and trains he would always look for the safest position to sit, with his back to a window. At work he would make throwing knives and whips out of plaited leather. He taught me a

---

[50] Loftus, John 1982 *The Belarus Secret*, p. 165.
[51] *Report on Antonovich-Zarechnyi*, 1–2, NARA, RG 263, CIA, Ostrowski, Radoslaw, E ZZ-18, B 98. Cited by Alexander, 2015 'Nazi Collaborators, American Intelligence and the Cold War', pp. 86–7.

form of karate and made me wear a belt and beret so that I looked like a little commando.[52]

Stan showed the impressionable boy a wartime Luger which he said he had used in combat and told him that he had once bayonetted a Russian commissar. Whether fantasy or fact it is impossible to know, and in one of the few interviews he gave, to a local radio station in 1994, he explained it away by saying: 'I tell him [John Kingston] what I saw, not what I did.'[53] Thus, apart from the fleeting appearance of Stan in the Marienfelde documentary, there is no available information to substantiate whether he had worked for SIS. Stan's claim, after he was first questioned by the police, that he had been trained by British intelligence and then parachuted back into Belarus '*during the war* [authors' emphasis]' wearing an SS uniform, is probably best consigned to the world of make believe.[54]

In one of their frequent telephone conversations, conducted in the pidgin English which Stan spoke throughout his life, Kingston challenged him with allegations he had heard from witnesses when he visited Slonim in 1996 in the company of one of the authors:

K. Someone from the church [the deacon Kazimir Adamovich] say you take people to kill. They say you shoot people.

C. (Laughs) Not true. Don't listen to them. It's plenty lies. I standing on the gate as a guard. I no shoot anyone. You like a Judas, you want revenge.[55]

Chrzanowski was first interviewed by the police in 1995 and thereafter on at least two other occasions. He did not deny being in Slonim for part of the period under investigation nor that he had seen naked people being herded through the city. At first he claimed that his only job was to guard a textile factory and that witnesses who had named him as a

---

[52] John Kingston conversation with Jon Silverman, 29 November 1995.
[53] Excerpt from *The Nazi Next Door* documentary.
[54] Kingston interview with author, 25 August 1995.
[55] Kingston interview with author.

killer had confused him with another man called Tollick, a known collaborator. Later, in an interview with the *Birmingham Post*, he said that he had been forcibly conscripted into the *Schutzmannschaft* to act as a guard but that he had never shot anybody.[56] (John Kingston's boyhood memory was different, that Stan admitted to having killed—but only 'partisans'.)[57] The police visited Canada and Israel in their search for evidence. When they showed wartime photographs of Stasik to residents in Slonim and were met with immediate recognition, they were satisfied that identification was not at issue. But the insuperable obstacle was finding at least two credible eyewitnesses who had seen Stasik kill. The investigation continued until well into 1996 but in December that year, John Kingston received the letter he had been fearing: 'The allegations have been thoroughly investigated by officers from this unit…the results have been passed to the CPS…they stated that there was no evidence which would afford a realistic prospect of conviction in this case.'[58]

Conclusion

Kingston received a letter from the Crown Prosecution Service on the same day that he'd heard from the police. It encapsulated the point of principle which goes to the heart of the question as to why so few war crimes investigations led to prosecutions:

> Allegations made under the War Crimes Act 1991 are considered in the same way as any other criminal prosecution by the CPS. The Act did not give the police as investigators and the CPS any *special powers or dispensation* [authors' emphasis] in either the investigation or the review of this type of case.[59]

A counter-view, expressed a number of times in this book is that it would be equally valid to argue that neither did the War Crimes Act tie

---

[56] *Birmingham Post*, 15 December 1996, p. 5.
[57] Kingston interview with author, 29 November 1995.
[58] WCU letter to Kingston, 13 December 1996.
[59] From RG Bland Special Casework Lawyer, (no ref.) 13 December 1996.

the hands of police and prosecutors and prescribe what evidence they would require in order to mount a prosecution. That was a matter of administrative decision-making and interpretation of the standard rubric that there had to be 'a realistic prospect of conviction'. A striking example of this 'immutable' policy was the decision to confine prosecutions to cases where it was indisputable that the victims were Jewish civilians. Clearly this was a 'dispensation' exercised by the CPS and Treasury Counsel outwith the terms of the War Crimes Act—but, of course, never disclosed.

By contrast, the Office of Special Investigations brought many cases in which the victims were not Jewish, including one where the perpetrator himself, a concentration camp *kapo*, Jacob Tannenbaum, was Jewish.[60] And in response to the argument that the OSI was not using the criminal law, unlike the UK, it is worth pointing out that, as a result of higher court rulings, the prosecutors were required to meet the threshold of 'beyond reasonable doubt' to win their denaturalization cases.[61]

In Germany's very different, civil law system, far greater evidentiary weight is placed on documents. Indeed, a preliminary inquiry conducted by the *Zentrale Stelle* is based solely on documentary evidence with no necessity for witnesses to be interviewed for a case to be passed to the Public Prosecutor. Even at trial, convictions have been obtained where the witness testimony can at best be described as circumstantial. And whereas in the UK, the prosecuting authorities have been wary of over-reliance on documents originating from the Soviet Union, Thomas Will said that some of the German war crimes trials 'had been possible only with the availability of documents obtained from Russian archives'.[62]

The final act of Stasik Chrzanowski's life played out without him being aware that, although there was no prospect of a trial in the UK, the case was not closed. Stasik died at the age of 96 in October 2017. At that stage, the Ludwigsburg investigators had been examining the documentary evidence against him, trawling through the National Archives at Kew, and were preparing to interview him at his home in Shropshire

---

[60] This case was unique in that the prosecution was launched after a fellow former inmate of the concentration camp spotted Tannenbaum, who had a reputation for sadism, in the street.

[61] *Klapprott v. United States*, 335 U.S. 601, 612 (1949) 89.

[62] Will interview with authors, 30 March 2022.

when they received news of his death. Thomas Will said: 'If he hadn't died at that point and we were determined to pursue the case, we would have applied for a European Arrest Warrant to have him transferred to a German jurisdiction.'[63]

Had such an application been made, the resulting legal confrontation between the erstwhile enemies of the Second World War could have been as incendiary as some of the debates which marked the passage of the War Crimes Act. The investigators of the *Zentrale Stelle* have continued their work and in 2021 alone, instigated eight new preliminary inquiries. At time of writing, in 2022, the Public Prosecutor's Office was handling nine war crimes cases. The passing of Stanislaw Chrzanowski went largely unmourned, even by his family. His stepson, John Kingston, survived him by only a few months and died in February 2018, the questions which had tormented him throughout his life unanswered.

[63] Ibid.

Afterword

Legacies and Holocaust Awareness

Introduction

Several months after the conviction of Andrzej Sawoniuk in 1999, the Board of Deputies of British Jews sent a letter of fulsome appreciation to Detective Superintendent Dermot McDermott of the WCU for the work carried out by officers since 1991:

> Your senior officers have kept us regularly informed of their progress, and it has truly been a heroic undertaking to bring such cases to court. In our experience, the police investigations have been painstaking, and we believe that no police force anywhere in the world could have done more to assemble the material. The fact that, in at least one case, the Unit was able to assemble evidence and prove its case to the satisfaction of a jury speaks for itself. The British Jewish community owes a great debt to the Metropolitan Police and the entire staff of the War Crimes Unit over the years for your magnificent efforts.[1]

With the hindsight derived from reading the disclosures in this book, it is possible that the Board might wish to revise or, at least, temper its praise. Some might even have preferred it if we had approached this inquiry in a spirit of outraged polemicism, to argue that prosecutors in the United Kingdom ducked an existential responsibility to go further

---

[1] Copy of letter, dated 19 October 1999 supplied to author by Det. Supt. McDermott, 29 August 2017.

Safe Haven: The United Kingdom's Investigations into Nazi Collaborators and the Failure of Justice.
Jon Silverman and Robert Sherwood, Oxford University Press. © Jon Silverman and Robert Sherwood 2023.
DOI: 10.1093/oso/9780192855176.003.0009

than they did: to put on trial men whose crimes were amongst the worst in recent recorded history and let a jury decide their guilt or innocence.

Lord Jon Mendelsohn, a former Westminster lobbyist and political organizer, who played an influential role in the campaign for a War Crimes Act, is highly critical of the legal authorities:

> All the problems can be attributed to the legal processes. It was a most inert environment. The lawyers were so conservative. You can't blame the government, nor the police. They were committed to the pursuit of prosecutions. The truth is that although the law changed, the practice of the law, the way it was interpreted, did not.[2]

Richard Matthews KC drafted the legal report published by the All-Party Parliamentary War Crimes Group which heavily influenced the Hetherington-Chalmers recommendations:[3]

> I had been impressed by what they were doing in war crimes cases in the United States regarding issues like the admissibility of hearsay evidence in certain circumstances and accepting documentary testimony which had been verified as recorded contemporaneously in the Soviet Union. We also thought it was imperative to speed up trials by doing away with the lengthy delays caused by committal hearings. But these changes were anathema to the legal establishment which was both small 'c' and large 'C' conservative in matters of procedure.[4]

The inclusion in several of our chapters of critical commentary from, *inter alia*, the United States and Israel, is evidence of the disappointment at the meagre outcome of the UK's war crimes investigations. David Fraser has pointed out that the War Crimes Act 'domesticated' the Holocaust, shrinking this prolonged cataclysm of suffering to acts of homicide or unlawful killing and excluding the concept of 'crimes against humanity': 'This domestication of the Holocaust within British

---

[2] Mendelsohn interview with author, 16 September 2022.
[3] 'Nazi War Criminals in the United Kingdom: The Law' prepared by a legal advisory committee and published in February 1989.
[4] Richard Matthews interview with author, 7 December 2022.

legal discourse resulted in an almost inevitable reduction of historically and morally complex events and categories into the rigid taxonomical structures of the law.'[5]

In truth though, Britain's common law system of criminal justice allowed for more flexibility than Fraser credits and it is worth examining how the intention behind the statute was crucially modified and diluted by those charged with implementing and interpreting the War Crimes Act.

On the day that the War Crimes Bill was published in March 1990, the Home Office minister, Earl Ferrers, made it plain that all the key procedural recommendations of the Hetherington-Chalmers Inquiry would be included because they were *already part of other criminal legislation*. This included the admission of live television evidence (para 9.34 of the Inquiry report) which had been introduced in the 1988 Criminal Justice Act. Powers to request evidence to be taken on commission abroad and the admissibility of video recordings of evidence taken abroad by letters of request (paras 9.37 and 9.38) were part of the Criminal Justice (International Cooperation) Bill, then before Parliament. He continued: 'The admissibility of documentary evidence, subject to appropriate safeguards as to the circumstances in which the evidence was taken and the fairness of its use in trials, was provided for in England and Wales by...the Criminal Justice Act 1988.'[6]

The Hetherington-Chalmers recommendation that cases should be transferred to the Crown Court without the delay of committal proceedings was already accepted in serious fraud cases. Regarding the admissibility of evidence from persons now dead (para 9.41), Ferrers said that the government believed that the courts could admit such evidence where it was safe to do so and that no change in the law was required.

Speaking in 1995, Sir Thomas Hetherington, a former Director of Public Prosecutions, expressed his frustration that none of the three *prima facie* cases highlighted in the secret annex to his Inquiry report had yet been the subject of charges: 'I am really puzzled by the delay. Yes, Scotland Yard [the War Crimes Unit] had a lot of work to do but

[5] Fraser, 2005 *Law After Auschwitz*, p. 288.
[6] HL Deb, 8 March 1990, vol. 516, cols. 1297–8WA.

they had quite a big team. I would have thought that before this, they would either have come to a dead end or there would have been [by the CPS] a decision to prosecute.'[7]

Perhaps then we should be looking, not at the framing of the legislation to explain the paucity of convictions but at the insistence of police and prosecutors, despite the uniqueness of the cases, to adhere to procedural precedent: the requirement for live eyewitness evidence, the disdain for testimony by document, and the testing of evidential strength by a lower court committal hearing even if it caused a delay fatal to an eventual trial. And even if these decisions could be justified to protect the integrity of jurisprudence, there is still a compelling case to be made that the characteristically British opaqueness of the war crimes process has done nothing to illuminate Holocaust scholarship nor to enhance wider awareness about the protection afforded by the UK to thousands who had willingly killed in the service of the Nazis.

At a time of burgeoning consciousness that the Holocaust challenged every core precept by which 'liberal' civilization defines itself, this was a glaring lacuna. But there is another question worth asking: was there a legacy from the War Crimes Act which could be said to have left its imprint on issues of crime and justice raised by those who seek refuge in the UK from involvement in conflict abroad?

The Damasevicius Case

By the end of the 1990s, even if the Board of Deputies was expressing satisfaction at the performance of the War Crimes Unit, there was a realization in Whitehall that legal limitations had prevented further potential prosecutions. In January 2000, Dr Efraim Zuroff, of the Simon Wiesenthal Center, wrote to the Home Secretary, Jack Straw, alleging that there were three former members of the Latvian Security Service (*Sicherheitsdienst*) living in the UK and a Lithuanian *Schutzmänner* who merited further investigation.

---

[7] Hetherington interview with author, 5 July 1995.

The Lithuanian was Julius Damasevicius, then aged 77 and living in the city of Nottingham. He had freely admitted voluntarily joining the Fourth Lithuanian Auxiliary Police Battalion shortly before Christmas 1942 in Vilnius and serving, with the rank of private, until 1944.[8] For much of 1943, he was a guard at a camp called Mykhailowka near Stalino (now Donetsk) in Eastern Ukraine. The camp held Soviet POWs, Ukrainians, and Jews who were exploited as forced labour on a major autobahn construction project, *Durchgangstrasse IV* (DGIV) linking Lemberg (now Lviv) in Western Ukraine with Stalino in the East. Research by Professor Hermann Kaienburg suggests that most of the 25,000 Jews employed on the project were shot in 1942 and 1943.[9] On Yom Kippur in 1942, all children under the age of fourteen, all pregnant women, the sick and the elderly were killed on the orders of *SS-Hauptsturmführer* Franz Christoffel. Other camp inmates were executed for infringement of arbitrary rules imposed by the guards.[10]

After the war, four members of the same unit as Damasevicius were convicted of war crimes in the Soviet Union, receiving sentences of between twenty and thirty years. And in the late 1960s, prosecutors in Germany conducted investigations into seventy of the German personnel on DGIV, thirty-nine of whom were resident in Germany.[11] By then, Christoffel had died but his deputy, Oskar Friese, was still living. However, he was saved from trial because of the German statute of limitations which, at that time, held that a prosecution, even for murder, was time-barred after twenty years had elapsed since the crime. (The restriction was later lifted.)

In an interview with one of the authors, Damasevicius said he was one of forty or fifty Lithuanian guards on the project and that his job was to escort prisoners to and from work each day and ensure that no one escaped. He admitted that:

[8] His name appears on a unit roster in the Lithuanian Central State Archive in Vilnius. File R683 series 1 folder 5.

[9] Kaienburg, 1996 'Jüdische Arbeitslager an der "Strasse" der SS', p. 37.

[10] Descriptions of the brutal conditions at Mykhailowka can be found in *The Grave is in the Cherry Orchard* (1961), the memoir of the Romanian-born artist Arnold Daghani, who survived incarceration there.

[11] Records of the investigations can be found in the archive of the *Zentrale Stalle* in Ludwigsburg.

Many of the Russian POWs died from the brutal conditions, of disease and hunger but the Germans were in charge of the camp and any ill-treatment came from them. There was a period in 1943 when I fell ill and went to Kaunas (in Lithuania) for treatment. If atrocities were committed, it may have been while I was away. I have nothing to hide. They are welcome to investigate me.[12]

After the Red Army had re-taken Ukraine, Damasevicius joined the ragtag detritus of collaborators—mainly Balts and Ukrainians—who retreated westwards with the Germans and were eventually taken prisoner by the advancing American forces in Belgium. He spent a year in a camp before being transported to the British occupied sector of Germany to work in a factory near Münster. The British government's initiative, Operation Westward Ho, in 1947, to provide the country with much-needed foreign labour, opened up a safe passage to the UK, with few questions asked:

I was interviewed in a prison camp in Germany about what battalion I had served in and for how long. We were asked who wanted to come to Britain to work and I arrived in 1947 with one or two other members from my battalion and worked first in a factory near Peterborough making railway sleepers and then for the London Brick Company as a cook.[13]

Deprivation of Citizenship

By the time the name of Damasevicius had been found on a battalion roster in the Vilnius archive in 2000, the dedicated War Crimes Unit at Scotland Yard had been wound up and its work taken over by the Anti-Terrorist Branch, SO13. Detectives interviewed him after contacting the war crimes prosecutor in Vilnius for more information, including witness statements. The Simon Wiesenthal Center supplied useful historical

---

[12] Damasevicius interview with Jon Silverman, 16 October 2000.   [13] Ibid.

background but without credible evidence of killing from eyewitnesses who could positively identify the suspect—unlikely in the context of a camp with a fluctuating population—a charge was always considered a remote prospect.

However, Efraim Zuroff's letter to the Home Secretary, Jack Straw, floated the suggestion that, if the threshold for a criminal prosecution could not be reached, other actions, such as deprivation of citizenship and deportation, should be considered against those collaborators who had lived in the UK with impunity. Straw, who had been heavily criticized for a somewhat supine response over the Latvian suspect Konrad Kalejs, was sympathetic to the argument:

> I am profoundly concerned about allegations of the kind you mention. The accounts which you and others have given involve allegations of horrific behaviour. I recognise that these accounts will be, even now, deeply distressing to the victims of such suffering and their families, and repugnant to decent people. I had already been considering, when I received your letter, what action I could appropriately take in such cases. You have raised in particular the powers to denaturalise and deport those who have been naturalised as British citizens. The powers of deprivation are set out in the British Nationality Act 1981, and deportation in the Immigration Act 1971. These have to be exercised according to statutory safeguards and other legal constraints, and I am examining their scope.[14]

Ironically, deprivation of citizenship and deportation had been options considered and rejected by the Hetherington-Chalmers Inquiry on the grounds that 'proceedings are likely to be lengthy and hold no guarantee of success. Furthermore, even if successful they do not result in punishment.'[15] It has to be said that a definition of punishment which excludes being uprooted from your home of half a century and expelled to another state in the full glare of media publicity is a strange one and would certainly be contested by prosecutors in the United States who

[14] Straw letter to Zuroff, 31 January 2000, HO 9704js.
[15] *War Crimes: Report of the War Crimes Inquiry* 1989 Cm 744 para 9.20, p. 95.

are proud of having used those same powers against Nazi collaborators for more than forty years. Even Canada, which did not have a distinguished record in prosecuting war criminals—not a single conviction was obtained—acknowledged in 1995 that the civil law route would be more productive and thereafter filed a handful of cases which led to judicial decisions to denaturalize citizens who had lied on their immigration entry forms.

Jack Straw set up an internal inquiry to examine the implications of using immigration and nationality powers against war criminals but by the time it had reached a conclusion, he had been moved to another government position and his post as Home Secretary taken by David Blunkett. In February 2002, Blunkett wrote to Efraim Zuroff outlining his views:

> Having had the opportunity to consider the work carried out by Home Office officials over the last two years I have concluded that insufficient importance is attached to the role of immigration and nationality legislation in this area. It is also clear from our experience with alleged Nazi war criminals that the United Kingdom needs to avoid repeating the mistakes of history by ensuring that those suspected of involvement in modern war crimes are not permitted to enter the United Kingdom. We also need, where it is appropriate, to take action against those already here *whenever their alleged involvement in the commission of atrocities has occurred* [authors' emphasis]. I believe that, if necessary, this should include taking measures to deprive an individual of British citizenship.[16]

Zuroff was highly encouraged, not to say elated, by Blunkett's words, as his exuberant use of capitals suggests:

> I think that it is unequivocally clear that he intends to use the proposed measures against ANYONE involved in atrocities REGARDLESS of WHEN THEY WERE COMMITTED!! The implications thereof

---

[16] Blunkett letter to Zuroff, 7 February 2002, HO 2506X2.

are quite far-reaching, although the number of Holocaust perpetrators who will be affected will depend on the speed with which their cases are handled once the new measures are adopted.[17]

Blunkett's pledge was partially fulfilled with the passage in 2002 of the Nationality, Immigration and Asylum Act which allowed deportation and deprivation of citizenship if behaviour was deemed 'seriously prejudicial to the vital interests of the United Kingdom'. By 2017, forty-five such orders had been made against people who had gained British citizenship through fraud or misrepresentation.[18] But not one collaborator who had whitewashed his past when entering the UK in 1946 or 1947 and lied again when interviewed for Operation Post Report in the early 1950s ever suffered that fate.

Holocaust Awareness

The War Crimes Act 1991, which was interpreted so narrowly, was synchronous with the expanding tide of Holocaust 'consciousness', that has seeped into every corner of cultural representation, becoming, in many ways, a paramount ethical signifier for our time. As Mary Fulbrook noted: 'The Holocaust has become a defining feature of contemporary self-understanding and values.'[19] In his study of the phenomenon, Andy Pearce asked:

> How do we account for this state of affairs, and what relation does it have to developments elsewhere? What are the aims and objectives of all this activity, how is it sustained, and by whom? In what ways are we really, truly 'conscious' of the Holocaust and how, if at all, does this consciousness affect our lives?[20]

---

[17] Zuroff faxed letter to Jon Silverman, 21 February 2002.
[18] HoC Briefing Paper, *Deprivation of British Citizenship and withdrawal of passport facilities* no. 06820, 9 June 2017.
[19] Fulbrook, 2018 *Reckonings*, p. 5.
[20] Pearce, 2014 *Holocaust Consciousness in Contemporary Britain*, p. 1.

To which we add one more question germane to the subject of this book. How do we fit the UK's belated application of the criminal law to the pursuit of war criminals into the framework of Holocaust consciousness?

War crimes trials derive much of their moral force from survivor accounts of suffering and intrinsic to the process of persuading the UK government that the law should be changed to allow perpetrators to be prosecuted was the amplification of the 'survivor voice' in society. In fact, that sentence should read 'survivor *voices*' because it would be a mistake to believe that, in the mid-1980s, those who lived through the Holocaust years in Europe and found sanctuary after the war in the UK were united in how they viewed their experiences or indeed 'status'. It sounds both cruel and crass to categorize survivors into a hierarchy of suffering, nevertheless it is true that, like George Orwell's typology in *Animal Farm*, some survivors were considered 'more equal' than others by dint of their 'backstory'. Invidious though it might seem, some of those who came through the camps believed, or were encouraged to believe by others, that their experiences were on a different plane qualitatively from those of slave labourers for example or those hidden by gentile families. On occasions, generating a greater awareness of the Holocaust in the 1980s meant also acknowledging the sensitivity of these divisions.

There was a myriad of groups to which survivors belonged. Probably the best established was the Yad Vashem Committee of the Board of Deputies of British Jews. It was chaired by Polish-born Ben (now Sir Ben) Helfgott, who had been brought to the UK as a 16-year-old in 1945 as one of the so-called Windermere Children and was then instrumental in founding the '45 Aid Society. This tight-knit collection of young men, who called themselves thereafter 'The Boys', exemplified a self-help ethos—many became successful businessmen, one or two of them, millionaires—which did not necessarily share a philosophy with other movements dedicated to the survivor 'community'. This strand of thinking focused on the legacy of psychological trauma left by the Holocaust and offered support and access to therapy.

By the 1980s, a generational divide was influencing awareness of the Holocaust in the UK. A new, younger, generation, some of them the grandchildren of survivors—awakened by the campaign for a war crimes act—was expressing a thirst for knowledge about the Holocaust and its perpetrators, which their elders had consigned to history. As one example, an Association of Children of Jewish Refugees was formed and through that body, the Manchester Second Generation established its own pressure group in November 1989 to lobby MPs for legislation:[21]

> Within a matter of days, we swamped schools, synagogues, social/ cultural organizations and local people with postcards publicizing the significance of the [war crimes] legislation. More than 2500 cards were posted to MPs and we are very proud that, according to the War Crimes Committee [*sic*] our activities were influential among ambivalent MPs...Like our contemporary group in Israel, we continue to act as a pressure group in respect of the prosecution of war criminals.[21]

The impact of such lobbying was most keenly felt amongst younger parliamentarians. In the House of Lords, which voted overwhelmingly against the War Crimes Bill three times, the older generation of wartime and post-war civil servants, diplomats, soldiers, and politicians were, in the main, hostile, believing that little of benefit would come from reopening old wounds and that there had been a compact after the war to move on from 'reckonings'. This view was not confined to the UK. In France, when the wartime leader of the pro-Nazi Milice, Paul Touvier, was discovered, after decades of being sheltered by the Catholic Church, President Mitterrand expressed distaste when he was put on trial: 'I have no sympathy for Touvier [But at that age] it's juridically absurd...I call that hounding people...They are more relentless now than fifty years ago. We were the ones who suffered and perhaps that's why we were not as harsh.'[22]

Holocaust Education

The organization which, for more than forty years, has been the principal conduit for disseminating Holocaust awareness, especially amongst young

---

[21] Tania Nelson, writing in the *Journal of the '45 Aid Society* No. 16, April Pesach 5753/1993.

[22] Short, Philip 2013 *Mitterrand: A Study in Ambiguity*, p. 557.

people, in the UK is the Holocaust Educational Trust (HET). It was established in January 1988 and, according to Lucy Russell, emerged from a shared belief in the need 'to educate the public in a period of renewed interest in the Nazi war crimes and the Second World War'.[23] HET was set up while the parliamentary All-Party War Crimes Group was pushing hard for the government to commit itself to framing legislation. As Philip Rubenstein explained, these two objectives, though linked, had to be kept separate:

> The war crimes campaign was finding it increasingly difficult to raise funds. It had a political objective and was therefore not eligible for charitable donations. A body with purely educational aims such as HET was eligible and it made sense to separate off the educational work and associated costs into HET. Of course, it had the added authority of a parliamentary base behind it.[24]

The long-time director of HET, Karen Pollock, confirmed the symbiosis between the war crimes campaign and the creation of an organizational structure to promote Holocaust awareness:

> Even now, we always acknowledge that HET was founded on the back of the war crimes bill going through parliament. Put simply, news stories about potential war criminals living in the UK can be translated into people talking about the Holocaust. And during our existence we have supported survivors called to be witnesses in trials. Most recently we supported a survivor who was a co-plaintiff in the trial in Germany of Oskar Groening, the so-called 'bookkeeper of Auschwitz'.[25]

The first step taken by HET was to write to the many organizations representing survivors and compile a directory of Holocaust resources. This required tact and diplomacy because, as Philip Rubenstein noted: 'Many of these groups were jostling for position in a crowded field

---

[23] Russell, 2006 *Teaching the Holocaust in School History*, p. 71.
[24] Rubenstein interview with author, 7 November 2022.
[25] Pollock interview with author, 7 September 2022.

and we certainly didn't want to ruffle any feathers. HET didn't go in for flag-waving.'

The figurehead behind both the War Crimes Group and HET—'the conductor who pulled the orchestra together', in the words of Jon Mendelsohn—was the Labour MP Greville Janner, who had been an investigator for the British army in occupied Germany. In his memoirs, he wrote: 'We must educate young people, in their schools and universities, through lectures and especially through visits to the dread horrors of Auschwitz-Birkenau. So we made up a cadre of Holocaust survivors, brave and ready to tell their stories in schools and institutions.'[26]

Janner's Polyanna-ish persuasiveness, for whichever cause he adopted, was undoubtedly a factor in HET quickly putting down firm roots, though, in relation to the war crimes objectives, he was chided by some of his fellow members of the All-Party Group for being more of a tactician than a strategist. They pointed out that, in a long parliamentary career, he had never held ministerial office, steered a bill through Parliament, or even undertaken a vote count.[27] As Rubenstein said:

When the Wiesenthal Center presented its list of alleged war criminals to the government in 1986, Greville never expected it to go anywhere and certainly not to lead to legislation. I was at the first meeting with the then Home Secretary, Douglas Hurd, in 1987 and it was clear to us that the issue of war criminals in the UK was like a bad smell which Hurd wanted off his desk as soon as possible. When he realised that the pressure to act would not relent, he eventually ordered the inquiry under Hetherington-Chalmers. Most of us were expecting the inquiry to be a whitewash. For Greville, it was at least an opportunity to keep the issue in the public eye.[28]

In this respect, a developing awareness of the Holocaust, partly stimulated through survivor voices and made more salient by arguments ventilated through the media over the proposed National Curriculum in teaching,

[26] Janner, 2006 *To Life!*
[27] Subsequently, Janner became the subject of a police inquiry into child sex abuse which led to charges in 2015. He died the same year.
[28] Rubenstein interview with author, 7 November 2022.

was undoubtedly helpful. Andy Pearce in his book *Holocaust Consciousness in Contemporary Britain* (2014) locates the cultural debate which preceded the adoption of the inaugural National Curriculum in 1991 within the polarized politics of the late Thatcher period. For our purposes, it is sufficient to note that the History Working Group's initial proposal for the compulsory elements of the curriculum was criticized for 'the omission of the two World Wars and related studies such as fascism'.[29] The campaigners for war crimes legislation saw this as an opportunity for some astute political lobbying, as Philip Rubenstein explained:

> The idea of a National Curriculum was controversial anyway because it was seen by some critics as a French import, imposing a top-down view of education. When the internal report of the History Working Group was leaked, it was obvious that there would be a degree of public and media outrage. We took advantage by organising a letter of complaint to the Secretary of State for Education, John Patten, signed by a host of distinguished soldiers, Field Marshals and the like, about the omission from the proposed curriculum of the two world wars. Patten was furious about the leak but, after several twists and turns, the government decided that the Holocaust should be part of the National Curriculum for fourteen to sixteen-year-olds.[30]

In Pearce's judgement, the concurrence of the campaign for war crimes legislation and the debate over the role of education were seminal developments:

> These two occurrences from 1991 – the War Crimes Act and the National Curriculum – changed the status of the Holocaust in British culture and society, helping to alter perceptions…In fact, both signalled the dawn of an institutionalization of the Holocaust: a process aligned to the formation of cultural memory, and one which would climax a decade later with HMD [Holocaust Memorial Day] and other events.[31]

---

[29]   Little, 1990 'A National Curriculum in History: A Very Contentious Issue', pp. 328–9.
[30]   Rubenstein interview, 7 November 2022.
[31]   Pearce, 2018 *Holocaust Consciousness in Contemporary Britain*, p. 60.

Bearing Witness

The willingness of survivors to appear in public forums in the 1980s marked a sea change from the immediate post-war years. Although it is a canard that they were, in the main, silent about their experiences at that time, society proved generally unreceptive to hearing horror stories from the European cataclysm. From the late 1940s onwards, written first-person accounts began to filter into the public realm but were regarded as a niche genre of publishing, of interest to a limited readership. The *Diary of Anne Frank* in 1952, by 'personalizing' the fate of Jewish families under Nazi oppression, struck a wider chord, eventually attaining a global resonance, reinforced by the more reflective works of survivors such as Elie Wiesel and Primo Levi. It was no accident that these were accounts from Western European inmates of the 'concentrationary universe', as Timothy Snyder has pointed out:

> After World War II, West European Jewish survivors were free to write and publish as they liked, whereas East European Jewish survivors, if caught behind the iron curtain, could not. In the West, memoirs of the Holocaust could (although very slowly) enter into historical writing and public consciousness.[32]

Levi's is perhaps the voice which has resonated most strongly with readers:

> I repress hatred even within myself. I prefer justice. Precisely, for this reason, when describing the tragic world of Auschwitz, I have deliberately assumed the calm, sober language of the witness, neither the lamenting tones of the victim nor the irate voice of someone who seeks revenge... only in this way does a witness in matters of justice perform his task, which is that of preparing the ground for the judge. The judges are my readers.[33]

---

[32] Snyder, 2009 'Holocaust: The Ignored Reality'.
[33] Levi, 1947/1987 *If This Is a Man/The Truce*, p. 382.

Some survivors had literal contact with judges when they gave evidence in court against alleged perpetrators and learned a harsh lesson that personal accounts were required to be subservient to the larger purpose of legal 'truth'. David Hirsh, who sat through the Sawoniuk trial in London, has written perceptively about the ways:

> in which the testimonies elicited were transformed from memoirs of the Holocaust by the norms and rules of the trial process into legally admissible evidence by the processes of cross-examination... For a survivor, the demand that the court makes, that it be allowed to take control of the presentation of memoir, to challenge it and to transform it into what it considers to be evidence, must be particularly difficult.[34]

At least the survivors in the Sawoniuk case 'had their day in court' even if their memories had to be tailored to the prosecution's needs. At Nuremberg, the voice of the victim was all but absent and, reflecting on the manner in which the UK's interpretation of 'legally admissible' evidence left a glaring accountability gap for the commission of thousands of crimes, Efraim Zuroff complained: 'That could only have happened if the victims were without any voice, or any advocates. And that, in my opinion, is a terrible tragedy.'[35]

As stated a number of times in this book, the individual investigations of the 1990s were foregrounded as murder inquiries, with the Nazi's genocidal campaign against the Jews implicit in the discursive framing of the War Crimes Act. In the words of Treasury Counsel, Sir John Nutting:

> I took the view that if you had a gravesite containing fifteen Jewish women, the only questions for a jury to answer were 'how did they die?' and 'was it connected to the abuse of the laws and customs of war?'[36]

---

[34] Hirsh, 2001 'The Trial of Andrei Sawoniuk: Holocaust Testimony Under Cross-Examination', p. 1.

[35] Zuroff interview with author, 29 August 2022.

[36] Nutting interview with author, 28 May 2021.

Exceptionally for a highly sensitive police-led inquiry, there was no attempt to erect a kind of cordon sanitaire to shut out those who had helped propel the legislation onto the statute book. As Jon Mendelsohn recalls:

> The All-Party Group, many of whom were not Jewish, worked closely with the police unit. We were useful in supplying names of survivors who could provide insights into what had happened in particular territories such as Belarus. We had dinner with Chief Superintendent Eddie Bathgate and his deputy David Sibley every six months or so and occasionally we would see the overall operational commander, David Veness and even the Commissioner, Paul Condon. In fact, the relationship was so close that I was invited to Bathgate's farewell dinner at the Yard. I was the only non-police guest present.[37]

After Bathgate retired in 1994, the Home Office reduced the funding for the unit in the mistaken belief that there were unlikely to be any prosecutions. But the decision was reversed after some discreet but effective lobbying. This unusual degree of access had another 'beneficial' consequence. In the early 1990s, some of the MPs on the All-Party War Crimes Group—especially those who were lawyers—were given regular updates by the then Attorney-General, Sir Patrick Mayhew. This included discussion, on confidential 'Privy Council' terms, of individual cases.

If some of this can be attributed to the growing significance of the Holocaust in the civic and cultural responsiveness of British institutions, it is noteworthy that a scrupulous 'separation of powers' was observed between pedagogy and justice, between the educational lessons to be learned from studying Nazi collaboration and the juridical process leading to a war crimes trial. Neither the aborted prosecution of Szymon Serafinowicz nor the full trial of Andrzej Sawoniuk were conceived of as anything other than exercises in legal accountability. Contrast that with the prosecution of the wartime Gestapo chief of Lyons, Klaus Barbie in 1987, framed as a 'pedagogic trial'.[38] It was exemplified by the decision

---

[37] Mendelsohn interview with author, 16 September 2022.
[38] Binder, 1989 'Representing Nazism: Advocacy and Identity at the Trial of Klaus Barbie'.

of the local authority in Lyons to encourage parties of schoolchildren to observe the proceedings.[39] In it, as Lawrence Douglas notes, the experiences of survivors were required to fit an ideological master narrative: 'The French prosecution was especially interested in presenting tales of atrocity through the testimony of political prisoners, casting the suffering of the nation not in terms of the bleak logic of helpless victimization but rather as the consequence of patriotic, heroic acts of armed resistance.'[40]

Conclusion

This book was not conceptualized as a finger-pointing exercise. Indeed, it is to the credit of both the war crimes police and lawyers that they invested so much time and effort in investigating the most complex 'cold case' in British legal history. At the outset, it may have appeared to them a hopeless task but they were rewarded by obtaining one conviction. Of course, set against the unfathomable enormity of the Holocaust, it can only be counted as a minor juridical 'triumph' and even the staunchest supporters of the war crimes legislation would concede that it was a case of 'too little, too late'. Conversely, those who opposed the bill felt that the outcome vindicated their view that it was a quest which the country should never have embarked upon.

Our intention has been to explain why more was not achieved. It is for the reader to decide whether the evidence presented in this book warranted a different approach. In any event, those hoping for legacies from this period would have to search hard to find any. In the wake of Rwanda's genocide of 1994—a rate of killing which even outdid the Holocaust—a number of *genocidaires* fled to the UK (among other European countries). During the Cold War, extradition requests from the Soviet Union were rejected because no treaty existed between the two countries. There is such a treaty with Rwanda but, in refusing to send them back, successive British governments have explained that

---

[39] One of the authors, Jon Silverman, reported on the trial for the BBC.
[40] Douglas, 2001 *The Memory of Judgment*, p. 196.

they could not be guaranteed a fair trial. Countries such as France and Belgium have used the principle of universal jurisdiction to hold their own trials of Rwandan suspects. Britain has not, although it seemingly does not find it incompatible with human rights norms to consider sending failed asylum seekers from all over the world to Rwanda.

In the third decade of the twenty-first century, ninety years after Hitler came to power fuelled by an insensate anti-Semitism, the Holocaust must, of course, continue to be a subject of memorialization and education. But if the UK's attempt to hold Nazi collaborators to account for their crimes tells us anything it is that there are some challenges which are beyond the capacity of the law to address.

Bibliography

Primary Sources

Australia, National Library of. Australia/Israel Review, 15 February–7 March 1995.

Australia, Special Investigation Unit. Affidavit of Juozas Knyrimas sworn on 6 October 1961, reference SIU 572.

Australian Attorney-General's Department. *Report of the Investigations of War Criminals in Australia*, Sydney, NSW, 1993.

Australian Government. Review of Material Relating to the Entry of Suspected War Criminals into Australia, 28 November 1986.

Birmingham, City Police, Chief Constable's Office. Application by Stanislaw Chrzanowski for naturalization, 12 June 1961. Ref: CID no 61/12813.

Charter of the International Military Tribunal. London, 8 August 1945. Charter V 'Powers of the Tribunal and Conduct of the Trial Art.19' Agreement for the Prosecution and Punishment of the Major War Criminals of the European Axis.

Chicago, US District Court. Case of Konrad Kalejs, 1 November 1998.

Crown Prosecution Service. *War Crimes: CPS Statement*, 13 October 1999.

Hatherill Report, The. 3 January 1940.

His Majesty's Stationery Office, The All-Party Parliamentary War Crimes Group, *Nazi War Criminals in the United Kingdom*, HMSO, 1989.

His Majesty's Stationery Office, Hetherington, Sir Thomas and Chalmers, William, *War Crimes: Report of the War Crimes Inquiry*. London: HMSO, 1989.

Home Office, UK Government Note from R. G. Jones to Frank W. Willis, 17 March 1972 HO Ref: Z40167 File ENs14/2.

House of Commons Briefing Paper, *Deprivation of British Citizenship and withdrawal of passport facilities* no.06820, 9 June 2017.

Shawcross, Sir Hartley. Britain's chief prosecutor at the International Military Tribunal at Nuremberg. *Trial of the Major War Criminals Before the International Military Tribunal Nuremberg, 14 November 1945–1 October 1946*. 42 vols. (Nuremberg Military Tribunal 1947), 3:92.

Straw Jack, Home Secretary statement re- 'Konrad Kalejs', 6 January 2000.

United States, Department of Justice. Post-trial brief on Konrad Kalejs prepared by the Office of Special Investigations, February 1995.

United States, Presidential proclamations 2655, 2656, 2657 which related to Japan, Germany, and Italy respectively.

University of Southampton, Special Collections, The head of *Einsatzgruppe A*, Dr Franz Stahlecker, Report, 29 September 1941, copy in Hartley Library Collection, MS 408_A1057 2/39, p. 468.

Archival Sources

Bundesarchiv Ludwigsburg, B162/2860.

Hansard

Hansard, House of Commons Parliamentary Debates, 28 October 1948, vol. 457, cc 272.

Hansard, House of Commons Debates, 19 March 1990, vol. 169, cc 950–1.

Hansard, House of Commons Parliamentary Debates, 18 March 1991, vol 188, cc 23–112.

Hansard, House of Lords Debates, 7 October 1942, vol. 124 cols. 583/584.

Hansard, House of Lords Debates, 7 October 1942, vol. 124 cc 585.

Hansard, House of Lords Debates, 15 May 1949, vol. 612, cc 376, 389–91.

Hansard, House of Lords Debates, 8 March 1990, vol. 516 cc1297-8WA.

Hartley Library

Hartley Library Special Collections, University of Southampton. Transcript of witness statements tendered in evidence in case of Serafinowicz, Simon. Archive file MS 408_A1057 1/9.

Hartley Library Special Collections, University of Southampton. Martin Dean Historical Briefing Paper dealing with the Mir and Turets Police Unit, 23 and 26 November 1991. Archive file MS 408_A1057 2/3.

Hartley Library Special Collections, University of Southampton. Police Exhibit No. HC/128. Archive file MS 408_A1057 2/5.

Hartley Library Special Collections, University of Southampton. Post Report no. 212543. Archive file MS 408_A1057 2/6.

Hartley Library Special Collections, University of Southampton. Material originated from the Oldenburg Public Prosecutor's Office, Lower Saxony, Germany, 1969 in connection with the trial of Max Eibner. Archive file MS 408_A1057 2/6.

Hartley Library Special Collections, University of Southampton. Reinhold Hein report to the Gendarmerie Regional Commander, Baranovichi, 6 July 1942. Archive file MS 408_A1057 2/9.

Hartley Library Special Collections, University of Southampton. Report 11 202 AR-Z 16/67 in connection with the trial of Max Eibner. Archive file MS408_A1057 2/10.

Hartley Library Special Collections, University of Southampton. Report by SS Haupsturmführer, Capt and squadron commander. Archive file MS 408_A1057 2/10.

Hartley Library Special Collections, University of Southampton. Archive file MS 408_A1057 2/30.

Hartley Library Special Collections, University of Southampton. Notes of case review by Martin Dean and Det. Supt. David Sibley. Archive file MS 408_A1057 2/35.

Hartley Library Special Collections, University of Southampton. Martin Dean report 23–27 November 1992. Archive file MS 408_A1057 2/35.

Hartley Library Special Collections, University of Southampton. Martin Dean note of case review 14 July 1994. Archive file MS 408_A1057 2/35.

Hartley Library Special Collections, University of Southampton. Martin Dean report 7 May 1994 Ref:5423. Archive file MS 408_A1057 2/35.

Hartley Library Special Collections, University of Southampton. Police Exhibit No: HC/134.

Hartley Library Special Collections, University of Southampton. Witness statements SOBLP89; SOBLP289; SOBLPX88. Archive file MS 408_A1057 2/35.

Hartley Library Special Collections, University of Southampton. Archive file MS 408_A1057 2/38 NS/136.

Hartley Library Special Collections, University of Southampton. Unused prosecution material in Serafinowicz case 380–841. Archive file MS 408_A1057.

Hartley Library Special Collections, Southampton. Exhibit HC/182. Archive file MS 408_A1057 2/41.

Hartley Library Special Collections, University of Southampton. Archive file MS 408_A1057 2/41.

Hartley Library Special Collections, University of Southampton. Martin Dean letter to Browning 13 July 1995. Archive file MS 408_A1057 2/43.

Hartley Library Special Collections, University of Southampton. Files of Polish Resettlement Corps, Hayes. Archive file MS 408_A1057 2/44.

Hartley Library Special Collections, University of Southampton. Letter from J. L. Irvine dated 18 February 1947 to unknown recipient. Archive file MS 408_A1057 2/44.

Hartley Library Special Collections, University of Southampton. Archive file MS 408_A1057 4/2.

Imperial War Museum

Imperial War Museum. Taped interview with Savile Geoffrey Champion, IWM. 2323, 1993.

Imperial War Museum, London. Taped interview with Lord Peter Eden, IWM. 17971, 4 April 1998.

Imperial War Museum, London. Taped interview with Ian Neilson. 18537, November 1998.

Tass (Russian News Agency) Eng.1648 FCO 28/2087 File no: ENs14/2.

International Military Tribunal, Nuremberg (IMT)

International Military Tribunal Nuremberg. Carl, Gebeitskommissar Carl report to Generalkommissar of Minsk, Wilhelm Kube, 30 October 1941; document PS-1104.

KGB Archive, Minsk

Minsk KGB Archives. Ivan Grigoryevich Lyakhov interrogation by Head of Section 3 of the Investigation Dept. of the MGB Directorate for Baranovichi province, 16 July 1951. Pp 1155–1169.

Lithuanian Central State Archives, Vilnius

Lithuanian Central State Archives, Vilnius. File R683 series 1 folder 5.

National Records of Scotland (Edinburgh)

National Records of Scotland. Collection AD 43/1/1.
National Records of Scotland. Collection AD 43/1/1/4.
National Records of Scotland. Collection AD43/3/11.
National Records of Scotland. File SIU 624/2, collection AD 43/3/12/1.
National Records of Scotland. File 3443/WCP 11/8, collection AD43/3/12/5.
National Records of Scotland. File 011/02, collection AD43/3/12/9.
National Records of Scotland. Collection AD 43/3/12/10.
National Records of Scotland. Collection AD 43/3/12/11.
National Records of Scotland. Collection AD 43/3/12/12.

United Kingdom Archives, Kew (UKNA)

UKNA CAB CM (48)47(3) and CP (48)151; CP(48) 159;CP(48)165.
UKNA CAB 65/44, November 1944.
UKNA DPP 2/13571, 6 November 1991.
UKNA DPP 2/13571.
UKNA FCO 28/2087. ENs 14/2. No. 2/2E.
UKNA FCO 28/2087K150A MA4, 18 April 1972.
UKNA FCO 28/20873, May 1972.
UKNA FO 371 24422/C2544 17.2.40.
UKNA FO 371 24422/C2901 26.2.40.
UKNA FO 371 26540.
UKNA FO 371 26540/11999.
UKNA FO 371 34367.8796/31/62KNA.
UKNA FO 371 64723 c15911/7675/180, 9 December 1947.
UKNA FO 371 65754, 21 January 1947.
UKNA FO 371 77060, CG 3545/15/184.
UKNA HO C39016/3, 20 June 1951.
UKNA WO 32/11726.
UKNA WO 32/12202.
UKNA WO 309 (JAG).
UKNA WO 309/1418.
UKNA WO 309/1816; GWDN: 7213–7215.
UKNA WO 311/8 4.9.44.
UKNA WO 311/8 4.9.44.
UKNA WO 311/61.

United Kingdom National Archives Storage Facility Hayes, Middlesex

Polish Resettlement Corps, files.

United States Department of Justice

United States Department of Justice. Deposition of Anton Gecas in case of Jurgis Juodis, 12 August 1982 C.A. No.81-1013-CIV-T-H.

United States Holocaust Memorial Museum

United States Holocaust Memorial Museum. Case of Viktor Bernhard Arājs RG-06.009.03, US Department of Justice, Office of Special Investigations, USHMM, Microfiche.

United States Holocaust Memorial Museum. Peter Black Oral History Interview USHMM Collections Division Archives Branch Accession no. 2000.169 RG No RG-50.030.0409.

United States Holocaust Memorial Museum. Collection of Erlean McCarrick, Accession no. 1997.A.0189 USHMM Shapell Center.

United States Holocaust Memorial Museum. Collection of Major Peter Clapham, governor of Lüneberg Prison. Accession no. 1994.A.0022. RG No.10.232.

United States Holocaust Memorial Museum, Martin Dean papers, Accession no. 2015.449.1.

United States Holocaust Museum. Detective Chief Superintendent Eddie Bathgate's First Historical Report, 1 June 1993. Christopher Browning Papers Box 18, USHMM Collections, Shapell Center. Bowie, MD.

United States Holocaust Memorial Museum. Encyclopedia.

United States Holocaust Memorial Museum. Vladimir Izvestnyi, Oral Interview, USHMM Collections Division Archives Branch. Oral History Accession no. 2003.456.29 RG No: RG-50.568.0029.

United States Holocaust Memorial Museum. Accession no. 1998.A.0221.10. RG No RG-50.473.0010.

University of Southern California

University of Southern California Taed Interview with Pearl Fiegler, 6 March 1995, USC VHA 1293.

University of Southern University. Taped interview with Henry Tauber, 8 April 1997, USC VHA 28006.

War Crimes Inquiries

War Crimes Inquiry Case number: 79 (Stanislaw Chrzanowski).
Wiesenthal, Simon Center Press Information, issued 3 January 2000.
Worldwide Investigation and Prosecution of Nazi War Criminals published by the Simon Wiesenthal Center Israel Office, Jerusalem/Snider Social Action Institute.

Wiener Library, London

Wiener Library Doct.Series, Metzner Affidavit, NO5530 1655/2713, 15 October 1947.

Yad Vashem, The World Holocaust Remembrance Center, Jerusalem
Yad Vashem Museum, Jerusalem. Statement of Aharon Harkarvi, no. 2104/96 SIU 5612 or PU443.

Published Primary Sources

Daghani, A. (1961) *The Grave is in the Cherry Orchard*. London: Eden Press.
Janner, G. (2006) *To Life! The Memoirs of Greville Janner*. Stroud: Sutton Publishing.
Levi, P. (1947/1987) *If This Is a Man/The Truce*. London: Penguin.
Lynton, M. (1998) *Accidental Journey: A Cambridge Internee's Memoir of World War II*. New York: Peter Mayer Publishers.
Michelson, F. (1981) *I Survived Rumbuli*. Washington, DC: United States Holocaust Memorial Museum.
Rogers, G. R. (1998) *Interesting Times*. Hope Valley, S. Australia: Garry R. Rogers.

Unpublished Material

Edelstein, B. (undated) in the collection of evidence prepared for the indictment of Viktors Arājs, 141 JS 534/60, pp. 6075–97.
Warner, F. (1985) *A Very Personal Account* (Private Publication).

Interviews, Emails, and Correspondence

Ackland, David. Letter to David Kingston, 22 April 1988.
Adamovitch, Father Kazimir. Interview with one of the authors, March 1996.
Angrick, Andrej. Email to one of the authors, 16 February 2022.
Bagley, Ivan Yacovlevich interview in Domachevo, 28 July 1997.
Bathgate, Eddie. Letter to John Kingston, 21 October 1991.

Bathgate, Eddie. Letter to John Kingston.

Bathgate, Eddie. Interview with one of the authors, 4 October 1996.

Bathgate, Eddie. Telephone interview with one of the authors, 24 July 2017.

Bland, Robert. Letter to John Kingston, 13 December 1996.

Bland, Robert. Interview with one of the authors, 3 September 1998.

Blewitt, Graham. Telephone interview with one of the authors, 17 February 2020.

Blunkett, David. Letter to Efraim Zuroff, HO 2506X2, 7 February 2002.

Cavendish, Anthony. Interview with Tom Bower BBC-2 'Newsnight', 11 December 1989.

Chuwen, Anthony. Interview with one of the authors, 14 May 1999.

Clegg, William. Interview with one of the authors, 28 April 2021.

Coates, Kay. Letter to Mr P. Shaw Home Office ref: C.45064/4, FCO ref:28/1156, on 30 January 1970.

Damasevicius, Julius. Interview with one of the authors, 16 October 2000.

Dean, Martin. Email to one of the authors, 20 May 1999.

Dean, Martin. Email to one of the authors, 2 February 2001.

Dean, Martin. Email to one of the authors, 14 February 2022.

Dean, Martin. Email to one of the authors, 11 April 2022.

Dean, Martin. Interview with both authors, 20 September 2022.

Dean, Martin. Email to one of the authors, 7 October 2021.

Drinkald, David. Email to one of the authors, 12 October 2018.

Drinkald, David. Interview with both authors, 25 August 2021.

Eden, Lord Peter. Interview with one of the authors, 13 October 2016.

Edgerton, Carolyn. Telephone interview with one of the authors, 5 March 2018.

Fry, Helen. Email to one of the authors, 11 February 2019.

Glees, Anthony Professor. Interview with one of the authors, 18 June 1996.

Goetzfrid, Alfons. Interview on 8 May 1996. Source: *Justiz und NS-Verbrechen* (Amsterdam: Amsterdam University Press, 2012) vol. 48, Lfd. Nr. 916, pp. 616–17.

Halpern, Sam. Interview with one of the authors, 28 June 1999.

Harrison, Paul. Interview with one of the authors, 13 September 1995.

Harrison, Paul. Interview with one of the authors, 27 June 1996.

Harrison, Paul. Email to one of the authors, 11 February 2022.

Harrison, Paul. Email, to one of the authors, 12 July 2021.

Hertz, J. H. Chief Rabbi to the UK and British Empire, cited in Antero Holmila, *Reporting the Holocaust in the British, Swedish and Finnish Press, 1945–50* (Basingstoke: Palgrave Macmillan, 2011).

Hetherington, Sir Thomas. Interview with one of the authors, 5 July 1995.

Kingston, John. Letter to the Secretary, War Crimes Inquiry, 11 April 1988.

Kingston, John. Letter to the War Crimes Inquiry, 15 May 1988.

Kingston, John. Interview with one of the authors, 15 August 1995.

Kingston, John. Interview with one of the authors.

Kingston, John. Interview with one of the authors, 29 November 1995.

Kingston, John. Conversations with one of the authors, February/March 1996.

Lee, Martin. Interview with one of the authors, 3 September 1998.

Lee, Martin. Interview with one of the authors, 17 May 2021.

McDermott, Dermott. Letter from British Board of Deputies, 19 October 1999.

McDermott, Dermot. Interview with one of the authors, 29 August 2017.

McDermott, Dermot. Email to one of the authors, 5 March 2018.

Mendelsohn, Lord Jon. Interview with one of the authors, 16 September 2022.

Milligan, Lord. Opinion *in causa* Antony Gecas, Pursuer, against Scottish Television PLC (Defenders), 17 July 1992.

Montgomery, John. Interview with one of the authors, 26 February 2018.

Montgomery, John. Interview with both authors, 16 November 2022.

Moore, Charlie. Interview with one of the authors, 19 February 2018.

Nutting, Sir John. Interview with one of the authors, 31 August 2020.

Nutting, Sir John. Interview with one of the authors, 28 May 2021.

Pollock, Karen. Interview with one of the authors, 7 September 2022.

Rosenbaum, Eli. Email to one of the authors, 28 April 1999.

Rosenbaum, Eli. Email to both authors, 5 March 2001.

Rosenbaum, Eli. Interview with both authors, 18 September 2022.

Rosenbaum, Eli. Email to both authors, 7 October 2022.

Rosenbaum, Eli. Email to both authors, 8 October 2022.

Rosensaft, Dr Hadassah, Belsen survivor, speaking at a conference in Washington in 1981 to mark The Liberation of the Nazi Concentration Camps 1945. *Eyewitness Accounts of the Liberators* US Holocaust Memorial Council 1987.

Rubenstein, Philip. Interview with one of the authors, 7 November 2022.

Ruxton, Gavin. Interview with both authors, 16 November 2022.

Sher, Neal. Interview with one of the authors, 25 June 1996.

Sibley, David. Email to one of the authors, 3 February 2018.

Sienko, Nicholas. Interview with one of the authors, 17 October 1996.

Soroka, Miriam. Interview in Jerusalem, 18 February 1990.

Southall, Nick. Email to one of the authors, 12 December 2018.

Stern, Guy, a former 'Ritchie Boy', interview with one of the authors, 29 March 2017.

Straw, Jack. Letter to Efraim Zuroff, HO 9704js, 31 January 2000.

Tomkins, Peter. Interview with one of the authors, 2 January 1997.

Tomlinson, Bob. Interview one of the authors, 13 August 2021.

Unnamed source in the SOI. Informal discussion with one of the authors, 5 January 2000.

Vlahovic, Rajka. Interview with one of the authors, 25 February 2020.

Will, Thomas. Interview with the authors, 30 March 2022.

Zuroff, Efraim. Letter (faxed), to one of the authors, 21 February 2002.

Zuroff, Efraim. Interview with one of the authors, 29 August 2022.

Internet Sites Accessed

BBC News Website, Janis Osis interview with one of the authors, accessed on the website, www.bbc.co.uk 'Latvia Killers Rehabilitated', 26 January 2000.

BBC News Website, Arnis Upmalis interview with one of the authors, accessed on the BBC News website, www.bbc.co.uk 'Latvia Killers Rehabilitated', 26 January 2000.

BBC Shropshire, 'Telford Pensioner Investigated for War Crimes'. https://www.bbc. co.uk/news/uk-england-shropshire-43441118- (accessed 30 March 2021).

Bergen-Belsen Trial Transcripts. http//www.bergenbelsen.co.uk/pages/TrialTranscript_ TrialContents.html (accessed 4 October 2017).

German Federal Court of Justice Decision 2 Ars 252/17 2AR 142/17.

Herald of Scotland. https://www.heraldscotland.com/news/12286078.war-crime-suspect-found-out-by-british/ 14 October 1997 (accessed 5 November 2021).

Herald of Scotland. Rabbi Abraham Cooper, Associate Dean of the Simon Wiesenthal Center in Los Angeles, 18 July 1992. https://www.heraldscotland. com/news/12641016.tv-company-cleared-of-libel-judge-brands-gecas-mass-murderer-and-war-criminal/ (accessed 5 May 2022).

Jewish Telegraphic Agency (Historical Archive), 28 April 1970. https://www.jta.org/ archive/britain-refuses-to-extradite-man-soviets-claim-murdered-ukrainian-jews-in-world-war-ii (accessed 18 April 2022).

Jewish Virtual Library. https://www.jewishvirtuallibrary.org/war-crimes-trials (accessed 20 June 2022).

Klapprott v. United States, 335 U.S. 601, 612 (1949).89.

Marienfelde Refugee Camp, 1953. https://www.criticalpast.com/video/65675045315

Moscow Declaration, The, published 1 November 1943.

Minister of Citizenship and Immigration v. Vitols Part IV.

R v. Turnbull [1977] QB224.

R v. Bow St Metropolitan Stipendiary Magistrate, ex parte Pinochet Ugarte (no. 2) (House of Lords), 25 November 1998 [2000] 1 at 84. AC 61.

United States v. Wittje, 333 F.Supp.2d 737,748(N.D.I11.2004)aff'd,422 F.3d 479 (7th Cir.2005).

Secondary Sources

Published Material

Aarons, M. (1989) *Sanctuary: Nazi Fugitives in Australia*. Melbourne: William Heinemann.

Abzug, R. H. (1985) *Inside the Viscous Heart: Americans and the Liberation of Nazi Concentration Camps*. Oxford: Oxford University Press.

Aldrich, R. J. (ed.) (1998) *Espionage, Security and Intelligence in Britain 1945–1970*. Manchester: Manchester University Press.

Anderson, M. and Hanson, N. (2022) *The Ticket Collector from Belarus*. London: Simon & Schuster.

Angrick, A. (2020) ' "Operation Blue," Einsatzgruppen D and the Genocide in the Caucasus', in C. Brooks and K. Feferman (eds.), *Beyond the Pale: The Holocaust in the North Caucasus*. Rochester, NY: University of Rochester Press, pp. 69–94.

Angrick, A. and Klein, P. (2009) *The "Final Solution" in Riga: Exploitation and Annihilation, 1941–1944*. Translated from German by Ray Brandon. Oxford: Berghahn Books.

Arendt, H. (1977) *Eichmann in Jerusalem: A Report on the Banality of Evil.* London: Penguin Random House.

Ashman, C. and Wagman, R. J. (1988) *The Nazi Hunters.* New York: Pharos.

Baranova, O. (2016) 'Collaborators, Bystanders or Rescuers: The Role of Local Citizens in the Holocaust in Nazi-Occupied Belarus', in A. Löw and F. Bajohr (eds.), *The Holocaust and European Societies: Social Processes and Social Dynamics,* pp. 89–104.

Barnes, J. (2021) Julian Barnes on *The Sense of an Ending*: 'I learned to do more by saying less', *The Guardian,* 12 June.

Bar-On, D. (1989) *Legacy of Silence: Encounters with Children of the Third Reich.* Cambridge, MA: Harvard University Press.

Bauer, Y. (2010) *The Death of the Shtetl.* New Haven CT: Yale University Press.

Bazhko, A. (1982) *Total Bankruptcy,* 2nd edn. Minsk: n.p.

Beresford, N. (2012) *The Belsen Trials, 1945–48.* Marston Gate, Buckinghamshire: Amazon Books.

Binder, G. (1989) 'Representing Nazism: Advocacy and Identity at the Trial of Klaus Barbie', *Yale Law Journal* 98, pp. 1321–83.

Bloxham, D. (2001) *Genocide on Trial: War Crimes Trials and the Formation of Holocaust History and Memory.* Oxford: Oxford University Press.

Bloxham, D. (2003) 'British War Crimes Trial Policy in Germany, 1945–1957: Implementation and Collapse', *Journal of British Studies* 42(1), pp. 91–118.

Bloxham, D. (2004) 'From Streicher to Sawoniuk: The Holocaust in the Courtroom', in Dan Stone (ed.), *The Historiography of the Holocaust.* Basingstoke: Palgrave Macmillan, pp. 397–419.

Bouwknegt, T. B. and Nistor, A.-L. (2019) 'Studying "Perpetrators" through the Lens of the Criminal Trial', in A. Smeulers, A. Weerdesteijn, and B. Holá (eds.), *Perpetrators of International Crimes.* Oxford: Oxford University Press, pp. 89–114.

Bower, T. (1981) *Blind Eye to Murder: Britain, America and the Purging of Nazi Germany—A Pledge Bet.* London: Warner Books.

Brandon, R. and Lower, W. (eds.) (2008) *The Shoah in Ukraine: History, Testimony, Memorialization.* Bloomington: Indiana University Press.

Bridgman, J. (1990) *The End of the Holocaust: The Liberation of the Camps.* Portland, OR: Areopagitica Press.

Browning, C. (1992) *Ordinary Men: Reserve Police Battalion 101 and the Final Solution in Poland.* New York: HarperCollins.

Browning, C. (2010) 'The Nazi Empire', in D. Bloxham and A. D. Moses (eds.), *The Oxford Handbook of Genocide Studies* in Bloxham. Oxford: Oxford University Press, pp. 407–25.

Campbell, B. (2018) 'Fermanagh War Hero Who Captured Suspected SS Butcher Dies at Age 98', *Belfast Telegraph,* 14 September. https://www.belfasttelegraph.co.uk/news/northern-ireland/fermanagh-war-hero-who-captured-suspected-ss-butcher-dies-at-age-98-37314604.html (accessed 23 June 2022).

Cesarani, D. (1992) *Justice Delayed: How Britain Became a Refuge for Nazi War Criminals.* London: Heinemann.

Cesarani, D. (2001) 'Getting Away with Murder', *The Guardian,* 25 April.

Crasnianski, T. (2016) *Children of Nazis: The Sons and Daughters of Himmler, Göring, Höss, Mengele, and Others – Living with a Father's Monstrous Legacy*. New York: Arcade Publishing.

Dallin, A. (1981) *German Rule in Russia, 1941–45: A Study of Occupation Policies*, 2nd edn. London: Macmillan.

Dean, M. (2000) *Collaboration in the Holocaust: Crimes of the Local Police in Belorussia and Ukraine, 1941–44*. New York: St. Martin's Press.

Dean, M. (2005) 'Soviet War Crimes Lists and Their Role in the Investigation of Nazi War Criminals in the West, 1987–2000', in Alfred Gottwaldt, Norbert Kampe and Peter Klein (ed.) *NS-Gewaltherrschaft: Beiträge zur historischen Forschung und juristischen Aufarbeitung*. Berlin: Hentrich.

Dean, M. (2008) 'Soviet Ethnic Germans and the Holocaust in the Reich Commissariat Ukraine' in R. Brandon and W. Lower (eds.), *The Shoah in Ukraine: History, Testimony, Memorialization*. Bloomington: Indiana University Press, pp. 248–71.

Dean, M. (2010) 'Crime and Comprehension, Punishment and Legal Attitudes: German and Local Perpetrators of the Holocaust in Domachevo, Belarus, in the Records of Soviet, Polish, German, and British War Crimes Investigations', in D. Bankier and D. Michman (eds.), *Holocaust and Justice: Representation and Historiography of the Holocaust in Post-War Trials*. New York: Berghahn Books, pp. 265–80.

Dodd, V. (2000) 'New evidence shows record of war crime suspect was not investigated', *The Guardian*, 6 January.

Douglas, L. (2001) *The Memory of Judgment: Making Law and History in the Trials of the Holocaust*. New Haven, CT: Yale University Press.

Dumitru, D. (2016) *The State, Antisemitism, and Collaboration in the Holocaust*. Cambridge: Cambridge University Press.

Epstein, B. (2008) *The Minsk Ghetto, 1941–1943: Jewish Resistance and Soviet Internationalism*. Oakland, CA: University of California Press.

Erren's Gerhard situation report, 25 January 1942, in E. Klee, W. Dressen, and V. Riess (eds.) *The Good Old Days: The Holocaust as Seen by Its Perpetrators and Bystanders*. Old Saybrook, CT: Konecky, 1991.

Ezergailis, A. (1996) *The Holocaust in Latvia 1941–1944: The Missing Center*. Washington, DC: United States Holocaust Memorial Museum.

Feferman, K. (2003) 'Soviet Investigation of Nazi Crimes in the USSR: Documenting the Holocaust', *Journal of Genocide Research* 5(4). pp. 587–602.

Feigin, J. (2006) *The Office of Special Investigations: Striving for Accountability in the Aftermath of the Holocaust*, ed. Mark M. Richard. Washington, DC: Department of Justice.

Finder, G. N. and Prusin, A. V. (2018) *Justice Behind the Iron Curtain: Nazis on Trial in Communist Poland*. Toronto: University of Toronto Press.

Frank, N. (2021) *The Father: A Revenge*. Hull: Biteback Publishing.

Fraser, D. (2005) *Law After Auschwitz: Towards a Jurisprudence of the Holocaust*. Durham, NC: Carolina Academic Press.

Fraser, D. (2010) *Daviborshch's Cart: Narrating the Holocaust in Australian War Crimes Trials*. Lincoln, NE: University of Nebraska Press.

Fritzsche, P. (2008) 'The Holocaust and the Knowledge of Murder', *Journal of Modern History* 80(3), pp. 594–613.

Fry, H. (2010) *Denazification: Britain's Enemy Aliens, Nazi War Criminals and the Reconstruction of Postwar Europe*. Stroud: The History Press.

Fry, H. (2017) *The London Cage: The Secret History of Britain's World War II Interrogation Centre*. New Haven, CT: Yale University Press.

Frydel, T. (2019) 'Ordinary Men? The Polish Police and the Holocaust in the Subcarpathian Region', in P. Black, B. Bela Rasky, and M. Windsperger (eds.), *Collaboration in the Holocaust and World War II in Eastern Europe*, Wien/Hamburg: New Academic Press, pp. 69–126.

Fulbrook, M. (2018) *Reckonings: Legacies of Nazi Persecution and the Quest for Justice*. Oxford: Oxford University Press.

Garrard, J. and Garrard, C. (2012) *The Life and Fate of Vasily Grossman*. Havertown, PA: Casemate Publishers.

Garrett, L. (2021) *X Troop: The Secret Jewish Commandos Who Helped Defeat the Nazis*. London: Chatto & Windus.

Gilbert, M. (1986) *The Holocaust: The Jewish Tragedy*. New York: Fontana/Collins.

Ginsburgs, G. (1966) *Moscow's Road to Nuremberg: The Soviet Background to the Trial*. Leiden: Martinus Nijhoff.

Glees, A. (1992) 'War Crimes: The Security and Intelligence Dimension', *Intelligence and National Security* 7(3), pp. 242–67.

Goldhagen, D. J. (1996) *Hitler's Willing Executioners: Ordinary Germans and the Holocaust*. New York: Alfred A. Knopf.

Gorycki, L. and Kapralsi, S. (2019) 'Patterns of Collaboration and Genocide Against the Roma: The Case of Poland during the Second World War', in P. Black, B. Bela Rasky, and M. Windsperger (eds.), *Collaboration in the Holocaust and World War II in Eastern Europe*. Wien/Hamburg: New Academic Press.

Haberer, E. (2005) 'History and Justice: Paradigms of the Prosecution of Nazi Crimes', *Holocaust & Genocide Studies* 19(3), pp. 487–519.

Halpern, S. (1996) *Darkness and Hope*. New York: Shengold Publishers.

Hasian, M. A (2006) *Rhetorical Vectors of Memory: National and International Holocaust Trials*. East Lansing: Michigan State University Press.

Hilberg, R. (1961) *The Destruction of the European Jews*. New Haven, CT: Yale University Press.

Hilberg, R. (1993) *Perpetrators, Victims and Bystanders: The Jewish Catastrophe 1933–1945*. London: Harper Perennial.

Hirsh, D. (2001) 'The Trial of Andrei Sawoniuk: Holocaust Testimony Under Cross-Examination', *Social & Legal Studies* 10(4), pp. 529–45.

Hitchcock, W. (2008) *Liberation: The Bitter Road to Freedom, Europe 1944–1945*. London: Faber & Faber.

Hutchinson, R. (1994) *Crimes of War: The Antanas Gecas Affair*. Edinburgh: The Mainstream Publishing Company.

Independent, The (1995) 'War Crimes Suspect Dies During Inquiry', 5 August.

Jeffery, K. (2010) *MI6: The History of the Secret Intelligence Service 1909–1949*. London: Bloomsbury.

Jensen, O. and Szejnmann, C.-C. (eds.) (2008) *Ordinary People as Mass Murderers: Perpetrators in Comparative Perspective*. Basingstoke: Palgrave Macmillan.

Jones, P. D. (1990) 'British Policy Towards German Crimes Against German Jews, 1939–45', *Leo Baeck Institute Year Book* 36(1), pp. 339–66.

Kagan, J. and Cohen, D. (1998) *Surviving the Holocaust with the Russian Jewish Partisans*. Boreham Wood: Vallentine Mitchell.

Kaienburg, H. (1996) 'Jüdische Arbeitslager an der "Strasse" der SS', *Heft* 1(96), pp. 13–39.

Kay, A. J. and Stahel, D. (2020) 'Crimes of the Wehrmacht: A Re-evaluation', *Journal of Perpetrator Research* 3(1), pp. 95–127.

Kemp, A. (1986) *The Secret Hunters*. London: Michael O'Mara Books.

King, C. (2012) 'Can There Be a Political Science of the Holocaust?' *Perspectives in Politics* 10(2), pp. 323–41.

Kinstler, L. (2022). *Come to This Court and Cry: How The Holocaust Ends*. London: Bloomsbury Publishing.

Kopasov, N. (2018) *Memory Laws, Memory Wars: The Politics of the Past in Europe and Russia*. Cambridge: Cambridge University Press.

Kushner, T. (1991) *Jews in British Society, Vol 2: The Jewish Image in Britain in the War*. Southampton: The Parkes Library.

Kushner, T. (2004) 'Britain, the United States and the Holocaust: In Search of a Historiography', in D. Stone (ed.), *The Historiography of the Holocaust*. Basingstoke: Palgrave Macmillan, pp. 253–75.

Kushner, T. (2008) *Belsen for Beginners: The Holocaust in British Heritage*. Basingstoke: Palgrave Macmillan.

Lawson, T. and Pearce, A. (eds.) (2021) *The Palgrave Handbook of Britain and the Holocaust*. Cham: Palgrave Macmillan.

Leader-Maynard, J. (2022) *Ideology and Mass Killing: The Radicalized Security Politics of Genocide and Deadly Atrocities*. Oxford: Oxford University Press.

Le Carré, J. (1969) *A Small Town in Germany*. London: Heinemann.

Lewis, S. (2015) 'Overcoming Hegemonic Martyrdom: The Afterlife of Khatyn in Belarusian Memory', *Journal of Soviet and Post-Soviet Politics and Society* 1(2), pp. 367–401.

Liddell Hart, B. (1951) *The Other Side of the Hill: Germany's Generals, Their Rise and Fall, with Their Own Account of Military Events, 1939–1945*. London: Macmillan.

Little, V. (1990) 'A National Curriculum in History: A Very Contentious Issue', *British Journal of Educational Studies* 38(4), pp. 319–34.

Littman, S. (1983) *War Criminal on Trial: Rauca of Kaunas*. New York: Jewish Gen Inc.

Loftus, J. (1982). *The Belarus Secret*. St. Paul, MN: Paragon House.

London, L. (2000) *Whitehall and the Jews, 1933–1948: British Immigration Policy, Jewish Refugees and the Holocaust*. Cambridge: Cambridge University Press.

Longden, S. (2007) *To the Victor the Spoils*. London: Robinson Publishing.

McKerron, I. and Grey, S. (1994) 'Nazi Mass Killer Was a British Spy', *Daily Express*, 3 February.

Marshall, R. (1990) *In the Sewers of Lvov*. Philadelphia, PA: Scribner's Book Company.

Masters, A. (1984) *The Man Who Was M: The Life of Maxwell Knight*. Oxford: Basil Blackwell.

Mullins, C. (1921) *The Leipzig Trials: An Account of the War Criminals' Trials and a Study of German Mentality*. London: H. F. & G. Witherby.

Nelson, T. (1993) 'Second Generation', *Journal of the '45 Aid Society* 16.

Overy, R. (2001) *Interrogations: The Nazi Elite in Allied Hands, 1945*. London: Allen Lane.

Pearce, A. (2014) *Holocaust Consciousness in Contemporary Britain*. Abingdon: Routledge.

Pendas, D. O. (2006) *The Frankfurt Auschwitz Trial, 1963–1965: Genocide, History and the Limits of the Law*. Cambridge: Cambridge University Press.

Perez, J. G. (2014) *Bergen Belsen Camp: Trial of Josef Kramer and 44 Others*. Createspace Independent Publishing Platform.

Plavnieks, R. (2018) *Nazi Collaborators on Trial during the Cold War: Victors Arājs and the Latvian Security Police*. The Holocaust and Its Contexts. London: Palgrave Macmillan.

Plesch, D. (2017) *Human Rights After Hitler: The Lost History of Prosecuting Axis War Criminals*. Washington, DC: Georgetown University Press.

Prusin, A. V. (2018) 'The "Second" Wave of Soviet Justice: The 1960s War Crimes Trials', in N. J. W. Goda (ed.), *Rethinking Holocaust Justice: Essays across Disciplines*. New York: Berghahn, pp. 129–57.

Redekop, V. N. (2008) 'A Post-Genocidal Justice of Blessing as an Alternative to a Justice of Violence: The Case of Rwanda', in B. Hart (ed.), *Peacebuilding in Traumatized Societies*. Lanham, MD: University Press of America, pp. 205–38.

Reydams, L., Wouters, J., and Ryngaert, C. (eds.) (2012) *International Prosecutors: The Politics of Establishing International Criminal Tribunals*. Oxford: Oxford University Press.

Russell, L. (2006) *Teaching the Holocaust in School History: Teachers or Preachers?* London: A & C Black.

Ryan, A. Jr (1984) *Quiet Neighbours: Prosecuting Nazi War Criminals in America*. Boston, MA: Houghton Mifflin Harcourt.

Seenan, G. (2001) 'Lithuania demands extradition of Nazi war crime suspect from UK', *The Guardian*, 20 February.

Sereny, G. (1995) *Into That Darkness: From Mercy Killing to Mass Murder*. London: Pimlico Publishing.

Shephard, B. (2005) *After Daybreak: The Liberation of Belsen, 1945*. London: Jonathan Cape.

Short, P. (2013) *Mitterrand: A Study in Ambiguity*. London: Bodley Head.

Silamikelis, V. (2002) *With the Baltic Flag: Through Three Occupations*. Riga: Jumava.

Silverman, M. and Yuval-Davis, N. (2002) 'Memorializing the Holocaust in Britain', *Ethnicities* 2(1), pp. 107–23.

Smith, S. D. (2002) *Making Memory: Creating Britain's First Holocaust Centre*. Fort Meters, FL: Quill Press.

Snyder, T. (2009) 'Holocaust: The Ignored Reality', *The New York Review*, 16 July.

Snyder, T. (2010) *Bloodlands: Europe Between Hitler and Stalin*. London: Vintage.

Solonari, V. (2007) 'Patterns of Violence: The Local Population and the Mass Murder of Jews in Bessarabia and Northern Bukovina, July-August 1941', Kritika: Explorations in Russian and Eurasian History 8(4), pp. 749–87.

Sorokina, M. (2005) 'People and Procedures: Toward a History of the Investigation of Nazi Crimes in the USSR', Kritika: Explorations in Russian and Eurasian History 6(4), pp. 797—831.

Tec, N. (1990) In the Lion's Den: The Life of Oswald Rufeisen. New York: Oxford University Press.

Tusa, A. and Tusa, J. (2010) The Nuremberg Trial. New York: Skyhorse Publishing.

Tyas, S. (2020) 'The Kaukasier Kompanie ("Caucasian Company"): Soviet Ethnic Minorities, Collaborators, and Mass Killers', in C. Brooks and K. Feferman (eds.), Beyond the Pale: The Holocaust in the North Caucasus. Rochester, NY: University of Rochester Press, pp. 95–117.

Üngör, U. U. (2019) 'Perpetration as a Process: A Historical-Sociological Model', in A. Smeulers, M. Weerdesteijn, and B. Holá (eds.), Perpetrators of International Crimes. Oxford: Oxford University Press, pp. 117–31.

Vīksne, R. (2005) 'Members of the Arājs Kommando in Soviet Court Files', in The Hidden and Forbidden History of Latvia under Soviet and Nazi Occupations, 1940–1991, Symposium of the Commission of the Historians of Latvia, vol. 14, Institute of the History of Latvia, pp. 118–208.

Walters, G. (2009) Hunting Evil: How the Nazi War Criminals Escaped and the Hunt to Bring Them to Justice. London: Transworld Publishers.

Ward, S. (1995) 'War crimes case is thrown into chaos', The Independent, 27 September.

Weinert, M. S. (2004) 'Cosmopolitan Law – and Cruelty – on Trial', Human Rights & Human Welfare 4(1), pp. 33–42.

Wells, L. W. (1978) The Death Brigade. The Holocaust Library (Published in the United States in 1963 under the title The Janowska Road).

Westermann, E. B. (2010) 'Killers', in P. Hayes and J. K. Roth (eds.), The Oxford Handbook of Holocaust Studies. Oxford: Oxford University Press, pp. 142–55.

Williams, A. T. (2006) A Passing Fury: Searching for Justice at the End of World War II. London: Penguin Random House.

Williams, Major D. (2006) 'The First Day in the Camp', in S. Bardgett and D. Cesarani (eds.), Belsen 1945: New Historical Perspectives. London: Portland Press.

Wilson, A. (2011) Belarus: The Last European Dictatorship. New Haven, CT: Yale University Press.

Zuroff, E. (1994) Occupation: Nazi Hunter. New York: Ktav Publishing House.

Zuroff, E. (2009) Operation Last Chance: One Man's Quest to Bring Nazi Criminals to Justice. New York: Palgrave Macmillan.

Zuroff, E. (2017) 'The Prosecution of Local Nazi Collaborators in Post-Communist Eastern Europe: A Squandered Opportunity to Confront Holocaust Crimes', Loyola of Los Angeles International Comparative Law Review 39(1), pp. 291–305.

Unpublished Material

Alexander, M. (2015) 'Nazi Collaborators, American Intelligence and the Cold War: The Case of the Byelorussian Central Council', MA thesis, University of Vermont.

Limbach, E. H. (2011) 'Unsettled Germans: The Reception and Resettlement of East German Refugees in West Germany, 1949–1961', dissertation submitted to Michigan State University.

Plavnieks, R. (2013) 'Nazi Collaborators on Trial during the Cold War: The Cases Against Viktors Arājs and the Latvian Auxiliary Security Police', PhD dissertation submitted to the University of North Carolina at Chapel Hill.

Movies, TV, Radio Broadcasts and Other Communications

Bland, Robert, CPS Special Casework Lawyer, briefing note, 15 December 1998.

Bloxham, Donald, speaking at a launch event at the Wiener Library, 19 April 2021 for the publication of *The Palgrave Handbook of Britain & the Holocaust*, ed. Andy Pearce and Tom Lawson: London: Palgrave Macmillan.

Brian Hayes Phone-In Programme, LBC Radio, 26 March 1990.

Clegg, William, speech at the British Academy of Forensic Sciences Friends' Dinner, Law Society, 26 February 1998, reported in *Journal of Medicine, Science and the Law*, 38(3).

Greenwood, Robert, KC, speech in Melbourne, 14 November 1994 reported in *Australia-Israel Review* 20(1) January 1995.

Report of the Senate Standing Committee on Legal and Constitutional Affairs, February 1988.

The Forgotten Nazi, Dir. Bob Tomlinson, Scottish TV, 2001.

The Next Door Nazi. Presented by Nick Southall, BBC Radio 4, 23 March 2021.

Watson, Peter, lawyer for Scottish Television, quote during defamation proceedings brought by Antanas Gecas in 1992.

Index